apm
association
project manageme

CW01099512

APM Project
Management
Qualification *(PMQ)*

Pull-out Study Guide Planner

Association for Project Management

Ibis House, Regent Park   **Tel (UK)** 0845 458 1944
Summerleys Road   **Tel (Int)** +44 1844 271 640
Princes Risborough   **Email** info@apm.org.uk
Buckinghamshire HP27 9LE   **Web** apm.org.uk

Association for Project Management is incorporated by Royal Charter RC000890
and a registered charity No. 1171112. Principal office as shown.

APM Project Management
Qualification Study Guide

APM Project Management Qualification Study Guide

Association for Project Management

MANAGEMENT

Association for Project Management
Ibis House, Regent Park
Summerleys Road, Princes Risborough
Buckinghamshire
HP27 9LE

© Association for Project Management 2020

All rights reserved. No part of this publication may be reproduced, stored in a retrieval system, or transmitted, in any form or by any means, without the express permission in writing of the Association for Project Management. Within the UK exceptions are allowed in respect of any fair dealing for the purposes of research or private study, or criticism or review, as permitted under the Copyright, Designs and Patents Act, 1988, or in the case of reprographic reproduction in accordance with the terms of the licenses issued by the Copyright Licensing Agency. Enquiries concerning reproduction outside these terms and in other countries should be sent to the Rights Department, Association for Project Management at the address above. All registered trademarks are hereby acknowledged and the publisher makes no claim to these trademarks.

British Library Cataloguing in Publication Data is available.

Paperback ISBN: 978 1 913305 06 2
eISBN: 978-1-913305-07-9

Cover design by Fountainhead Creative Consultants
Typeset by RefineCatch Limited, Bungay, Suffolk
in 10/14pt Foundry Sans

Contents

Figures and tables

Tables

Introducing APM

The Association for Project Management (APM) is the only chartered body for the project profession, with over 30,000 individual members and more than 500 organisations participating in our Corporate Partnership Programme.

As a registered educational charity, we are committed to developing and promoting the value of project management in order to deliver improved project outcomes for the benefit of society.

There are a number of ways in which you can benefit from what we do, including:

- membership;
- qualifications;
- chartered status;
- publications;
- events.

Inspiring positive change – our vision and mission

Our vision for the profession is ambitious, challenging and radical. Above all, it reflects what society expects: A world in which all projects succeed with project management as a life skill for all.

Our mission is: inspiring communities to deliver meaningful change for societal benefit by advancing the art, science, theory and practice of project management.

Our objectives

- **Chartered standard** – We are the chartered body for the project profession, leading the way in setting and maintaining a universally high standard for the project profession. This includes chartership, wider continuing professional development (CPD), qualifications and best practice knowledge share. Our objective is to successfully position, develop and launch the chartered standard to become the accepted benchmark standard for project professionals.

- **Membership growth** – We are the membership body for the entire project profession, for all sectors, all locations, all stages of career and all individuals. Our objective is to accelerate the growth, diversity and global reach of our membership by engaging with new sectors and communities.

- **Knowledge and research** – We are the leading source of knowledge and insights designed to facilitate discussion, inspire improvement and assist application. Our objective is to advance the art, science, theory and practice of project management and the profession, supported by an innovative knowledge and research programme.

- **Organisational innovation** – We listen – to our members, to our partners and to the world around us – in order to remain responsive, relevant and sustainable in a constantly changing world. Our objective is to define and build the association as the model of a sustainable professional body for the 21st century.

- **Collaborate and engage** – We work to raise awareness of the project profession as a route to the delivery of public good. Our objective is to accelerate the universal adoption of project management by people delivering change through collaboration and partnerships.

About the author

Raymond Stadnik has over 30 years' experience of delivering change within a wide range of organisations throughout the world. Part of that time he has focused on developing the competence of people either through classroom-based training or more intensive coaching events.

Raymond has now brought that experience to bear on the production of the *Project Management Qualification Study Guide*. The guide attempts to follow the APM project life cycle format as closely as possible, suggesting a study timeline that mirrors a project timeline.

"A timeline is a very important feature of any project. The study guide should be written taking timing into account. Sections of the guide should start with organisational context, strategy, concept, planning, execution, handover and closure. Then benefits and outcomes. There are two choices here for the learner; study project management academically topic by topic, or as an unfolding project, building as it progresses. The latter option may also be more in line with any project management experience a user may have already observed. From a teaching perspective, candidates who have studied project management using a timed sequence, that mirrors an actual projects sequence, achieve greater exam success."

Raymond Stadnik FAPM, author.

1 Study planning

1.1 Using this guide

This study guide has one main objective: to support you in your study for the APM Project Management Qualification (PMQ). It is also hoped that this guide will act as a reference after your success has been rewarded and that it will occupy a deserved place on your bookshelf helping you to solve your real-life project management dilemmas for years to come.

If you are using this guide as a means of self-study, it is expected that 60 hours would be a good average time to devote to becoming exam ready. This time includes planning, reading and attempting the quick quizzes and some sample questions found in Chapter 3.

Even with very little practical project management experience this guide and the associated APM materials will be everything you need to develop an effective study plan for the PMQ exam. Provided of course you apply sufficient personal effort to execute your plan.

When you first view this guide, the syllabus, candidate guidance and any other available material you are planning to use, you might think that there is a lot of different numbering that may not seem to be connected. Well, you are not alone; that's probably a common first challenge experienced by most people wanting to tackle a substantial subject like project management. It is, however, essential that you do get to grips with the complete structure very early on and incorporate this into your study planning. These introductory pages will help bring all the different components together.

PMQ learning structure

The most important document for an initial review is the APM Project Management Qualification Syllabus: learning outcomes and assessment criteria aligned to the *APM Body of Knowledge 7th edition*. You can download the syllabus from the APM website. The syllabus highlights the 11 learning outcomes that describe the knowledge you are required to demonstrate, at a sufficient level, to be awarded the PMQ qualification. The learning outcomes contain 67 assessment criteria. The purpose of the assessment criteria is to show learners what specific knowledge is being examined for each learning outcome. Ultimately, you will be tested for the required level of knowledge through individual exam questions.

The content of this learning guide will help you to accumulate the necessary insight to demonstrate your knowledge to the required level for this qualification. There are 20 study areas contained in the study guide. Each study area fulfils the knowledge requirements for one or more of the assessment criteria. The relationship between the study guide, assessment criteria and learning outcomes is shown in Figure 1.1.1.1.

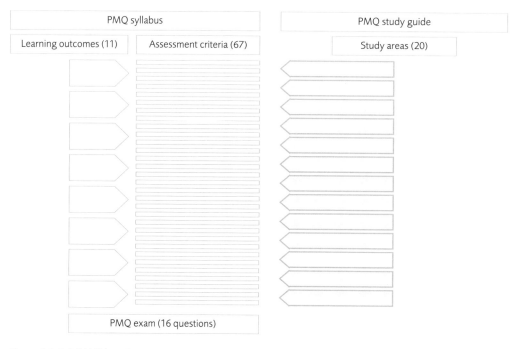

Figure 1.1.1.1 PMQ learning structure.

Study guide planner (see pull-out at front of book)

To help you plan your study and monitor your progress the PMQ study guide planner can be used. It shows the 20 study areas grouped into the three main chapters of the guide and mapped to the learning outcomes from the syllabus. As you complete the study of a particular subject you can then tick it off on the planner, keeping track of your progress. You will find that the study areas are overlaid onto the project life cycle showing how the subjects relate to the sequence of a project. This is not a strict rule of thumb but provides a very rough sequence to help you see how a project might develop, which you will find helpful if you do not yet have any practical project management experience. In reality a lot of the subject areas discuss processes and frameworks that are probably happening simultaneously and throughout the whole life cycle rather than starting and stopping as the study guide suggests. See the study guide planner as more of a revision aid rather than an example of a project plan.

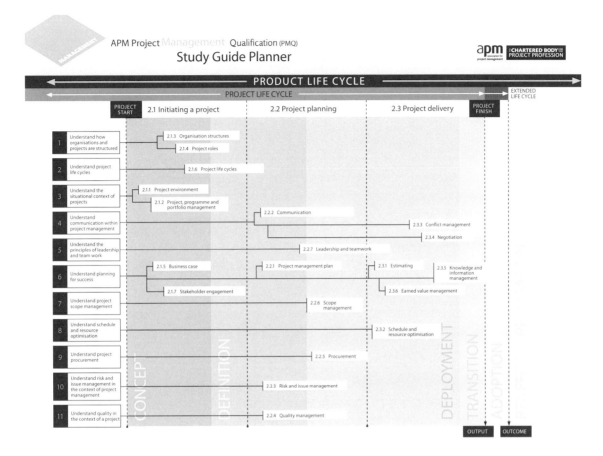

Figure 1.1.2 Pull out study guide planner

Other supporting documentation

As well as the syllabus you are advised to download *APM Project Management Qualification, Guide for Candidates*. This will provide you with information concerning the exam procedures, exam marking and notifications.

You should also download the latest version of the PMQ examination sample paper. This contains examples of exam questions, some of which regularly appear in live examinations. This paper will give you a feel for the actual exam and build your familiarity with the paper prior to your exam day.

Other helpful documents are also available from the APM website, such as indicative content for each of the assessment criteria, which is a guide to the type of responses a candidate could make for each assessment criterion. Visit the PMQ information section of the qualifications page of the APM website. Information is regularly updated and published to help and support candidates taking the exam.

APM Body of Knowledge 7th edition

This study guide and the supporting documentation will assist you in studying for and sitting the PMQ exam. You may also consider purchasing the *APM Body of Knowledge*. While this is not strictly necessary for PMQ study, as a lot of the content of this study guide is taken directly from the *APM Body of Knowledge*, you might find some of its other topics and content of interest in the future.

1.2 How to study

You will have your own preferences and approaches to the way you learn, and they will influence the way you select and use this material. Many candidates find that self-study is just as effective as classroom-based courses, while for others the discipline and self-motivation required for going it alone is just too demanding.

There are many benefits therefore in deciding first off how you are going to plan and schedule your studies in relation to all the other activities in your daily life. By thinking about these aspects now, you are likely to gain through having a more enjoyable and meaningful learning experience. This in turn will improve overall effectiveness and enable you to adopt a more flexible approach to answering questions.

Before you commence your study of the material it might be worthwhile reviewing some of the APM documentation suggested in the previous section – 'Using this guide' – in order to become familiar with the structure of the exam. It might also be useful to review Section 3.2 and see how exam questions are typically structured.

Suggested approaches

Consider the relationship between practice and theory, investigate typical projects in your working environment, or do some online research of projects that you hear about on your local news or in the press. This type of research will allow you to appreciate the connection between the theory you are currently studying and common practice out there in the real world.

After completing each subject try and look for opportunities where you can apply some of the tools and techniques that you are learning. In addition to theoretical study, application and appropriate feedback are essential for effective learning. There are likely to be opportunities to apply theory in your workplace, in social activities and in the home. For example, a work-based project, a club project or a DIY project.

You may be able to review past projects and discuss project management performance with experienced project managers within your organisation or friends and family members who may work in a project environment. You can obtain feedback on your own study performance from peers, colleagues and supervisors, and there may be opportunities to form study groups or social networks where there are others who are also studying for the PMQ.

All of the activities discussed above can enhance your learning experience significantly. However, you will need to be proactive in identifying opportunities and include them in your learning plan. Remember that a plan means nothing until it is executed; ensure you take action.

Setting personal learning objectives and realistic targets

On average, the core study time required is about 60 hours including reading, quizzes and answering sample questions. Additional time will be required for any optional learning activities, revision, attendance at coaching workshops and final exam preparation.

The targeted time frame for study is only a suggested outline and may vary considerably depending on personal time constraints and any previous experience of the subject matter. It is therefore important to establish the feasibility of the target date you have set for taking the examination and allow adequate study time. The key note here is to be realistic. If you dive into study trying to get to the exam as soon as possible, your approach may not take account of all the other activities, that up to this point have gone by unnoticed and now they too are making demands on your time. This is when you start missing your goals, become disheartened and the plan is now in shreds. The opposite can be just as challenging, where you purchase the guide, don't bother with a plan but start reading from page one expecting to complete the guide at some point in the future. Months go by and guess what? You still haven't read past page 10 and you have read page 8 about 50 times!

What is needed of course is a balanced approach that allows you to study, work and carry on your social and family life as normally as reasonably possible. Tell your friends, family and work colleagues what you are doing and the commitment you are expecting to make to gain a very worthwhile qualification. They will, I am sure, be glad to support you and of course join in the celebrations when you get a great pass in the exam.

Using common learning techniques

Mind mapping

A mind map is a powerful graphic technique, which provides a universal key to unlock the potential of the brain. It harnesses the full range of cortical skills – word, image, number, logic, rhythm, colour and spatial awareness – in a single, uniquely powerful manner. In so doing, it gives you the freedom to roam the infinite expanses of your brain. A mind map can be applied to every aspect of life where improved learning and clearer thinking will enhance human performance.

Widely used in learning, mind maps were first originated in the late 1960s by Tony Buzan. Mind maps are now used by millions of people around the world – from the very young to the very old – whenever they wish to learn or use their minds more effectively. Mind maps can be applied to most of life's situations that involve any learning or thinking.

If it has been some time since you have studied, you might find mind maps helpful to consider. An online search of 'mind maps' will give you more information to consider.

Prompt lists and checklists

If you are new to project management, the amount of terms and sheer volume of material may seem a little overwhelming. Breaking down larger concepts into lists can often be a good way of taking control of the material. Starting with each of the larger subject areas a hierarchy of related terms can be developed, then breaking these down into more associated terms.

Lists of terms can be useful and lists of questions or prompts can also aid learning. Ideally if you have a daily commute, using lists is an easy way to revise and can be a break from reading and then re-reading the material.

Flash cards

"A picture paints a thousand words" is a commonly quoted saying to describe the effect of visual imaging and its use in creating visual representation as a substitute for lengthy text-based information. When these images are created by learners and placed on small cards, they act as aid memoirs when used systematically to revise and learn fundamental concepts. Learners report increased success rates in exams when flash cards are used.

Flash cards can be used to show images or very short text descriptions and can be created by hand or on a computer and then printed for use. There are also a number of free-use software applications that will allow the development of digital flash cards that can be reviewed on either a phone or laptop. An online search of 'flash cards' will provide some insight into this potentially powerful learning aid.

Study groups

If you work for an organisation where project management is a common practice then the chances are that there may be others learning project management at the same time as you. Ask those around you if they know of anyone and discuss your course generally with your colleagues. They may be interested in what you are doing, so much so they may also decide to study for a project management qualification.

Preparing and studying with others may mean that you can share ideas, test each other and discuss some of the more practical applications of project management within your organisation. It is often satisfying to share areas of learning that you may find difficult with others who may also find the same areas challenging. Jointly you are able to piece together the solution and gain the satisfaction of solving what was seen as a learning obstacle.

2 Study areas

2.1 Initiating a project

Organisations operate in a dynamic context, full of uncertainty, novelty and turbulence. This section identifies just how organisations can use projects, programmes and portfolios in order to enhance performance, bring about change and enable organisations to adapt, improve and grow. Project-work therefore represents intentional investment in development, enhancement and improvement.

The need for investment emerges from the aspirational plans and an overarching purpose that transpire from the strategic intent of an organisation, reflected in each project's business case. Project-work encompasses strategic investments that enable assets, structures, systems, activities and capabilities to be formed, maintained or enhanced so that the organisational plans and ambitions can be realised.

Organisational change is introduced through projects, programmes and portfolios in order to deliver business value. The business value is accrued through the realisation of benefits that result from project-work. Benefits are part of ensuring that investments are made to deliver value to the organisation. This normally applies even when the project is being done by a supplier or contracting organisation, or if the work is needed to maintain current capability or in order to conform to new regulations or directives so that smooth business operations can be allowed to proceed.

The successful deployment of change, the support of new behaviours and the utilisation of new capability, resulting in the realisation of benefits, involves engaging with, promoting and working with diverse communities and groups. To ensure that value is created and sustained, organisations need to consider and address the full investment life cycle ensuring that forecasted benefits materialise.

Delivering strategy is enabled through the use of projects, programmes and portfolios. Portfolios structure investments in line with strategic objectives, while balancing, aligning and scrutinising capacity and resources. Programmes combine business-as-usual with projects and steady state activity dictated by strategic priorities. Projects are transient endeavours that bring about change and achieve planned objectives. Together, they combine to deliver the beneficial change required to implement, enable and satisfy the strategic intent of the organisation.

Stakeholders, those individuals or groups who have an interest or role in the project, programme or portfolio, or are impacted by it, cannot by definition be 'managed'. Rather, depending on their stake, and the role that ideally, they will play, the people involved in the work, from sponsor to team member, are part of the effort to keep the stakeholder appropriately engaged and influenced to do the right things. This is not easy work and benefits from a facilitative approach rather than assuming that 'command-and-control' approaches will be effective.

This section is the start of the learning journey and includes:

2.1.1 Project environment

2.1.2 Project, programme and portfolio management

2.1.3 Organisational structures

2.1.4 Project roles

2.1.5 Business case

2.1.6 Project life cycles

2.1.7 Stakeholder engagement

2.1.1 Project environment

It is relevant that the first section of a learning resource on project management considers the reasons why that project may need to exist in the first place. An initial thought is that the organisation is faced with a constantly changing environment that is creating problems, opportunities or business needs requiring some degree of response if threats are to be minimised, opportunities exploited and business needs effectively addressed.

Every project is a response to a changing environment. Within that environment are the factors that influence and impact projects.

Figure 2.1.1.1 How the environment influences an organisation

Organisations must develop a strategic approach to managing change. Projects deliver the beneficial change required to implement, enable and satisfy the strategic intent of the organisation. Practically this will be achieved by deploying new assets, functions, capabilities, processes, structures and systems. The environment is the driving force for the project. It is important for the project manager to understand how these drivers are likely to influence the project. It may impact how they deliver the project, what they deliver, who is involved and when it needs to be delivered. Early on in the project the answers to some of these questions may be uncertain. As a result, planning needs to be flexible, options need to be effectively evaluated and various scenarios assessed in order for the project to emerge as the optimum solution to what might be a range of diverse needs.

Tools and techniques used to determine factors which influence and impact projects

The impact of infrastructure, the physical environment, mitigating the potential adverse impacts of other projects and the project's technology are just some of the factors the project manager must take into account when planning the delivery of a project. Shorter term practical implementation impacts of the project as well as its conceptual development and consequent long-term impacts also need to be fully considered. In addition, project managers also need to be attuned to the internal aspects, such as the cultural, organisational and social environments of the project's sponsoring organisation.

Understanding this environment includes identifying the project stakeholders and their ability to affect its successful outcome. This means working with people to achieve the best results, especially if the project is based in a highly technical or complex environment. Therefore, it is essential that the project manager and the project team are comfortable with, and sympathetic towards, their physical, technological, cultural, organisational and social surroundings. The objective is influencing the project environment in a positive way or changing the way the project is being delivered, all with the aim of gaining a better reception of the change the project is designed to introduce.

Resistance to change may be evident among some of the stakeholders, while others may have vested interests, personal or group agendas that are only indirectly related to the project. Timely identification and categorisation of these interests proactively means that the corresponding risks, which are otherwise likely to undermine the success of the project, can be significantly reduced. Failure to take such an approach could inevitably lead to a less than optimum project outcome.

Every project team member needs to develop the attitude that, just as they are stakeholders, every other project stakeholder is also important. There should be a commitment to service and creation of a project management environment in which every decision and action is designed to make the stakeholder's experience better than it would have been had the project not been implemented. It requires a focus on the quality of the stakeholder's experience at every stage of the project.

PESTLE

There are a number of common forms of environmental analysis from simple external/internal factors analysis to using a more specific framework. One of the more common forms of analysis for the project environment is PESTLE analysis, a management technique to help project management understand the environment in which the project operates.

PESTLE analysis is a popular method of examining the many different factors affecting an organisation and the project – the external or internal influences on success or failure. The impact of these factors on the project may be differentiated in six ways:

- Political – Current and potential influences from political pressures.

- Economic – Local, national and world economic impact.

- Sociological – The effect of changes in the needs of society.

- Technological – New and emerging technology.

- Legal – Local, national and world legislation.

- Environmental – Local, national and world environmental issues.

The six factors may be applied to the whole of the organisation, or to specific business areas, or to a specific project and could consider external only, internal only or both, in order to contemplate the likely effects. Business areas could include:

- customers
- the industry/marketplace
- competitors
- supply sources
- internal capability

- technology
- intermediaries
- stakeholders
- time
- governance requirements.

Following PESTLE analysis, an organisation would most likely have a number of options available as to how the desired objectives could be achieved. One strength of a business case for a project is that a number of options have been considered and that there is evidence to show that the organisation has not become over reliant on a single idea, when there may be other more favourable options available.

SWOT analysis

The purpose of SWOT analysis is to use an established framework to systematically understand the strengths, weaknesses, opportunities and threats that each project option may face. SWOT can be particularly powerful uncovering opportunities that the project may be well placed to take advantage of but that the project team may never have considered when using other forms of comparison. Similarly understanding weaknesses of the project options allow for the best approach to be considered in advance, allowing a pro-active approach avoiding threats that would otherwise catch the project team unawares.

These two forms of analysis can be used in very different ways: PESTLE can be used to consider the environment and to establish options for consideration; SWOT may be used as an evaluation tool to test the options being considered and so is more of a comparative analysis. SWOT can be used in a wide variety of situations where a comparative analysis is required. One example of how it might be used in a project is within the concept phase of the project life cycle to evaluate the project options being considered at that point. It can also be used for uncovering the strengths and weaknesses of the organisation in relation to the project and in addition isolate the threats and opportunities that may exist in that relationship.

Both PESTLE and SWOT analysis could be used with good rigour but still raise more questions than answers. Caution should always be expressed when appraising the outputs of traditional models. The increasing level of uncertainty that exists and the combination of economic unknowns with political, social and environmental concerns regarding the proposed actions and their longer-term implications may require new ways of engaging with uncertainty.

VUCA

The US military coined the term VUCA to reflect the 'volatility, uncertainty, complexity and ambiguity' of general conditions and situations associated with a multilateral world following the end of the Cold War in the early nineties. The term has been widely adopted to represent increasingly vulnerable and unpredictable contexts. The key implication of VUCA conditions is that there is an inherent uncertainty that makes it difficult to predict and plan with great accuracy. The rigidity that comes from expecting full and perfect knowledge is unsustainable and unattainable in turbulent environments. Uncertainty defies anticipation and detailed planning. VUCA seeks to give a perspective of the project to enable managers to identify emerging opportunities, respond to new conditions and address shortfalls and differences in outcomes, avoiding the classic mismatches between plans, models and reality, translating into poor project performance.

Figure 2.1.1.2 shows an example of how an organisation might use VUCA to understand the risks in particular project situations. The two causative factors, level of confidence in outcome and current knowledge are combined and rated high or low. If the organisation has high confidence in outcomes and high level of knowledge it should consider if there is any volatility in the situation, could interest rates suddenly rise, or the costs of materials fluctuate unexpectedly for example. The risk here could originate from complacency and the project becomes exposed to uncontrolled change.

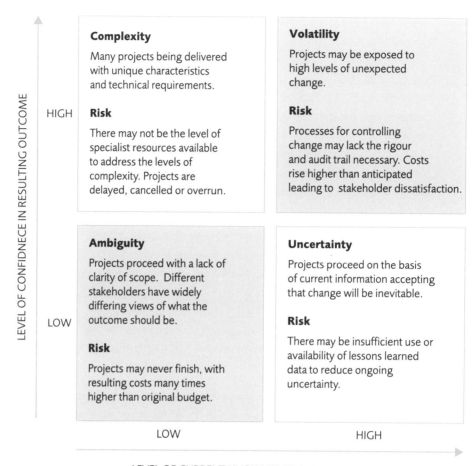

Figure 2.1.1.2 Example of VUCA applied to project examples

In the opposite scenario, low confidence and low available data, there is likely to be ambiguity and therefore the project is likely to have difficulty delivering requirements to the satisfaction of stakeholders unless it can use a robust process for defining requirements more reliably. At the heart of VUCA is the development of a learning culture for greater levels of preparedness, anticipation, evolution and pro-active intervention. A failure to process and manage learning is one of the major causes of projects failing to perform to the required degree.

Impact of the legal and regulatory environment on projects

This section is not about turning the project manager into a legal expert, far from it. Effective project management is about having an awareness of critical areas of the project and also being able to know who else may have the relevant expertise and when they need to become involved to provide the necessary support. Understanding some of these factors will provide an appreciation of how they are likely to impact the project.

Working conditions

Employees' working conditions are set out in the basic foundation of employment law. This law regulates the relationship between employers and employees. It governs what employers can expect from employees, what employers can ask employees to do, and employees rights at work. Areas covered by employment law include all types of discrimination, disability provisions, dismissal of employees and grievance procedures, working hours, leave entitlement, employment contracts and pay. The project manager must first determine the applicable legislative requirements and ensure that the necessary training and communication is conducted in order for all project personnel to understand their duties of compliance. Acting in a compliant manner may influence decisions on how work is allocated, who is allocated and how the performance of that work is then managed, ensuring that targets and objectives are judged to be realistic and fair. Ultimately the project manager must create the right working conditions for the project in accordance with legislation.

Management of risk in the workplace

There is a key duty of the project manager which also extends to all project personnel and that is to understand the risks in their area of work and take the necessary steps to highlight these and take proactive measures to manage these risks to an appropriate degree. Individuals must utilise sufficient knowledge to understand their main duties to be compliant with the law. All employers must protect the health, safety and welfare at work of all their employees, as well as others on their premises, including temporary and casual workers, self-employed, clients, visitors and the general public. All workers also have a duty of care for their own health and safety and that of others who may be affected by their actions at work. All workers must cooperate with employers and co-workers to help everyone meet their legal requirements.

The focal point for health and safety in the project will be the health, safety and environmental management plan. It will outline the safety requirements and the duties required for compliance, such as procedures for risk assessments, training, availability of suitable protective clothing and environmental impact. The project will have to ensure that all aspects of workplace risk are budgeted for in addition to the overall budget for completing the work.

Governance

The sponsor is the person accountable for ensuring that the work is governed effectively and delivers the objectives to meet identified needs. The project manager must be sufficiently aware of the practices underpinning project-based working to be able to provide a high degree of assurance to the sponsor that the work is being managed effectively, responsibly and sustainably. This will allow the sponsor to make informed decisions about whether the business case is likely to be realised and to take the most appropriate resulting actions.

Governance will impact how the project is managed, the processes the project will use and how project status will be assured and reported when the project is being delivered. The project manager must understand the governance framework required and how the resulting management approach must be tailored to provide confidence to stakeholders that the project is being managed in a compliant manner.

Sustainability

Sustainability is concerned with balancing the environmental, social, economic and administrative aspects of project-based work to meet the current needs of stakeholders without compromising or overburdening future generations. Sustainability involves both individual and organisational responsibility to ensure that outputs, outcomes and benefits are sustainable over their life cycles and during their creation, disposal and decommissioning. Sustainability is relevant across all areas of project-based working. For example, the procurement team seeking opportunities to buy from sustainable sources and to make the supply chain more efficient.

Even minor players in a project-based team can have an influence, however small, on sustainability and may therefore be expected to think creatively and act responsibly in their day-to-day work. This may be something as simple as reducing unnecessary travel or the use of paper. Sponsors and stakeholders, especially those with seniority, can put in place mechanisms to identify, monitor and reward working practices that support sustainability. They can also influence wider stakeholders and challenge aspects of sustainability. Project managers must seek and follow the environmental guidelines of the commissioning organisation. Once they understand the requirements, they should monitor and report team adherence and ensure that their risk strategy incorporates impacts to sustainability.

2.1.1   Learning summary

The section of the guide that you have just read will provide you with the learning necessary to be assessed against the following PMQ learning outcome and assessment criteria:

3. Understand the situational context of projects.

3.6 *Explain tools and techniques used to determine factors which influence and impact projects (including PESTLE, SWOT and VUCA).*

Understanding why the project is being carried out is key to the ultimate success of the project. It can impact how the project is delivered, who might be involved, what is delivered and when is best for all of this to happen. There are two main techniques for determining the factors which influence and impact projects. PESTLE is used most often to generate the specific options that should be considered and then SWOT to do a comparative analysis of these options. The strongest, less weak, most opportunistic and less threating option can then be chosen.

VUCA on the other hand showed an appreciation of the higher-level aspects of the environment that may also affect which projects are carried out. Learners may have experienced PESTLE and SWOT before but may not have seen VUCA related specifically to a project environment. Figure 2.1.1.2 provides a simple example of the VUCA considerations in relation to projects. The wide-reaching aspects of this analysis not only touch individual projects but the environment, culture and capabilities of the organisation.

3.7 *Explain the impact of the legal and regulatory environment on projects (such as the impact on working conditions, risk management, governance and sustainability).*

The project manager is not an expert in the legal or regulatory environment but an expert in the project management domain. However, part of that expertise must be a solid appreciation of the legal and regulatory environment relating to the project being delivered. Knowing this environment is important but perhaps more important is knowing when and who to consult when a potential legal and regulatory problem is likely to arise. Learners should understand the paradoxes in this area, rigorous safety may be seen by some to be too constraining, taking a journey by train takes twice as long as flying and time is of the essence. Whatever opinions exist the governance of the organisation, as implemented by the project sponsor must overrule opinion. This assurance will ensure that stakeholders remain committed to the project throughout its life cycle.

2.1.2 Project, programme and portfolio management

Projects are unique, transient endeavours, undertaken to bring about change and achieve planned objectives, which can be defined in terms of outputs, outcomes or benefits. A project is usually deemed to be a success if it achieves the objectives according to its acceptance criteria, normally within an agreed timescale and budget. Project-work is conducted across normal organisational functional areas, setting up a temporary organisation, drawing on the skills, expertise and knowledge of the organisation, as well as third parties, where appropriate.

Projects normally use capital expenditure to acquire, upgrade and maintain assets, services, products and capability. Projects may also need to take into account the ultimate requirements for decommissioning and disposal.

In some settings, it is possible to find arrangements involving multiple projects running in parallel, or related to one another, to provide support or to build additional capabilities. Multiple concurrent projects may require prioritisation in terms of scheduled deployment, importance of primary deliverables or the availability of key resources, skills, or individuals.

Differences between projects and business-as-usual (BAU)

The term business-as-usual (BAU) refers to an organisation's normal day-to-day operations. It can also be referred to as steady state. Projects contrast with BAU in a number of ways. It is important for the success of the project that the project's unique characteristics are recognised and that the most appropriate structures, management and controls are put in place.

Feature	Projects	Business-as-usual
Purpose	Achieve objectives then terminate	Sustain the organisation to achieve its business purpose and goals
Timescale	Limited, temporary in nature, pre-defined start and end points	Ongoing no defined end point
Outcome	Unique product or service	Repetitive, non-unique product, service or result
People	Temporary teams, formed across organisational boundaries to meet project needs. May not be aligned with organisational structure	Teams formed within organisational structure and aligned to suit functional demands
Management	Dedicated manager appointed for the duration of project only, may not have direct line authority over project team	Long term formal management, direct line authority over functional unit personnel

Table 2.1.2.1 Differences between projects and BAU

Typically, a project's objective is to deliver outputs, for example a software solution, a building, a process or a service. The project team transitions the outputs to an internal or external client to deliver the desired outcomes and benefits. Sometimes, the project also includes the work required to deliver outcomes and benefits. In such cases, the project team leads more of the work to deliver the changes required by the client to realise the project's intended benefits.

BAU on the other hand uses the products of the project to realise the benefits. It is unusual for projects to deliver any benefits into the organisation during their deployment (unless there is some form of phased roll-out, or a delivery contractor benefits by being paid to deliver specific phases).

All projects trade the triple constraints of time, cost and quality in achieving the defined scope of the project within the defined tolerance for risk.

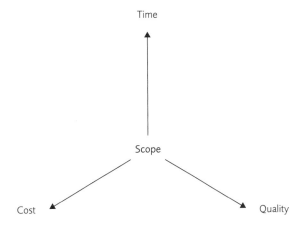

Figure 2.1.2.1 Triple constraints of time, cost and quality

Project managers must understand the relative priorities of time, cost and quality as an important part of the decision as to which life cycle approach will suit best.

Differences between project, programme and portfolio management

Project, programme and portfolio management is concerned with managing discrete packages of work to achieve objectives. The way the work is managed depends upon a wide variety of factors. The scale, significance and complexity of the work are obvious factors; relocating a small office and organising the Olympics share many basic principles but offer very different managerial challenges. Scale and complexity are not the only factors. Managing a major infrastructure development for delivery to a client will need a different approach from internally managing the merger of two banking organisations.

A good distinguishing factor is often to look at the nature of the objectives. Objectives may be expressed in terms of outputs (such as a new HQ building), outcomes (such as staff being relocated from multiple locations to the new HQ), benefits (such as reduced travel and facilities management costs) or strategic objectives (such as doubling the organisation's share price in three years).

Commonly, work of a lesser scale and complexity, leading to an output, is referred to as a project. Work that combines projects with change management to deliver benefits is considered to be a programme, while a collection of projects and programmes designed to achieve strategic objectives is called a portfolio. However, some undertakings that only deliver outputs may be very large and complex, while some work that delivers benefits and encompasses the management of change may be relatively small and straightforward. Small organisations will have strategic portfolios that are nowhere near as complex and expensive as, say, a large government IT project.

Although projects, programmes and portfolios are often spoken of as being mutually exclusive approaches, they are actually just convenient combinations of managerial tools and techniques used to describe typical sets of circumstances. The concept of projects, programmes and portfolios should be thought of as just points on a gradual scale of managing effort to deliver objectives.

Relationship between programmes, projects and strategic change

Strategy implementation, often recognised as the hardest part of the strategy process, is delivered through the execution of strategic projects and programmes and the realisation of their targeted benefits. From an executive perspective, project-work is an essential part of making strategic investment work. The key focus is on the creation of value through projects that will enable meaningful execution of both deliberate and emergent strategies. This implies extending the scope of interest around projects and programmes to incorporate the realisation of benefits that will justify the investment and fulfil the criteria outlined in the business case.

Programmes are unique and transient strategic endeavours, undertaken to achieve beneficial change and incorporating a group of related and business-as-usual (steady-state) activities. They can be defined as coordinated projects and change management activities combined to achieve beneficial change. The distinction between projects and programmes depends on context and the guiding criteria between them often relates to the complexity of scope and the addition of change activities. The need for significant improvement will be consistent with the organisation's strategy, and programmes will help to deliver elements of that strategy.

Projects, programmes and portfolios tend to flow out of strategic decisions made by the organisation and can therefore be viewed as strategic investments that enable other activities and capabilities to be developed. Figure 2.1.2.2 shows how the organisation in response to the environment has set its strategic objectives for change, which could involve a number of structural choices from portfolios to programmes to projects. Portfolio management is mainly focused on the selection and prioritisation of projects and programmes within the capacity to deliver. Programme management then focuses on the coordination of projects and business-as-usual with particular emphasis on the achievement of beneficial change.

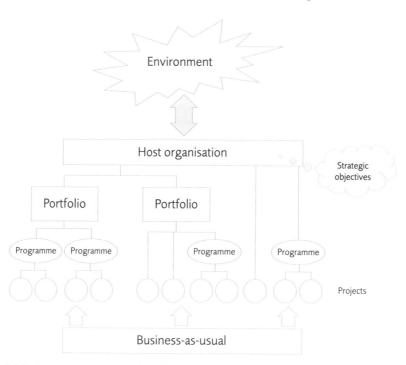

Figure 2.1.2.2 Projects, programmes and portfolios situated to deliver strategic change

Ultimately it is project-work that is concerned with the ability to enact the organisational strategy by enabling benefits to be realised so that the intended value can be accrued. These projects could be part of a programme or directly part of a portfolio. Projects could also be delivered as single entities by the host organisation because there is no advantage in them being part of a programme or portfolio, but they are still required to be delivered to fulfil the organisations strategic objectives. Senior leaders within the organisation are able to demonstrate how each project or programme that they fund contributes to the overall strategy. Where projects or programmes cannot be justified or aligned with the organisational strategy, their continued operation and purpose can be questioned. It is worth noting that supplier organisations managing projects for their clients on a commercial basis may have a different strategic justification for conducting commercial work. Project work may also be needed as an enabler to maintain existing capabilities or assets, ensure compliance with newly introduced legislation or satisfy other professional requirements or business imperatives.

Situations where the use of programme management may be appropriate

Programmes typically combine new deployment with some elements of business-as-usual. Consequently, they utilise capital expenditure to acquire assets, services, products and capability, alongside operating expense incurred as a result of performing normal business operations. Programmes are often defined as delivering change, and would typically incorporate the full utilisation of benefits to satisfy the business case. The overall measure of success will be determined by the actual realisation of the expected benefits, which frequently involves the use of capabilities or facilities created by the programme in an ongoing, business-as-usual manner.

Programme management may be appropriate if the organisation wishes to achieve the following:

- More effective delivery of change – project interdependencies are managed to greater effect allowing them to have the greatest chance of delivering their benefits without adverse effect on business-as-usual. It is likely that projects within the programme will have a complex set of dependencies and outputs, which would be more difficult to deliver as individual projects.

- Increased responsiveness to strategic initiatives – filling the gaps between strategies, business cases and projects. The programme level view will look for synergies between individual project business cases in order to yield a greater return from the projects as a programme rather than if each project had delivered independently.

- More effective management of resources – through prioritisation and project integration allowing for resource conflicts, within individual projects, to be managed at a programme level ensuring that those projects that are of priority get first call on resources to maximise benefits realisation within business-as-usual.

- Better management of risk in a wider business context – contingencies that are applied to projects on an individual basis may lack economies of scale. If these risk contingencies are applied at a programme level, the overall contingency amount may be reduced as common responses made at this level may influence several projects simultaneously. This will typically benefit the organisations where there were a number of higher risk projects being delivered.

- More efficient coordination and control – by defining roles and responsibilities for managing the programme and application of a uniform process to initiate, accelerate/de-accelerate and terminate projects within the programme. Bringing together common processes for delivering scope will result in a greater likelihood of those projects being more fully utilised by the organisation, once they are delivered.

- Increased focus on obtaining strategic benefits – by having an insight into the strategic goals and needs of the organisation, projects can be directed into business-as-usual in a combined way that has the best chance of achieving any benefit synergies that may not be apparent if projects were delivered singly out with the programme.

If an organisation is under challenge in attempting to deliver a range of projects in different areas of its business, effective programme management becomes a critical success factor.

Situations where the use of portfolio management may be appropriate

Portfolio management is used to select, prioritise and control an organisation's programmes and projects, in line with its strategic objectives and capacity to deliver. Their goal is to balance the implementation of change initiatives and the maintenance of business-as-usual, while optimising return on investment.

Portfolios are used to structure investment decisions. They can be managed at an organisational or functional level to optimise strategic benefits or operational efficiency and address a number of major questions:

- What are the projects and programmes needed to deliver the strategic objectives, taking account of risk, resource constraints and affordability?

- Is the organisation capable of delivering them effectively and efficiently?

- Are the full potential benefits from the organisation's investment capable of being realised?

For organisations implementing portfolio management, the following situations would be where the use of such a process would be most appropriate:

- Where there is a need for the organisation's projects and programmes to be more aligned with its key business objectives, including those of profitability, customer service, reputation, sustainability and growth.

- When the organisation's financial controls, financial planning and expenditure review processes need to be applied to both individual projects and the portfolio as a whole.

- When assurance is required of how the mix of projects continues to support strategy and take account of changes to external factors.

- Where the need exists for the organisation to effectively discriminate correctly between activities that should be managed as projects and other activities that should be managed as non-project operations.

- A need for assessment and addressing of risks associated with the project portfolio, including the risk of corporate failure needs to be highlighted and monitored.

- Provide verification that projects and programmes are consistent with the organisation's existing capacity and capability.

- To allow the organisation's engagement with project suppliers to encourage a more sustainable portfolio by ensuring their early involvement and by a shared understanding of the risks and potential rewards.

- Provide more evidence that the organisation's engagement with its customers and engagement with the sources of finance for its projects encourages a sustainable portfolio.

- Assurance that the impact of implementing a project portfolio is acceptable to its ongoing operations.

Applying portfolio management allows organisations to:

- drive priorities for change by adopting a high level 'whole picture' view of their business and how it must react to change;

- make the best decisions using information that is clear and representative of the true potential effect of key business drivers;

- use the most appropriate resources to achieve the best results with the least amount of wasted effort.

Corporate leaders are accountable for demonstrating profitability and return on investment, and therefore view project work as a critical part of delivering that investment and contributing to the overall benefit of the organisation. Portfolios play an important part in maintaining the alignment between project work and strategic objectives and in enabling the realisation of the benefits that underpin the successful capture of the intended value and securing the return on investment.

2.1.2 Learning summary

The section of the guide that you have just read will provide you with the learning necessary to be assessed against the following learning outcome and assessment criteria:

3. Understand the situational context of projects.

3.1 *Differentiate between projects and business-as-usual (BAU).*

In some organisations where there is a very high intensity of projects being delivered it can sometimes seem as if there is no BAU. It is as if delivering projects is actually BAU. All organisations must have a BAU despite the number of projects being delivered. It is BAU that is the legal entity, provides financial management, human resources services such as recruitment and payroll, marketing, which may be the reason why projects are being delivered in the first place, and of course the legal structure, which pays taxes and ensures regulatory compliance. Learners should become familiar with their organisation structure out with individual projects and think of that as BAU.

3.2 *Differentiate between project management, portfolio management and programme management.*

At its simplest form one organisation could have a single portfolio containing one or more programmes that support the strategic vision and intent of the organisation. Each programme is then broken down into its constituent projects, all of which will be undertaken in addition to the normal operations of the organisation. Management of the relationships between the programmes, projects and BAU is normally the responsibility of a senior management team within the organisation concerned, who will be carrying out portfolio management.

3.3 *Outline the relationship between programmes, projects and strategic change.*

Projects deliver outputs, programmes deliver outcomes and portfolios make sure that everything that is delivered is delivered in the most efficient way and prioritised in relation to the strategic objectives of the whole organisation. Programmes deliver strategic benefits, but they are only able to do that if each project within the programme yields the benefits as stated in the business case for that project. Without programme management each project would be delivered when it was completed. Without that coordination of delivery, projects would risk 'colliding' with each other as BAU struggle to cope with the number of projects being delivered at any one time. The effects could be delays in projects reaching their operating levels, lack of synergies in delivery of projects, lower levels of benefits realisation than expected, poor return on investment and higher operating costs.

3.4 *Describe situations where the use of programme management may be appropriate.*

Programmes are groups of related projects and business-as-usual (or steady-state) activities that together achieve beneficial change for an organisation. Programme management activity ensures that the selection of projects and other work in business-as-usual is structured in way that ensures benefits can be delivered incrementally over time. It is almost like the programme manager is the 'air traffic controller' of the organisation's projects, making sure that they are delivered in the most efficient way possible. Actions taken by programme management might mean slowing projects down, speeding others up and even stopping some to ensure that benefits realisation is maximised, taking advantage of all opportunities that may exist to exploit available synergies.

3.5 *Describe situations where the use of portfolio management may be appropriate.*

Portfolios are groupings of projects and/or programmes managed at an organisational or functional level in order to select, prioritise and control deployment in line with strategic objectives and the capacity to deliver. The goal of portfolio management is to balance change initiatives and business-as-usual while optimising return on investment.

The rationale for a portfolio is fundamentally different from that of a project or programme. Where projects and programmes are focused on deployment of outputs, and outcomes and benefits, respectively, portfolios exist as coordinating structures to support deployment by ensuring the optimal prioritisation of resources to align with strategic intent and achieve best value. It is common for portfolios to exist as a mechanism for ensuring delivery of organisational strategy when this relies on the deployment of programmes and projects in multiple functions and business units.

2.1.3 Organisation structures

The organisation structure defines the reporting and decision-making hierarchy of an organisation and how project management operates within it.

Organisations have multiple functional departments within them, such as finance, IT and human resources. These functions provide the structure within which resources and processes are brought together to perform work. Project management cuts across functional boundaries, and the ease or difficulty with which this occurs is influenced by the way the organisation is structured.

Differences between types of permanent and temporary organisation structures

Organisational structures define how roles, responsibilities and power are assigned and controlled to achieve strategic objectives, and how information flows between different levels of management.

For routine/operational work, the chosen 'permanent' organisational structure provides a relatively stable environment to support decision making and the flow of information across the organisation. Most organisations adopt a matrix-type structure, with individual operational units supported by functions that set policy and manage controls across each part of the operation.

Projects are temporary endeavours and therefore, by definition, have a temporary structure established by the people in the permanent organisation to manage activities and resources to deliver specific objectives within predetermined time frames. Temporary structures adopted for projects, programmes or portfolios typically do not adopt the same structure as the permanent organisation, but need to be coordinated.

Project managers work across both temporary and permanent structures and the ease or difficulty with which this occurs is influenced by the way the organisation aligns and balances its organisational structures and resourcing strategy. As project-based working spans functions, it is vital that the accountability of both permanent and temporary structures is clearly communicated. The choices of permanent to temporary organisation structures lie on a continuum with the permanent functional structure at one extreme and project at the other. At the middle point there is the matrix structure, one of the most common temporary structures used to manage projects, where authority is balanced between functional and project manager. The relative authority between functional manager and project manager determines where the particular choice of organisation structure lies on the continuum as shown in Figure 2.1.3.1.

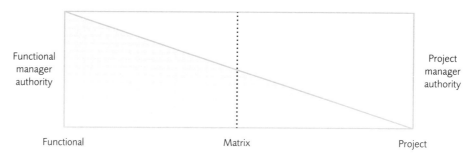

Figure 2.1.3.1 The continuum of organisation structure to manage projects

Functional structure

In this structure, people are divided into groups largely along functional lines and work together to carry out the same or similar functions. In organisations where the functional divisions are relatively rigid, project work can either be performed within a functional department itself or handed from one functional team to another in order to complete the work.

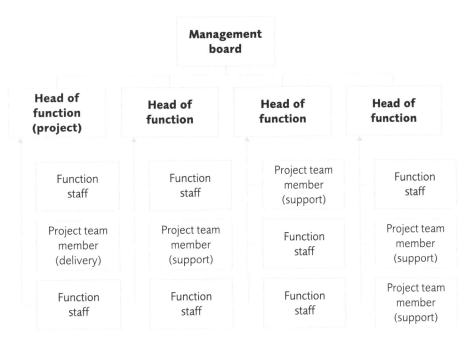

Figure 2.1.3.2 Project management within a functional structure

The head of the functional area would take overall responsibility for project delivery. A member of the department would be assigned to deliver the project, acting as the project manager, although may not carry that title, most probably they would maintain whatever title accompanies their role within the department. The funding would come directly from the operating budget for the department, but there may be a supplementary fund provided directly by the board of the organisation if the degree of change was a one-off exception. In this respect the head of the department is acting as project sponsor.

The strength of this approach is that the people with the technical skills in the department are delivering a project requiring these skills. The project is actually very close to business-as-usual (BAU) but has the characteristics of a project in that it has time, cost and quality constraints. The main weakness of this approach is setting of priorities between the project and BAU, considering that staff may not appreciate project working, particularly if the project has a low visibility within the overall department or organisation. Depending on the culture of the organisation, it is common that functional departments work in silos and so may be unwilling to supply resources to support projects in other parts of the organisation, especially if they feel their department has very little to gain from the project.

Matrix structure

The matrix structure is one of the structures most commonly found in projects. Team members may report to different managers for different aspects of their work on the project. Team members are responsible to the project manager for their part in the project, while their functional line manager will be responsible for other aspects of their work such as appraising their performance, training and routine day-to-day tasks. The project manager may be appointed from one of the functional areas or may be contracted into the organisation just for the period of the project duration.

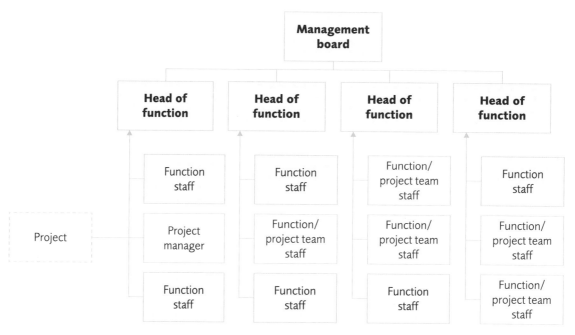

Figure 2.1.3.3 Project management within a matrix structure

In this form of organisational structure staff are assigned to the project to perform their role within it; once this duty has been completed, they would return to the main organisation structure and continue their role there or be assigned to start working on another project.

The strength of this approach is that the project is likely to be visible to the whole organisation, rather than just an individual department as in the functional structure. It also creates the need for organisations to manage resources more effectively to the degree that project work does not adversely affect BAU. Staff become aware of project working and movement from project to project becomes the norm.

While the matrix structure is particularly effective its common disadvantage is that when an individual is working on the project, they are reporting to the project manager as well as their functional line manager (dual reporting) and there can be conflict of priorities. The solution commonly in solving the two-boss problem lies undoubtedly in ensuring the existence of good interpersonal relationships as well as regular effective communication between all areas of the organisation, which results in more complex communication channels than would exist in a functional structure, for example. Along similar lines the project manager is usually not the line manager of the project team members and so has no structural power to wield to get things done. The matrix structure relies on project managers understanding how they can influence others in the absence of organisational authority within line management.

Project/product structure

In this structure the organisation is made up of projects, each having a project manager or project director, depending on the size of the project, reporting directly into the board of what is often a holding company. The structure consists of groups of people who are all dedicated only to the project assigned and report to the project director on a daily basis. All work is project related and once the project is completed (projects using this structure may last for many years) that part of the organisation ceases to exist.

	Management board		
DIRECTOR PROJECT A	**DIRECTOR PROJECT B**	**DIRECTOR PROJECT C**	**DIRECTOR PROJECT D**
Project A team member	Project B team member	Project C team member	Project D team member
Project A team member	Project B team member	Project C team member	Project D team member
Project A team member	Project B team member	Project C team member	Project D team member

The main strength of this structure is focus on the project, there is no other objective such as BAU, loyalty is absolutely to the project. Projects may have their own equivalent of BAU service functions such as procurement, finance, human resources as well as specialist technical expertise. Clear project processes combined with well-defined roles and responsibilities mean that teams become technically proficient.

In this type of structure, the strengths can become the weaknesses. The very strong job security while the project is being carried out is then a weakness at project completion when there is no longer a requirement for the people who were employed in delivery. Projects can also become very insular and not communicate with each other this can lead to underutilisation of staff overall as availability in one project is not used to solve a need in another. Once each project is completed, teams will leave on mass and the organisation may not get the opportunity to maintain the learning gained by the individuals while working on the project.

2.1.3 Learning summary

The section of the guide that you have just read will provide you with the learning necessary to be assessed against the following learning outcome and assessment criteria:

1. Understand how organisations and projects are structured.

1.1 *Differentiate between types of permanent and temporary organisation structures (including functional, matrix and project).*

Learners should appreciate the reasons why certain structures exist and why one type of structure may be considered more suitable than another. Also, it could be possible for a single organisation to adopt all three structures in different situations and to deliver effectively under varying circumstances.

Typically, the low-level complexity and value of the project make the functional structure ideal for a small, mainly internal project, which although has typical project characteristics is in reality very close to business-as-usual activity. The level of project process discussed throughout this study guide would be unlikely to be needed for these types of projects. The matrix structure has projects that alternatively may need considerably more project process application. The widest range of projects that would be internal or carried out for clients of an organisation (external), could be delivered effectively using a matrix structure. The key aspect is visibility of the project to the wider organisation and that two management structures exist alongside each other, the delivery organisation functional structure and the project organisation structure, both of which are integrated using matrix principles.

Finally, the project/product structure, which is the least common as it would only be the largest of enterprises that would justify this type of structure or where the project was particularly high value, complex and had multiple parties involved in its creation. Here the project is the organisation structure, there is no other entity involved in project delivery. An online search will show some of the classic examples of these types of projects, which go into history as examples of mega enterprises lasting for years and costing billions.

2.1.4 Project roles

One of the biggest challenges faced by the project manager in creating the project organisation is defining the roles that are necessary – a decision that will be informed by the scale of the project to be delivered. In most cases the project sponsor and project manager are required. Thereafter a number of other roles may be considered based on the project's needs. The project has a different culture from the day-to-day organisation. Most of the roles are cross-functional team activities, where the traditional organisational hierarchy dissolves. Distinct roles need to be clearly defined and the relationship between them fully established; this not only promotes teamwork but ensures a complete coverage of responsibilities and ownership. A typical project organisation structure is shown in Figure 2.1.4.1.

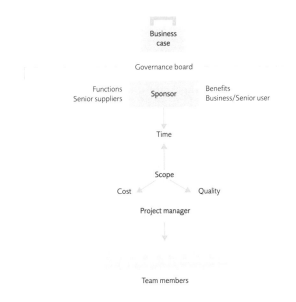

Figure 2.1.4.1 Example project management roles and structure

The role and the key responsibilities of the project manager

The project manager's role is to plan, organise, staff, motivate, evaluate, direct, control and lead the project from start to finish and to deliver the project objectives.

Project manager responsibilities include:

- delivering the project to time, cost and quality/performance priorities;
- making timely decisions to ensure project success;
- communicating with the sponsor, informing them of progress and seeking direction when necessary to aid success;
- managing sponsor and user expectations;
- defining and planning the project through the creation of the Project Management Plan;
- monitoring and controlling project progress;
- building, leading and motivating the project team throughout the project;
- ensuring work packages are allocated and the responsibilities identified;

- keeping the sponsor and senior management informed of progress/problems/issues;

- initiating reviews and assisting the sponsor in the decision to terminate the project, if justified;

- communicating and acting as prime point of contact with team members, other organisations, contractors, suppliers and operations representatives, etc.

The role and key responsibilities of the project sponsor throughout the project

The sponsor is the individual considered as the primary risk taker and has ultimate accountability and overall responsibility for the project. The sponsor will most likely have managed the project through the concept phase, once the business case has been approved a project manager will be appointed to take over delivery of the project. The sponsor still remains accountable for ensuring that the project's benefits are realised, when the project is handed over to operations.

The sponsor is a member of and has the delegated authority of the steering group, as a chairperson, to assist with business management and project management issues that arise outside the formal duties of the steering group. The sponsor also lends support by advocacy at senior level and ensures that the necessary resources (both financial and human) are available to the project. The project champion, corporate client, functional head of department may have the same responsibilities as a project sponsor in some projects.

Sponsor responsibilities include:

- being the arbiter for user and stakeholder requirements through chairing of the steering group;

- determining the relative priority of time cost and quality;

- initiating the project and ensuring a project manager is appointed;

- monitoring high-level project progress and making control decisions when necessary and when escalated by the project manager;

- monitoring the project's business environment and reviewing the business case at gate reviews;

- keeping senior management informed of project progress;

- terminating the project if necessary, after a gate review;

- providing ongoing support to the project manager;

- liaising with the programme manager if the project is part of a programme;

- developing and maintaining ownership of the business case.

Other roles within project management

Users

User(s) are accountable for specifying operational requirements and for accepting and operating the deliverables to achieve the defined benefits.

User(s) responsibilities include:

- identifying project requirements, ensuring objective separation of 'musts' and 'wants';

- identifying project constraints and dependencies;

- accepting and operating the deliverables;

- providing practical assistance and guidance through a user representative or senior user as part of the steering group structure, if it exists;

- assisting the project manager with handover/acceptance;

- informing the project manager of any operational changes that may influence delivery;

- actively participating as a member of the project team.

Project team members

Project team members may stay with the project throughout its life or may only join the team to carry out a specific task. The primary role of the project team is to support the project manager in managing the project to meet its objectives, by providing the combined expertise to allow the project objectives and scope to be correctly identified and achieved.

Specific responsibilities may include:

- managing communication with stakeholders as assigned in the communication plan;

- managing sections of the work breakdown structure (identifying tasks, estimating, monitoring, problem solving, ensuring completion of quality, on time and within budget);

- acting as risk owner and effectively managing risk within their area of expertise;

- supporting the project manager and other team members in solving project-wide problems (acting as action owners);

- contributing to the evaluation of the project at all stages and reviews;

- reporting progress of their assigned tasks in a timely manner.

Project steering group/board

A project steering group, also known as the governance board, project board or steering committee, is the key body within the governance structure that is responsible for the business issues associated with the project that are essential to ensure the delivery of the project outputs and the attainment of project outcomes. This includes approving the budgetary strategy, defining and realising benefits, monitoring risks, quality and timelines, making policy and resourcing decisions, and assessing requests for changes to the scope of the project that have potential to impact the business case.

The membership is often determined by the project sponsor, who normally chairs group meetings and may consist of:

- the organisations business unit managers/owners;

- representatives from selected key stakeholders;

- experts from within the organisation; and

- external, independent representatives, who may be quality auditors, consultants, specialist consultants or representatives from other agencies;

- representatives from key suppliers to the project, these could be internal or external;

- representatives from the user population.

MANAGEMENT

The project manager is not a member of the steering group, but is 'contracted' by the steering group to ensure the work of the project is undertaken as agreed, whereas the steering group provides support, guidance and the executive oversighting of progress. The project manager will normally attend meetings of the steering group to answer any questions raised by members.

An additional resource (such as a project team member or administrative staff) may attend to assist the project manager by recording the minutes and decisions of the meeting. Collectively, a steering group's role is to:

- take on responsibility for the project's feasibility, business case and achievement of outcomes;

- ensure the project's scope aligns with the agreed requirements of the business owners and key stakeholder groups;

- provide those directly involved in the project with strategic guidance on project business issues;

- ensure effort and expenditure are appropriate to stakeholder expectations;

- ensure that strategies to address potential threats to the project's success have been identified, costed and approved, and that the threats are regularly re-assessed;

- address any issues that have been escalated from the project manager and assess any major implications for the project;

- keep the project scope under control as emergent issues may force changes to be considered;

- reconcile differences in opinion and approach and resolve disputes arising from them;

- report on project progress to those responsible at a high level, such as executive management groups; and depending on the nature of the project, take on responsibility for progressing any organisation wide issues associated with the project.

It is really only large projects that would justify the inclusion of a steering group within the structure; however, all projects, regardless of scale, would need to ensure compliance with whatever governance framework the host organisation required.

Product owner

Often categorised as a part of the overall 'supplier' input, the product owner's main contribution is to lead the focus on product development. Very much part of an agile approach, they have strong expertise and deep knowledge of stakeholders needs and can act as the intermediary between stakeholders and those team members delivering the project.

Product owner responsibilities include:

- defining goals and creating vision for the operability of the project's outputs;

- acting as the on-site customer for iterative or agile projects;

- communicating with stakeholders to ensure that the project remains aligned with business objectives;

- providing feedback to the project team on iteration planning, task dependencies, constraints, priority and progress in relation to business needs;

- establishing priorities for scope, budget and time with relation to stakeholder requirements and accepting incremental delivery;

- acting as the primary communication link between stakeholders and teams, ensuring stakeholder buy-in linking major decisions with strategy and providing clear instructions and an outline of deliverables to product developers;

- evaluate progress providing feedback to the team on delivery performance and advising if continuation is feasible.

2.1.4.1 The project management office (PMO)

When an organisation is responsible for delivering many simultaneous projects there will be management tasks that are common to all of these projects. Other common areas could include information management, services for governance, reporting and general administration. It could benefit an organisation if these common needs could be brought together to form a central core of services to all projects the organisation delivers. This could be achieved through the creation of a project management office (PMO).

The functions and benefits of different types of project office

There are many variants of such a structure that could provide support for projects, programmes and portfolios: project management office, programme management office or portfolio management office, depending on what is being supported. The personnel may range from a single person to a large team containing many different roles and specialists including, among others:

- estimators;

- planners and schedulers;

- cost engineers;

- subject matter experts;

- assurance staff;

- configuration managers.

The payback gained by any organisation undertaking considerable investment in a PMO could be improved deployment support, process improvement and increased resource flexibility. In addition, PMOs can provide access to services that might never be justified for a single project, for example:

- Controls and reporting – collecting, analysing and presenting progress information and managing interdependencies.

- Assurance – audits, health checks and reviews to support decision gates and change control.

- Centre of excellence – improving processes, tools and techniques; embedding best practice through training and support; and measuring capabilities to review progress and target higher levels of maturity.

- Specialist support – provision of specialist skills such as risk; quality, planning or finance resources as role models to other project professionals.

- Information management – document management and access to information, tools and services.

There are three typical ways that PMOs are organised and funded (Figure 2.1.4.2):

Embedded PMO: Where the majority of PMO functions are delivered under the control of the project/programme/portfolio manager, with only organisation-wide elements such as processes defined at a higher level. Effective on large projects that need lots of support and can justify the investment.

Central PMO: Where the majority of PMO functions sit outside of the project teams, providing a service to multiple projects. Effective when there is a portfolio of small projects, where flexibility is valued more than management control.

Hub-and-spoke PMO: A hybrid form with a central enterprise or portfolio PMO linked to satellite PMOs within individual projects and/or programmes. Effective when there are clear roles and responsibilities between managers and the PMO to ensure processes and information are managed effectively.

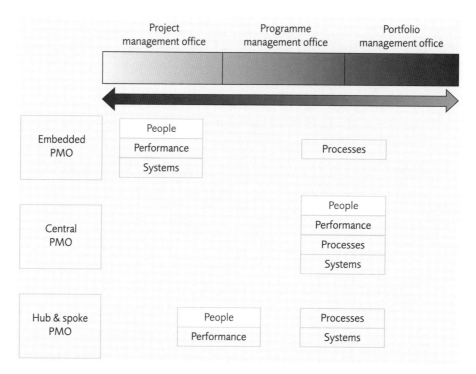

Figure 2.1.4.2 Different forms of PMO

2.1.4.2 Governance

Governance is the framework of authority and accountability that defines and controls the outputs, outcomes and benefits from projects, programmes and portfolios. It is the mechanism whereby the investing organisation exerts financial and technical control over the deployment of the work and the realisation of value. Just about everything that is covered in this guide falls into the domain of governance and particularly this section, describing responsibilities and support structures for the project is very much originated from the organisation's governance of project management principles.

Why aspects of project management governance are required?

When effectively implemented, governance provides confidence to all stakeholders that projects are being managed well and that the most appropriate financial and technical controls are being exerted to ensure that the deployment of effort has the best chance of leading to a realisation of value.

The part of governance that is most applicable to projects originates from business change governance. Another part is corporate governance, which sets out the responsibilities of those individuals who establish the vision, mission and strategy of the whole organisation: the board. They will provide the necessary leadership to put governance into effect, supervising the management of the business and reporting periodically to shareholders. Corporate governance is therefore about what the board of a company does and how it sets the values of the company, to be distinguished from the business-as-usual governance that focuses on the day-to-day operational management of the company by full-time departmental managers.

For listed companies in the UK, corporate governance forms part of a legal requirement, and the UK Corporate Governance Code sets out standards of good practice in relation to aspects such as leadership, effectiveness, accountability, remuneration and relations with shareholders.

The governance of project management will be implemented in each individual project as a result of the organisations policies. This will influence each project in a number of ways, for example:

- Projects will have a relevant business case to secure funding and assess initial and ongoing feasibility.

- All projects will follow a recognised project life cycle, used to transfer governance to each project through phases with various control points, such as gate reviews, audits and evaluation reviews.

- Organisations will seek to agree a structured methodology for the delivery of projects ensuring that there is consistency of practice throughout the whole organisation.

- Clearly defined processes and documentation, maintained throughout the delivery of the project, such as the project management plan, will ensure that all project management activities are undertaken to best practice principles.

- More effective decision making at stage gates, ensure the sponsor can initiate a review of the project taking account of the current environment and impact of change.

- Reporting and escalation routes with clearly defined roles and responsibilities will ensure prompt attention and control of risk and issues.

- Effective quality management ensuring the effective use of quality assurance and independent audit.

When governance is working well, it provides sufficient reporting and control activities to ensure that the sponsor and other senior leaders/stakeholders are kept informed of relevant progress and are provided with the information they need to make decisions about future investment in the project, programme or portfolio.

2.1.4 Learning summary

The section of the guide that you have just read will provide you with the learning necessary to be assessed against the following learning outcome and assessment criteria:

1. **Understand how organisations and projects are structured.**

1.3 *Explain the role and key responsibilities of the project manager.*

While learners may be familiar, through personal experience, with the role of the project manager it is often the case that this title is used widely by organisations as a catch all. It might be that after reading through a learning resource like this that a vast array of wider-ranging responsibilities become apparent. Realising that the project manager is more of a generalist than a focused technical expert is often a challenging part of the role especially to those who may have entered project management with a strongly focused technical background.

Having an insight into how the project manager will have ownership of and form the PMP, when this will happen and who else might be involved is powerful knowledge in this area. Accept that there will be a degree of dependency the project manager will have on other stakeholders, and while some will see this as a vulnerability of the role, it does in reality make for a most successful project outcome.

1.4 *Differentiate between the responsibilities of the project manager and the project sponsor throughout the project.*

The role of the sponsor is often not fully understood. Learners should see that there are some distinct differences between sponsorship and project management. The role of sponsor is to implement strategic decision making for budget, benefits, risk and the realisation and maximisation of value as documented in the business case. The project manager on the other hand is more tactical, getting the work done. The relationship between these two key players in the project team should not be seen as a line management relationship; in most cases the sponsor will not be the boss of the project manager. The relationship should be more of a partnership where both parties are clear on their distinct responsibilities through different phases of the project life cycle.

1.5 *Describe other roles within project management (including users, project team members, the project steering group/board and the product owner).*

The project team will be formed by a number of clearly defined roles. These roles all have distinct responsibilities. See the project organisation structure as evolving rather than being an all or nothing. As the project progresses through concept into definition, more and more additional roles will become necessary. The expertise and insight each provide adds value to the overall management task.

1.6 *Describe the functions and benefits of different types of project office (including project/programme/portfolio management office (PMO), embedded PMO, central PMO and hub-and-spoke PMO).*

The overarching theme of this section is to illustrate how the provision of a solid project-supporting structure is essential for project success. Clear responsibilities and governance are essential but, in some cases, this support may also be extended to a PMO. Not all organisations will have a PMO, the nature of the projects they do, just don't merit that level of investment. But for those that do, the key aspect here is that it can vary widely in its size, capability and the role it provides to projects, programmes and in some cases even to the portfolio level. There is no 'one size fits all'. Learners should be familiar with the common aims of the PMO and think about how projects in their own organisations could benefit from a single source of project support, if it were justified of course.

1.7 *Explain why aspects of project management governance are required (such as the use of: policies, regulations, functions, processes, procedures and delegated responsibilities).*

Governance of project management is often not directly visible on a day-to-day basis to the project manager, although that's the way it should be. There is a perception that governance equates to the rules and bureaucracy that burden the project, slow down decision making and ensure that every box is ticked even when a tick was unnecessary. What learners should appreciate is that governance is there to support project management, improve performance, to assist in decision making and, rather than being seen as something different from project management, it is in fact *project management!* Of chief importance is the way governance manifests itself in the day-to-day running of the project from processes and procedures, roles and responsibilities and conformance to standards of risk and quality management, through to reporting and managing information.

2.1.5 Business case

The business case provides justification for undertaking a project or programme. It evaluates the benefit, cost and risk of alternative options and provides a rationale for the preferred solution. The earliest phase of the project life cycle provides the opportunity for the project to evaluate the options that may be available. These options would have been generated by a review of the environmental stimulus creating the need to consider a change in the first place; the environment is creating the problem, opportunity or business need that the change should address.

How does each project business case help an organisation?

All organisations, either private or public must require accountability for how funds are used and the level of returns gained from these funding decisions. The business case provides a recognised framework by which project spending proposals can be recorded, reviewed and audited to learn lessons about how efficiently the organisation is deploying funds to achieve its targeted returns.

The business case will be referred to throughout the project in order to make decisions about the continuing viability of supporting the change initiative. It will be used during reviews and act as a baseline for checking ongoing viability of the project. These reviews will be carried out at the end of major project phases and prior to starting phases all with the intention of avoiding continuing investment when perhaps there appears to be no reasonable way that the project will achieve the returns that justify such funding. A decision to terminate a project could be for a number of reasons. A changing economic environment may cause increases in the cost of providing funding and therefore increase overall costs to an unacceptable level. The output being delivered may be forecast to not deliver the benefits that were planned. Societal trends may mean that the output is no longer a desirable commodity for the intended user population.

Business case and strategy

The approach, to ensure that the decision to approve a business case is most valid, should take account of several different viewpoints. Typically, there are five key questions that need to be answered in order to consider any proposed change requiring significant financial investment:

- How does it support or fit with the long-term strategic goals of the organisation? (Strategic case)

- Does it represent the optimum value for money or can a greater return be gained elsewhere? (Economic case)

- What are the factors that influence the commercial viability of the proposal and can they be sensibly realised? (Commercial case)

- Is the level of funding required actually available either through existing capital reserves or borrowed funds and what impact does this have on the overall affordability of the proposal? (Financial case)

- How will the change be delivered and by whom and do we have the existing capability to deliver such an extent of change? (Management case)

This multi-dimensional approach, known as the Five Case Model and shown in Figure 2.1.5.1, is used by the British Government in the guidance it provides internally to those who have the responsibility for making investment decisions.

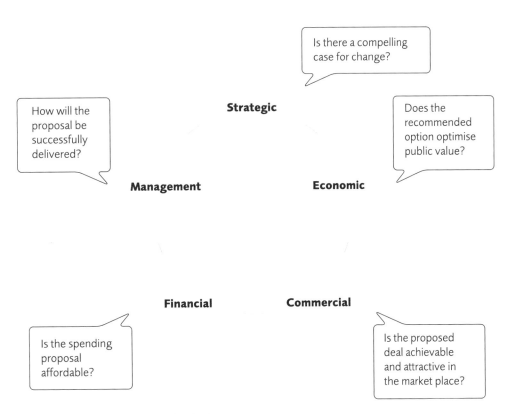

Figure 2.1.5.1 Five dimensions used in the business case

The majority of the effort in business case production will usually be at its greatest within the concept phase of the project life cycle. Early concept may form a strategic outline case (SOC), further refined to become the outline business case (OBC) and finally towards the end of the phase where the final business case (FBC) is agreed and funding approved.

Who is involved in developing and producing the business case?

As well as a structured approach to business case development, the views of key stakeholders will also be essential. This will ensure that the business case that has been approved is seen as a realistic proposition by those who may have influence in resulting project deployment and actual transition of the output into operational use and subsequent benefits realisation.

The following stakeholders may be involved in business case development and contribute to its content:

Project steering group (project board) – The members of the project steering group are often made up of corporate management who in their monitoring of the organisation's external or internal business environment have defined a need to consider that change options should be explored.

Project sponsor – Appointed by the steering group and considered as the owner of the business case, the sponsor will lead its development during the concept phase of the project. At the end of concept, the business case may be approved by the steering group and funding released in order that the project proceeds to detailed planning in the Definition phase.

Project manager – While there may be a sound business case from a financial point of view, this becomes meaningless if there has been no recognition of how the resultant project is going to actually be managed and delivered. The project manager will be appointed by the sponsor and

MANAGEMENT

will contribute detail about the reality of delivering such a change. In some cases, where the project is a smaller internal project within a functional department of the organisation, the project manager may write the business case under the direction of the functional manager. In this case the project manager may solicit the input of others in the organisation to form the business case content, but it should always be the functional manager (in effect the sponsor) who will remain accountable for the business case realising the benefits planned.

Other business case contributors

An effective business case results from the consideration of alternative options but added to that must be the number of stakeholders who may influence either the project output or benefits realisation when the output becomes operable. Other key contributors could be:

- Users – they will be key to providing the sponsor with insight as to how the output will be operated within business-as-usual. It is their perspective that will add most value to the project and be key to benefits realisation.

- Business analyst – may be an internal role or brought into the organisation as an external consultant, and provides a vital link between the project, its stakeholders and both the internal and external environments. A strength of a skilled business analyst is the experience they may have gained in other projects and the implementation of these lessons learned in planning a new project.

- Subject matter experts – these stakeholders could provide expertise in such areas as procurement, human resources, finance, specific technical areas and process application.

- Suppliers – can sometimes be used as a blanket term when describing some of the roles above. Any stakeholder who has the capacity to input significant detailed knowledge to make the writing of the business case possible and to add value to the decision making, could be considered a supplier. This term will also extend to suppliers in the traditional sense, providers of resources, materials and equipment, for example.

Taking account of this wide range of contribution can increase the objectivity, impartiality and stability of a business case throughout the life cycle of the project.

Typical business case content

At the highest level the business case will show the level of investment required, the change intended and the resulting benefits. An environmental analysis may show the distinct background and business drivers stimulating the organisation at this time. The detail of how this is documented can vary depending on the business sector of the sponsoring organisation and the level of accountability expected. There are, however, some fundamental aspects that would be common to most business situations.

Background/situation – this will capture the essence of why the project is needed. Information such as environmental analysis, market situation and the output of any research studies that have been carried out. The information in this section should be quite categoric as to the problem, opportunity or business need the project is intended to address.

Benefits – crucial to ultimate feasibility. Full agreement of how the benefits will be realised, measured and the stakeholders involved.

Budget – the funds that are expected to be consumed as a result of delivering the project. There may also be contingency allowances taking account of uncertainties. As the project progresses further through its life cycle more granular cost estimates will be produced and reflected to the business case budget. This information should be sufficient for stakeholders to understand the operations and sustainment required to utilise the new project and enable the acceptance and use of the benefits.

Risks – the longer the timescale of the project, the more difficult it may be to identify the level of uncertainty and the most effective approach. Business case risks are most important to identify. If they can't be mitigated at this stage, it may mean that the project is abandoned, or a less risky strategy pursued.

Options appraisal – the strength of any business case is increased when a full range of possible options has been considered. This shows that the organisation has not become embedded into a single tracked idea, but that it has reflected on what other options may be possible with the available funds. The do-nothing option may also be considered. When the final business case is ultimately produced, it is approved not only on the basis of being a good idea in itself, but that in relation to alternatives it was the strongest option. It is common that options will be subject to a financial appraisal considering relative costs in relation to time and the phasing of return value. Options appraisal is a major part of justification for the chosen option to proceed.

Additional content – as well as the above the business case may also document information on timeline, success criteria, stakeholders, constraints, assumptions, dependencies and details of any plans.

Importance of a business case throughout the project life cycle

When a business case for a project is weak or ill defined, that project will always have difficulties in being subsequently delivered, and is unlikely to realise the benefits that justify the committed investment. A valid business case, therefore, is not just vital in deciding options; it should be used throughout all phases of the project to monitor the feasibility of continuation and the ongoing viability of the project output at the time of its completion. The business case should be considered as a contract between the project and the business so that stakeholders are clear on what benefits should be achieved once the project has delivered the outputs. It is important therefore for the business case to be used throughout the life cycle to confirm continuation of the project. The business case will be used in the following phases:

Concept – the business case should be considered as the launchpad for the project, fully justifying the investment and stating explicitly why the project should be delivered and its importance to the sponsoring organisation.

Definition – as a response to the business case, the appointed project manager will develop the project management plan (PMP). A thorough business case will ensure that an effective PMP will be developed acknowledging the project manager's acceptance that the defined success criteria and related performance requirements are indeed a realistic proposition. The business case will be used at gate reviews to ensure continued viability of the project.

Deployment – at various stages of deployment, plans will be implemented and performance verified through testing and assurance. As outputs are developed it is important to establish the feasibility of subsequent outcomes and benefits post transition. Reference to the business case is key to the most effective decisions being made and continuation confirmed.

Transition – it is at this phase where most funding has been consumed and it is hoped that the intended output is likely to achieve the outcomes and benefits the business needs. The business case will be important here as the main reference to review how the benefits are being realised compared to what was expected by stakeholders as documented in the business case.

2.1.5.1 Benefits management

In most cases a project is initiated in order to deliver change and beneficial outcomes to the sponsoring organisation. The business case documents a detailed account of the decision making that has underpinned the project to the point where benefits realisation is possible. Benefits realisation is the practice of ensuring that benefits are derived from outputs and outcomes and is essential to support the achievement of the business case.

Once the outputs have been handed over or transitioned into business-as-usual, these need to be used to realise the benefits that the organisation invested in. This may be at the end of the work, or during the work in the case of projects and programmes that use an iterative life cycle and are able to deliver intermediate benefits early and incrementally, potentially by concentrating on creating a minimum viable product.

Adoption is dependent on the recipients of the change being ready to accept and use the outputs in the intended way. Ongoing support is usually also needed to ensure that new routines are established that use the new process/system/product/ways of working in the intended way. Some organisations manage this work through their normal business operations. Others choose an 'extended life cycle' deployment approach for a single project or programme that ensures that accountability and governance of the investment stays with the change team until fully embedded.

Organisations that are committed to driving through the realisation of benefits devise methods for managing benefits, which involve tracking and measuring the benefits that were promised at the last decision gate and included in the business case. It is at the point of adoption that any failure to keep the business case up to date in the light of changes during the process will be highlighted – the type or quantum of benefit may well change over time and expectations need to be managed through governance.

During its development the business case should contain detail of the upfront plan for any supplemental activities and additional considerations necessary in order for the project output to be in the optimal state for benefits realisation to be possible. Income expected and any operational costs connected to additional activities, including capital expenditure, should also be considered.

Benefits management is the identification, definition, planning, tracking and realisation of benefits. A project that is only responsible for delivering outputs interfaces with the entity responsible for delivering the benefits. This may be a programme, portfolio or business-as-usual organisation.

During the investment appraisal of project options, the business case for the project depends on stakeholders, such as business change managers reflecting enough to accurately attribute benefits at the right level – avoiding aspects that yield value being missed or 'double-counted'.

A benefits management plan ensures that there is a proactive management approach to maintain a focus on benefits driven change throughout the entire project life cycle. The relationship between the project or programme manager and the business change manager is crucial. The delivery of outputs and the management of change must be closely coordinated. Benefits management is an iterative process with five main steps as illustrated in Figure 2.1.5.2.

Figure 2.1.5.2 Benefits management process

Benefits management plan – this explains how benefits will be managed. It sets out policies for aspects such as measurement, roles and responsibilities, priorities and key performance indicators (KPIs).

Identification – requirements are captured from sources such as the project mandate and stakeholders. Benefits depend on the delivery of outputs and the achievement of outcomes. At this stage benefits are recorded together with justification and outline measurement criteria.

Definition – the project manager should be aware of just how benefits will be realised when the project reaches transition into operational use. The interrelationships between these need to be understood through benefits modelling and mapping. Each benefit (and disbenefit) should be documented in terms of priority, interdependencies, value, timescales and ownership.

Planning – this step involves capturing baseline measurements and agreeing targets. Baseline measurements identify the current performance of an operation so that improvements can be measured. The benefits plan illustrates the timeline and milestones for realising benefits, including any dependencies on project outputs or interactions between benefits.

Tracking – the project manager and the sponsor agree what benefits are tracked and how. This happens in early life cycle to enable the necessary baseline measures to be set up. Some benefits are tracked using qualitative indicators, for example customer satisfaction scores, in addition to financial or non-financial quantification, for example increased revenues or percentage increase in proposals that are converted into sales. The sponsor is accountable for ensuring that benefits tracking and reporting is effective as a part of good governance. This applies irrespective of whether benefits are being realised as planned or not.

Realisation – benefits happen when something changes. This usually involves permanently changing attitudes and behaviours as well as physical changes. While implementing change, new opportunities for additional benefits should always be sought. Long-term actions and monitoring for continued realisation should be documented as part of the handover to business-as-usual.

Effective benefits management is needed in all projects as an additional activity required to translate requirements that have been expressed in terms of benefits and manage them to successful deployment and realisation.

MANAGEMENT

2.1.5.2 Investment appraisal

One of the most difficult aspects for those responsible for making an investment decision is the measurement of the returns that need to be achieved by that investment for it to be considered worthwhile. There are various characteristics of the project that add to this difficulty, such as long timescale and the level of uncertainty. Different stakeholders will also have different views of what value means to them as far as their interest in the project.

Whether the investment is being made in the public, private or charities sector, the sponsor makes the case for how best value can be realised by deploying capital, operational expenditure and human resources to ultimately deliver an output with sufficient capability to return that investment. Private organisations almost always make their investment decisions based on financial consideration due to the requirements for financial self-sufficiency. Public organisations and charities are often more concerned with value-for-money service, affordability, non-financial considerations or maximising the benefits for a set budget, with the funding derived either from government or donations.

Investment appraisal techniques used by a project manager

The sponsor will attempt to balance all the necessary factors involved in developing the business case, but when evaluating the available options purely from a financial view point, there are a choice of financial appraisal techniques to evaluate and compare investment decisions, including absolute monetary values such as net present value (NPV) and relative indicators such as the internal rate of return (IRR). Organisations typically have defined hurdle rates in percentage terms for investments that represent the minimum target return on investment.

Net present value

This technique seeks to examine the value of the benefits that are likely to be received as a result of the output of the project going into use. These values are estimated each year of operational life for a period that is established as feasible for benefits realisation. At the end of this period it would be likely that the output would go into the termination phase and would no longer be yielding benefits.

A simplistic form of analysis could then ask whether, if all the years of return values were summed, that total amount would be more, less or equal to the amount that has been invested in producing the output in the first place. This calculation is simplistic because it ignores the fact that the initial investment capital will have cost the sponsoring organisation additional expense in either interest or opportunity cost. The longer that capital is outstanding the more the total costs of using the capital are accrued.

NPV seeks to identify the relationship between the original investment and the returns, taking account of time and opportunity cost, and is often referred to as calculating the time value of money. It does this by reducing the returns by an amount equivalent to what would have been gained by the investment had it been used in an alternative way or reducing the returns in relation to the cost of borrowing the capital. This reduction is referred to as discounting. The reduced returns are referred to as the discounted cash flow. The actual discount rate chosen is either the interest rate charged for the capital or the return rate expected by an alternative opportunity.

Consider the following simple example. You have £1,000 capital and can choose to invest it at 10 per cent per annum return or keep it in a safe place. Supposing on this occasion you decided to do the latter. At the end of that first year you would still have your £1,000 capital but could have gained £100 more had you invested. The fact that there was an alternative opportunity that you rejected has reduced the value of your capital amount through an opportunity cost. The extent of that reduction can be calculated as £1,000/£1100 = 0.909, which in effect means that the value of your £1,000 is now £909. If you continued your decision through to a second year, the comparison is now with the investment gaining a second year of compound interest, £1,000/£1210 = 0.826 and a third year, £1,000/£1331 = 0.751. What we have actually calculated is the discount factors for a 10 per cent investment providing returns over a three-year period. From purely an opportunity cost viewpoint your £1,000 after three years is now worth £751. It is important to note that you still have your £1,000 capital but have failed to gain the equivalent of £331 over that period. Discount factors for different time periods and interest rates can be predetermined and exist in discount tables or within financial software.

Table 2.1.5.1 shows the practical application of discount factors to calculate the NPV for an investment of £750,000 with variable returns (income) each year over four years at a discount rate of 10 per cent per annum.

Year	Income (£)	Discount factor	Present value (£) (Discounted cashflow)
1	50,000	0.909	45,450
2	500,000	0.826	413,000
3	250,000	0.751	187,750
4	100,000	0.683	68,300
Total	**900,000**		**714,500**
		Original investment	**−750,000**
		NPV =	**−35,500**

Table 2.1.5.1 Application of discount factors to calculate NPV

This example shows the real strength of using NPV and discount factors. The less financially astute might have considered the total income of £900,000 and accepted this investment bearing in mind that this figure is £150,000 more than the original investment. A good deal? Well, not if the cost of using the £750,000 capital is 10 per cent. In fact, this project would lose the investor £35,500, which is the NPV. This final figure of NPV can be negative as this example, or positive, which would mean the investment is yielding more than the discount rate, or zero, which would mean that the cash flow is yielding exactly the same rate as the discount factor being used to calculate the NPV.

Internal rate of return

Another technique that can be used to consider an investment from a slightly different point of view is internal rate of return (IRR). It calculates the average per-period rate of return on the capital invested. It is useful for comparing various investment options with equal timing and equal risk. Organisations will often have a target rate of return or hurdle rate that needs to be achieved as a minimum, before an option is pursued. This target rate will also take account of other factors such as risk, margin, inflation, currency exchanges and any other aspect known at the time of the appraisal. More specifically the IRR is the discount rate that causes an investment's NPV to be zero. In Table 2.1.5.1 above the NPV is a negative value, which means the actual IRR will be below 10 per cent. The actual return rate can be calculated graphically as shown in Figure 2.1.5.3 where we can see that if the option is calculated at different return rates, by trial and error we can define the point at which the NPV is zero. At this point we have found the IRR.

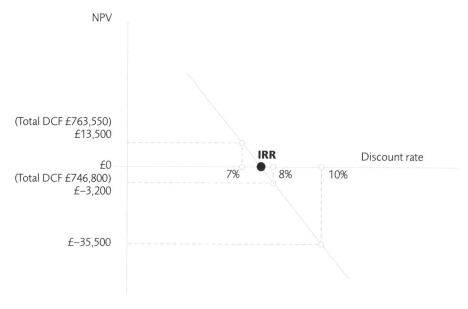

Figure 2.1.5.3 The relationship between NPV and IRR

The graph shown highlights the following trend, as the example is trialled at a higher discount rate the NPV would become more negative. The opposite is true when a lower discount rate is used when at seven per cent the NPV becomes positive, it has crossed the zero NPV axis. What can be concluded here? Our example is only feasible if the cost of borrowing was at seven per cent or lower, or that the opportunities available were yielding seven per cent or less. The exact IRR could be calculated at around 7.8 per cent.

The task of doing lots of trial and error work for a large-scale investment would be very tedious and time consuming and so in practical terms that work would be completed by using appropriate software commonly available in the market for such calculations.

The section of the guide that you have just read will provide you with the learning necessary to be assessed against the following learning outcome and assessment criteria:

6.   **Understand planning for success.**

6.1   *Explain the importance of a business case throughout the project life cycle.*

Learners should understand that although the business case is created as an output of the concept phase it is used and referred to throughout the life of the project. Different stakeholders will have contributed to the business case in addition to its owner, the project sponsor. The information contained in the business case will be used to evaluate the project at various points in the life cycle in order to make decisions about the ongoing viability of the project and its likelihood of ultimately delivering the benefits required to justify the funds being consumed.

6.2   *Explain what is meant by benefits management (including identification, definition, planning, tracking and realisation).*

Even if the project delivers its output on time, on budget and to the quality requirement, all of this effort will have been in vain if the subsequent output cannot realise the benefits that are defined in the business case. A suitable benefits management process will ensure that there is due consideration, upfront, for exactly how benefits realisation will be conducted.

6.3   *Explain investment appraisal techniques used by a project manager (including internal rate of return (IRR) and net present value (NPV)).*

Benefits realisation takes time to achieve and that time reduces the value of benefits the longer they take to be realised. This is commonly considered in two ways: NPV, which identifies the residual value once the initial investment has been recovered, taking the cost of the capital into account; and IRR, which identifies the rate of return achieved from the value inflows for a project. This enables project options to be compared against an organisation's target rate, allowing an objective decision to be made as to whether an option should be considered from a financial point of view.

2.1.6 Project life cycles

Life cycles are fundamental to the management of any project. Often organisations will set a standard approach for deployment, depending on the desired outputs, benefits and outcomes that are expected. Aspects of uncertainty, novelty and the risk appetite of the organisation may also influence the life cycle decision. The choice of deployment approach will also play a key part in selecting the most suitable form of life cycle, and thereby determine the stages involved in organising project work and indicate how they are interrelated and sequenced.

Differences between linear, iterative and hybrid life cycles

Whatever life cycle is chosen, it will provide a structure for governing the progression of the work by acting as an important management tool. It will focus on the allocation of resources, the integration of activities, the availability of key individuals, the support of timely decision-making and the mitigation of risk. Additionally, the life cycle also allows the provision of control and governance mechanisms matching the life cycle structure. Consequently, it is important that sponsors and project managers understand the characteristics and specific features of the selected approach.

Approaches to deployment range between highly predictive and highly adaptive settings. The choice between predictive and adaptive philosophies is largely influenced by the availability of knowledge. More predictive approaches tend to rely on knowledge known at the start, allowing work to proceed in a sequential manner, while adaptive contexts imply that new knowledge is created as the work progresses, which is then used to inform and guide the remaining effort. Adaptive approaches allow more key stakeholders to contribute and shape the development process.

Linear life cycles

In a linear life cycle the initiative progresses through a sequential series of steps or phases. In a project each phase would provide only partial capability until the final desired state is reached, usually at the end of the last phase. This is suitable for stable, low-risk environments.

A typical linear life cycle encompasses multiple phases as shown in Figure 2.1.6.1:

Concept – development of an initial idea through initial studies and high-level requirements management, and assessment of viability, including an outline business case.

Definition – development of a detailed definition, plans and statement of requirements that include a full justification for the work. It would be typical of a project management plan to form the output of this phase.

Deployment – implementation of plans and verification of performance through testing and assurance to realise intended outputs, outcomes and benefits.

Transition – handover, commissioning and acceptance of outputs to the sponsor and wider users, culminating in formal closure.

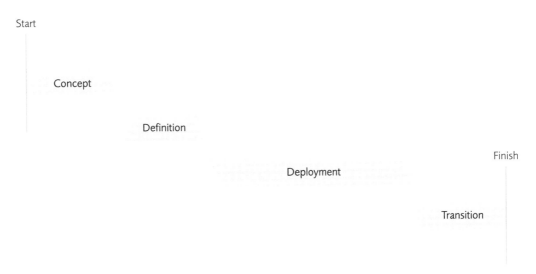

Figure 2.1.6.1 Linear project life cycle

The linear approach aims to be highly structured, predictable and stable, providing a transparent format for managing contracts and allowing maximum control and governance over the process. It works particularly well for the deployment of well-understood and clearly defined outputs trading time, cost and risk to achieve the right scope and quality. On the other hand, it assumes the availability of relatively perfect knowledge upfront, while being resistant to change and inflexible in terms of corrections and rework. It also implies a long sequence, culminating in the ultimate handover. Dividing knowledge into distinct phases in this way can often create silos and knowledge barriers between the phases, particularly when different delivery agents will deliver different phases. Those carrying out work in the deployment phase may have a tendency to blame activity in the previous phase for any problems they encounter while delivering their assigned workload. In addition, they may have very little incentive to pass on learning to help those delivering pieces of work further on in deployment.

Iterative life cycles

Iterative life cycles are most commonly used in agile development projects. Agile is a family of development methodologies where requirements and solutions are developed iteratively and incrementally throughout the life cycle. The life cycle used in an agile approach is composed of several iterations allowing the deployment of initial capability, followed by successive deliveries of further value. They are based on the idea of concurrency, or simultaneous engineering, where different development steps are allowed to be performed in parallel. Iterative life cycles repeat one or more of the phases before proceeding to the next one, and manage uncertainty regarding the scope by allowing the objectives to evolve throughout the life cycle as learning and discovery take place. Prototypes, timeboxes or parallel activities are utilised to acquire new insights, obtain feedback or explore high-risk options. The scope of this activity depends on the level of uncertainty and the organisational risk appetite. The duration may extend throughout deployment.

There are six phases in an iterative life cycle and these are shown in Figure 2.1.6.2. During the pre-project phase, iterative life cycles begin by developing a high-level vision. Feasibility and foundation phases ensure that the finer detail is uncovered during the cycles of iteration. The evolutionary development phase allows the specification and design to run in parallel and so, 'fast tracks' to deployment. Iterations are thus used to progressively elaborate and improve understanding based on client interaction with learning between the iterations. Iterations are applied when the goals are clear but the means of achieving them are not. The rapid deployment of smaller, partial solutions becomes the basis for gaining fast feedback and new insights about what needs to be done. Iterations are often conducted through working prototypes which stakeholders utilise as the basis for adaptation and improvement. The deployment phase seeks to bring the evolving solution into operational use either fully or using an incremental solution, which delivers partial requirements, utilising user experience to form the next solution increments. The final phase, post-project, identifies whether in fact the solution has delivered the benefits to the degree required to achieve the business case.

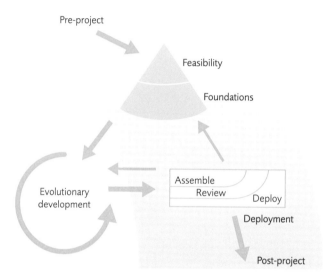

Figure 2.1.6.2 Iterative development in dynamic, agile context
Source: The DSDM Agile Project Framework Handbook, 2014

Overall, using iterations allows earlier return on some of the benefits that have already been implemented while validating the concepts and engaging users. Similar notions can be explored in the context of structuring and managing programmes, where iterations can also accommodate tranches and chunks of business-as-usual. A tranche is a sub-division of the deployment phase of a programme designed to enable an incremental approach to development of outputs, outcomes and benefits.

Hybrid life cycles

There is no single life cycle model that would suit all applications. The choice is dependent on what the organisation is trying to achieve and what aspects of the project are important. Hybrid life cycles therefore enable a pragmatic mix of approaches, typically fusing together elements from predictive and adaptive perspectives to create a new model or approach. For example, utilising iterative or agile methods for early requirements gathering, where the uncertainty is greatest, and following it up with incremental or sequential processes, which would be derived from the two previously mentioned life cycle models as shown in Figure 2.1.6.3, to formalise deployment.

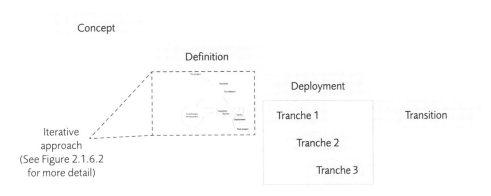

Figure 2.1.6.3 Hybrid programme life cycle

The use of prototyping, timeboxing or iterative thinking offers tested methods for experimentation and risk reduction. Adding iterative elements to 'predictive' projects can enhance deployment in stages, support the generation of insights, underpin the realisation of an early benefit stream, and validate some of the ideas much earlier within the cycle. Blending, merging or mashing of life cycles, ideas, principles, practices and methods can apply equally to programmes and portfolios. Building agile working into a project or programme can offer increased efficiency and flexibility. However, it also requires great skill and clarity when using multiple different systems of working.

Why projects are structured as phases in a linear life cycle

There are a number of reasons why projects are better managed in a life cycle, phased structure. The following are often cited:

- Improved planning of work – the life cycle allows phases to be broken down typically into stages, work packages and finally to specific activities. This shows the specific work elements in a more visible way, allowing improved planning decisions to be made. Near term stages may be detailed and later stages outlined. This is more efficient since later stages may be more subject to change.

- Clearer identification of priorities – the partitioning of work means that the staged (or phased) structure enables focus to be maintained on important factors appropriate to the characteristics of each stage.

- More effective risk assessment – thorough risk assessments can be conducted at the end of each stage and used to support go/no go decisions. Stages ensure that project management focuses on the most critical areas of risks.

- Greater estimating accuracy – stages provide a clearer basis for estimates to be established, which are more accurate when work is viewed in more granular way. Forward estimates can take account of efficiency variations and shortfalls. Any estimating error can then be more easily targeted when work is being carried out.

- More representative performance management – stages provide opportunities to review achievement and recognise success. Smaller shorter-term stages (e.g. sub-stages in deployment phase) can provide early feedback of success to the project team, which can lead to increased overall motivation.

- Greater adoption of continual improvement – as each unit of work is delivered there is an opportunity to learn lessons and then feed these into the upcoming work. Each stage enables feedback on performance and effectiveness of processes. This enables improvements to be considered on a continual basis throughout the complete delivery of the project, not just at the end, which is often more common but less effective to the current project.

- Improved control – the sponsor and project manager can review objectives and tolerances and make appropriate changes to ensure effective control. Gate reviews for example can provide the sponsor with an opportunity to review the project to consider termination if the objectives or benefits cannot be achieved, or changes to baseline requirements need to be considered to allow the project to continue.

- More effective stakeholder communication – enables stakeholders to be updated on project status. This is especially useful in ensuring the integration of the wider stakeholder community as well as those involved in day-to-day activity.

Differences between a project life cycle and an extended life cycle

Depending on the scope of a project and what it is delivering, the life cycle chosen can present a number of considerations. Some projects will be part of a programme and will be concerned with coordinating the delivery of multiple outputs. Some projects will work as standalone projects and would be primarily concerned with delivering their outputs only. Other projects will be expected to incorporate the management of change and the realisation of benefits and hence require a greatly extended life cycle. Where a contractor is working for a client, the contractor's 'project' may simply be the deployment and transition phases of the client's project and will include the capability for benefits realisation. In these circumstances the client is responsible for operating the outcomes in a manner that will obtain the desired benefits. In this case the host organisation must ensure attention is given not only to managing the project to closure but focusing attention on the operational phases also, effectively extending the life cycle.

Extended life cycles ensure that accountability and governance of the investment stays with a single organisation until the change is fully embedded by offering the missing connection to benefit realisation, while preventing the formation of knowledge boundaries between project teams and operations.

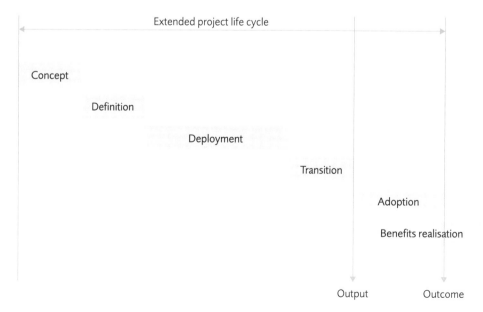

Figure 2.1.6.4 Extended life cycle

Recognising that many projects are initiated in order to deliver change and beneficial outcomes to organisations, life cycles can incorporate a further phase named 'benefits realisation' that may proceed up to the achievement of the business case.

An additional underpinning phase is also required in order to realise benefits as new outputs need to be made available and accessible to potential users. This may need to be enabled and operated separately. The additional activities included in the extended life cycle, encompass:

- Adoption – operations and sustainment required to utilise the new project and enable the acceptance and use of the benefits.

- Benefits realisation – realisation of the required business benefits.

The principal implication of extending the end of the life cycle to incorporate benefits realisation is that there is a need to start upfront, planning for the supplemental activities and incorporate additional considerations during the concept and definition phases. There are income and operational costs connected to the additional activities as well as capital expenditure considerations, which will be addressed during the concept and definition phases.

The benefits of conducting reviews throughout the life cycle

A review is a critical evaluation of a deliverable, business case or project management process. Reviews are one of the principle mechanisms by which the quality of deliverables, performance of the management process and the on-going viability of the work are assured. They may take many forms and occur at many different levels within the project environment, but essentially investigate one of three aspects of a project:

- Deliverables – a review can be a procedure for quality control of products delivered by a project or programme.

- The business case – the continued desirability, viability and achievability of the work should be reviewed at set points in the life cycle. This type of review can result in premature closure of projects and programmes.

- Management processes – in this instance a review is part of project assurance to check that the work is being well managed.

Decision gates

The purpose of decision gates is to conduct a review and confirm viability of the work across the chosen life cycle. In a linear life cycle, decision gates are event-driven, at the end of a phase of work. In the case of an iterative life cycle, they are time-bound. Many projects or programmes adopt a hybrid life cycle with a combination of main decision gates at the end of major phases of work, supplemented by interim review points to reflect the iterative nature of the development. The typical placement of decision gates in a linear life cycle is shown in Figure 2.1.6.5.

MANAGEMENT

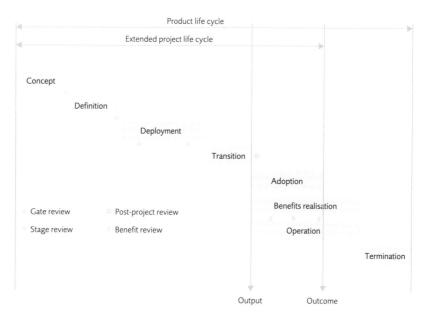

Figure 2.1.6.5 Typical decision gates and other reviews within a product life cycle

In all cases, the sponsor and the wider governance board are accountable for the decision to continue the work. Reviews in advance of decision gates ask four key questions:

- What has been achieved?

- What is required for the next stage?

- What are the key decisions to be made?

- Is the business case still viable, i.e., can the desired benefits be achieved for an acceptable level of cost and risk?

Within a standalone project, the decision gate is dealing only with the continued viability of that project's business case. In programmes and portfolios, decisions will include whether to rephase or terminate existing projects or initiate new ones. Between decision gates, the sponsor is accountable for ensuring authorities are in place to prevent the team working out of compliance and at risk. Decision gates may also be used to request relevant authorities for the work, such as a financial or procurement authority.

Benefits reviews

A benefits (realisation) review is carried out during benefits realisation and is a formal review of a programme or project, typically conducted 6–12 months after handover and commissioning of the deliverables. These reviews may be repeated throughout the operational life of the product. This review is used to answer the question: Did we achieve what we set out to do in business terms, and if not, what should be done? For a construction, development or procurement project, a review is undertaken when there has been time to demonstrate the business benefits of a new service or building. For a major programme of change there will be several reviews over time. A benefits realisation review is an essential component of the benefits management process. It checks whether benefits, including these set out in the business case have been achieved and identifies opportunities for further improvement.

Audit

This is normally undertaken by an independent body, internal or external to the organisation but independent from the project. An audits objective is to provide assurance to the sponsor that the project is being managed using the agreed governance and process. Audits can be undertaken by a Project Management Office should one exist, and they form the foundation of assurance, providing confidence to stakeholders that the project is likely to achieve its objectives and realise benefits.

Other reviews

The type of reviews that an organisation decides to adopt will very much depend on the life cycle model used, the project being delivered and the needs of the various stakeholders involved. There are a number of other reviews that could be adopted, and shown below is an example of how reviews could be carried out in relation to the project life cycles.

Stage reviews

These reviews evaluate the progress of the project and should be considered as part of the normal monitoring and control points within a project. They can be undertaken by some form of assurance function or by the project manager and their purpose is to discover whether, or not, the project is being managed effectively and to encourage learning while doing, continual improvement. They should be included in the project schedule by the project manager and they will use the project management plan as their base reference. The post-project review will use the information contained within these reviews to form a complete picture of project management performance. Common areas reviewed could be risk, estimating accuracy, safety, team performance and quality, for example.

Post-project review

The project manager is responsible for arranging a post-project review (PPR) that will take place shortly after the project is formally completed (end of transition phase). If the project is terminated early, the PPR will be conducted at the point of termination. The prime objective of the PPR is to learn lessons that may be appropriate to recommend improvements to other project management teams. A review document will be produced to describe the impact of approved changes on the project management plan, any benefits that can be assessed at this time and confirm that the quality of work done during the project meet the quality expectations of the customer.

Reviews must be conducted in an open manner. Organisations must be prepared to learn; to get most value, reviews should be conducted openly and participants must be prepared to make constructive criticism. It is only in this way that real lessons will be learned or improvements to business processes and supporting infrastructure made.

All recommendations must be sufficiently robust for the organisation to be able to act upon them. Importantly, both project management and supporting business operations should be included in recommendations for incorporating into the organisation's guidelines for developing good practice.

Why projects may close early

If projects exist to bring about planned objectives, then it follows that as circumstances change over time, not all projects are able to achieve those organisational objectives. In such a situation, it is logical to close the project early to divert investment away from something that is no longer a priority, towards a more useful opportunity.

The use of decision gates is one way in which the governance process ensures that investment does not continue if there is no longer a viable business case. However, for governance to be effective, the culture of the organisation needs to be one where early project closure is seen as a positive decision, not a failure.

Many sectors understand this and the concept of 'failing fast' is built into planning and decision-making processes, for example in drug development, where many promising compounds will enter the portfolio but those that will not make it through full clinical trials and come to market are stopped as early as possible. Many projects may look promising but cease to become so when more information is known. It is not wrong to start something when the outcome is uncertain. It is wrong to continue when there is evidence that sufficient value cannot be created to justify the level of investment being considered.

Sponsors of projects, programmes and portfolios are responsible for developing governance approaches that help the decision to close projects early. For the sponsor to make such a decision the project will always be seen within the context of the overall change and benefits sought, and would not be viewed as failure but as an opportunity for better utilisation of resources.

2.1.6   Learning summary

The section of the guide that you have just read will provide you with the learning necessary to be assessed against the following learning outcome and assessment criteria:

2. **Understand project life cycles.**

2.1 *Differentiate between linear, iterative and hybrid life cycles.*

Learners should see firstly that life cycles are a fundamental feature of project management, secondly that there is no one life cycle better than another. The life cycle that an organisation decides to use will be influenced by characteristics of the project. The linear life cycle is probably the simplest to view and the starting point for most organisations to gain experience of the life cycle approach. For some the choice might be a more iterative approach, which is very much an agile approach where value may be drawn from the process in an evolutionary way. The linear life cycle draws its value at the end. Both options have their strengths and so organisations in practical terms may want to use aspects of both in a more combined way, and so the hybrid life cycle will exist.

2.2 *Explain why projects are structured as phases in a linear life cycle.*

There are clear benefits here in structuring the project in a life cycle form. They allow planning to be more reliable. A whole range of project management activities are greatly assisted by viewing the project in this more granular way; improved risk identification, estimating accuracy, performance review, quality management and reporting are all enhanced in their effectiveness when used in a life cycle.

2.3 *Differentiate between a project life cycle and an extended life cycle.*

Delivering the project within its life cycle will demonstrate how the project manager has performed in relation to the objectives of time, cost and quality. What happens next? Well, this is where focus changes to how benefits are going to be realised and where processes, such as benefits management, apply. As far as the life cycle is concerned it is now said to be extended to show that there will be a time period where various operational activities will take place to ensure that users will interact with the output and benefits will be realised. For a truly successful project both life cycles are equally important.

2.5 *Explain the benefits of conducting reviews throughout the life cycle (including decision gates, benefits reviews and audits).*

Reviews are essential to good project management practice. They provide the basis for stakeholder management, communication and effective governance. Reviews help organisations to assess the contribution of projects to business objectives – these objectives and the metrics that will be applied to measure their

MANAGEMENT

achievement should be stated in the organisation's business and supporting strategies. All reviews will generate learned lessons, feeding them into the organisation's project management processes and procedures for future projects. Reviews should be a key part of project management, enhancing project management performance and contributing to the long-term maturity of the organisation. Reviews in themselves may even initiate change, in the way that the organisation and its people work.

2.6 *Explain why projects may close early.*

Historically there are many projects that, if reviewed, should not have continued through to deliver an output. They were recorded in project management folklore as spectacular failures. A simple online search will reveal the culprits. As in all cases hindsight is a terrific thing to have; however, a lot of these projects were considered viable at one time, so why did they continue to fail. Projects are about people and if those people have worked hard to get the project to a certain point, there is most commonly an emotional attachment and a reluctance to admit defeat. What is most important here is that there are distinct opportunities created in termination of projects. Future learning, redirection of funds and new opportunities emerging can often provide greater returns than the losses experienced when a project is closed earlier than planned without providing the benefits defined in the business case.

Stakeholders are persons, groups or institutions with interests in a programme or project. Primary stakeholders are immediate communities of interest, often they will be described as internal stakeholders, particularly if they are involved directly with the implementation of the project. Secondary stakeholders (usually external stakeholders) are the intermediaries in the process, and may often include government agencies and other institutional bodies.

Groups or individuals closest to the project may not actually think of themselves as stakeholders, because they feel they own the management processes, for example the project manager and team. A rule of thumb for ensuring that key stakeholders have been included in the process is to question whose support or lack of it might significantly influence the success of the project. This is a particularly good test for where groups may claim to speak for a wider representation than may actually be the case, and whose capacity to articulate their concerns might easily cause other groups to be overlooked.

The relationship between stakeholder analysis, influence and engagement

If our ultimate goal is stakeholder engagement, we need to look first at each stakeholder and their relationship to the project. Different types of relationships need different kinds of approaches; some need more activity than others. Stakeholders similarly can be quite specific, such as individuals or geographically identifiable groups of people. Others may be less visible, and we must think more laterally about how we are going to establish and maintain a relationship with them.

Stakeholder analysis starts with the identification of a project's key stakeholders and assessing their interests in the project and the ways in which those interests affect project riskiness and viability. It contributes to project design by identifying the goals and roles of different groups, and by helping to formulate appropriate forms of engagement with these groups. Developing a sound stakeholder environment means understanding the needs of stakeholders, both perceived and in reality. A typical approach could include the following considerations:

- understanding the role of the various stakeholders, and how this information may be used as an opportunity to improve both the perception and reception of the project;

- identifying the real nature of each stakeholder group's business and their consequent interest in the project;

- understanding their behaviour and motivation towards the project;

- assessing how they may react to various approaches and communication;

- identifying the characteristics of the stakeholders' environment and development of appropriate responses to facilitate a good relationship;

- responding to the stakeholder's motivation in relation to the project;

- determining the key areas that will have the most impact on the successful reception of the project.

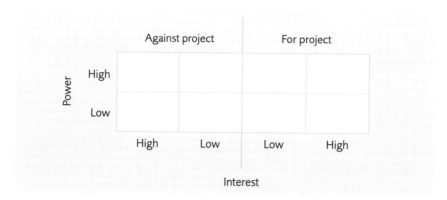

Figure 2.1.7.1 An approach to capturing analysis of stakeholders

Ultimately project management must take into consideration all parties whose actions may change the course of the project. The objectives of these stakeholders involved in a project are unlikely to be aligned, for example the aim of the sponsoring organisation is to minimise the cost of the project and that of the delivery contractor is to maximise profit. Project managers should be aware of all stakeholders and their likely objectives. They will find it difficult to please all of them because of the often-conflicting objectives. Political skill will be a useful attribute to assure maximum satisfaction among the stakeholders. Figure 2.1.7.1 shows how the analysis of stakeholders could be captured and reviewed.

Environmental groups are perhaps a good example of stakeholders who often will have a direct and categoric opposition to the project, regardless of how it is eventually implemented. For example, the decision whether to build a Terminal 5 at Heathrow Airport, London, was held up for more than ten years by one of the most complex public inquiries ever mounted in Britain.

Having identified the various stakeholders, each may be assigned to a category according to their relative ability to influence the project. Three distinct tasks are envisaged, namely:

- identification and mapping of relevant stakeholders;

- analysis of their interests in and relative power over the project or programme;

- developing an outline action plan defining how each stakeholder group will be managed throughout the life cycle of the project and the likelihood of them supporting the project.

Power is a factor that is closely associated with influence. Each stakeholder is analysed as to their degree of importance according to their level of power and therefore their ability to influence the project. Appropriate members of the project team can then prioritise their efforts accordingly to maintain the necessary stakeholder engagement, thus giving rise to the best chances of ultimate project success. If the project is large enough, or the stakeholder linkages are sufficiently intense, the project team's stakeholder engagement efforts may be assigned to a specific group within the project team. Assignments of such kind would be fully recorded in the project's communication plan. This plan will assign specific responsibilities to those who will conduct communication and the overall engagement strategy of how information about the project will be conveyed to those who need that information, which could be external stakeholders, such as the general public, for example.

The importance of managing stakeholder expectations to the success of the project

Carrying out such an in-depth analysis of stakeholders will consume resources, and to justify this consumption the project manager must acknowledge the importance of managing stakeholder expectations and how that will influence overall success of the project, particularly in the following areas.

Enabling more effective risk management

Once stakeholders are identified and analysed it will help with the management of risks within the project including their identification and assessment. For example, if there are a significant number of negative stakeholders, or a key stakeholder is found to be negative, the risk in the project will be high. Once this is established it can be mitigated and reduced. Similarly, if the right stakeholders are brought into the team, they will help with risk identification and the risk within the project can be more accurately assessed.

Improved communications planning

Not everybody needs to know everything, but everybody needs to know something. The results of the analysis will define the key communication requirements. These requirements are essential to assure effective engagement. This is especially true if the key interests of the stakeholders have been gathered in terms of time, cost, quality, scope and benefits. Not only can the appropriate level of information be ascertained but also where the information will come from and how it will be transmitted.

Ensuring a productive team is formed

Knowing which is the most appropriate engagement strategy to adopt for stakeholders – either partnering, being consultative, needing to be involved or simply kept informed – will help to define whether or not they need a place on the team. The outputs of the analysis should indicate likely stakeholder relationships that might be most productive for the project being considered.

Those seen as partners may play a key role as suppliers and members of the steering group depending on their interests and level of seniority. Engagement strategies for stakeholders in other areas may ultimately encourage them to be partners also. Similarly, if there are many stakeholder groups that need to be consulted this may mean that a team needs to be formed to complete these activities.

Enabling effective engagement actions to be initiated

Once identified it is possible to apply a further analysis to the stakeholders to develop an engagement strategy for dealing with the stakeholders concerned. Effective engagement improves the chance of achieving objectives by having a positive influence on stakeholders' behaviours to:

- use and sustain positive interest; or

- minimise or remove negative interest.

Effective engagement requires the project team to focus on understanding stakeholder perspectives and to address these in order to achieve the intended outcomes. Putting in effort to explore stakeholder points of view has the dual benefit of building understanding of the issues and building relationships.

Increased likelihood of project being accepted

There are stakeholders who are important, particularly when the project reaches the handover, as they will decide whether the output should be accepted or not. Identifying these stakeholders from the onset and fulfilling their needs will be a big step in ensuring stakeholder satisfaction is sufficient to warrant the product being accepted into the operational environment.

2.1.7 Learning summary

The section of the guide that you have just read will provide you with the learning necessary to be assessed against the following learning outcome and assessment criteria:

6. Understand planning for success.

6.11 *Explain the relationship between stakeholder analysis, influence and engagement.*

There are several distinct parts to understanding an effective approach to stakeholders. They must be identified first of all. Previous projects can yield valuable lessons. The analysis process looks at the power a stakeholder is likely to have; this allows the level of influence to be gauged. An additional question remains, however, and that is what is their level of interest in the project? And is that interest positive or negative? A stakeholder analysed to have high power, high interest and negative attitude to the project may need intensive engagement from the project manager, and possibly the project sponsor, to try to change their attitude towards the project. Whereas if a stakeholder group analysed to have low power, high interest and positive attitude to the project may need regular engagement with just enough information to keep them onside. Stakeholder analysis allows the project to develop the most appropriate engagement strategy, which will be different for different types of stakeholder. The communication plan will be essential in ensuring the level of engagement is maintained throughout the delivery of the project.

6.12 *Explain the importance of managing stakeholder expectations to the success of the project.*

For the project manager and team, the big question is, what is the payback for taking such time and resources to ensure stakeholders are assured of a project delivering for them? The challenge here, of course, is that each stakeholder may have a different view for what they expect from the project. A thorough analysis of stakeholders and an effective communication plan are most important here. They allow the project to proceed without disruption, help with risk management, communication, team building, engagement and ultimately acceptance of the output. Stakeholders underpin the project, if they are not happy with the result the risk is that it will not be accepted and so benefits realisation will not be achieved. Project management history is full of examples of such projects.

2.2 Project planning

Section 2.1 identified the high-level expressions of stakeholder vision. It is now necessary to consider just how that need is likely to be delivered through to a detailed statement of work for the chosen solution. This continuation of the journey involves a number of steps of refinement: exploring objectives; detailed requirements; success criteria; measurable benefits; best value options; scope definition and acceptance criteria for each element of that scope. This work builds a firm foundation for detailed planning.

The linear progression from high-level expressions of need and benefit in an early business case through to the specification of detailed requirements, scope and acceptance criteria is well understood. For many projects, this remains a value-creating process, especially for large scale, highly technical projects, where rework is expensive and does not justify an iterative approach.

The emergence and growing popularity of iterative approaches requires us to think about defining outputs in a different, more adaptive way. The danger, however, is to assume that the approaches designed to build in agility and flexibility do not require the discipline to define some things clearly, for example benefits that justify the investment or the acceptance criteria for deliverables.

Taking forward the definition of outputs into detailed planning requires a focus on multiple areas, the success of which is dependent on the integration of those areas into the baseline project management plan. Depending on particular project objectives and the life cycle chosen, different approaches to planning time, resources and cost, in the context of risk can be adopted.

Groups of people with a common aim are called a 'team' on the assumption that the people will not only cooperate with each other but also collaborate to innovate and perform. Effective project-based working relies on effective teamwork, often carried out in a context where teams are temporary, multidisciplinary and, occasionally, also geographically dispersed. Leading a group of people so they can become a high-performing team is skilled work and some would argue that it is the most important skill that a project professional needs to develop.

This section continues the learning journey and includes:

2.2.1   Project management plan

2.2.2   Communication

2.2.3   Risk management

2.2.4   Quality management

2.2.5   Procurement

2.2.6   Scope management

2.2.7   Leadership and teamwork

2.2.1 Project management plan

The project management plan (PMP) is the output of the definition phase of the project and integrates some or all fundamental components of scope, schedule, cost, risk, quality and resources. The project manager owns the PMP. Once each of these management components have been planned and integrated this will form the deployment baseline, which along with the PMP are approved at the decision gate associated with the approval of significant costs on the project. Some projects may have an integrated baseline review to provide assurance prior to approval. The approval of the deployment baseline is a good time to reconfirm the boundaries of the project – both what is in and out of scope, and how the project interfaces with other projects or business-as-usual activities in a programme or strategic portfolio. Any lack of 'fit' would require rework of the integrated plan prior to approval – either to adjust scope or to make provision for a different amount of cost contingency to take account of exposure to risks, and to fund risk responses that are not built into core scope.

The project can then proceed to the deployment phase where the deployment baseline will be used for progress monitoring and implementation of change control.

The relationship between the deployment baseline and the development of the project management plan in linear and iterative life cycles

Depending on particular project objectives and the life cycle chosen, different approaches to planning time, resources and cost, in the context of risk can be adopted. When using a linear life cycle approach, the assumption underpinning integrated planning is that all the work can be defined, estimated, scheduled, risked, resourced and costed. This may be to different levels of granularity in the near term than the long term – nevertheless, a baseline can be established from which deployment can be managed and controlled, and the planned value is then understood for the whole project. Unexpected issues will inevitably arise during deployment, but this does not negate the need for the best plan possible before work starts.

When using an iterative life cycle approach, a baseline plan is still required, but the assumptions underpinning the plan are different, with flexibility and agility built into the thinking. In an iterative project life cycle, the baseline resources and schedule are determined, but the achievement of scope and quality may vary from the plan as teams may have autonomy to re-prioritise tasks and act on new knowledge. Any work not achieved in the time allocated is returned to an existing backlog allowance, to then be planned into the future schedule or removed from the project.

Linear life cycles treat scope and quality as the driver and calculate the consequential consumed time and cost. Iterative projects commit to set resources over limited periods to deliver products that are developed over successive cycles. Many organisations use a hybrid linear/iterative approach to projects and programmes most of the time. The challenge is to plan in the most effective way to give the investing organisation the best possible chance of achieving the objectives and benefits described in the business case.

The importance of producing a project management plan

The PMP is the consolidated plan for the project and as such communicates the details of the approved project plans to stakeholders. It has been produced through a facilitated exercise led by the project manager with the engagement of all key stakeholders who will be involved in the deployment of the project. Figure 2.2.1.1 shows the different stakeholders that may need to contribute to producing the PMP. The PMP will then act as a reference source for all other stakeholders.

Figure 2.2.1.1 Different stakeholders that may need to contribute to producing the PMP

It is important to have as much continuity as possible throughout deployment. Achieving this can often be difficult particularly if the project resources are procured under a specific contract and are not considered as employed staff. In circumstances like these there can often be a large amount of staff turnover. This transient flow of resources should not adversely affect the project if the PMP is available, up to date and used as the main induction material for new members of the team.

The PMP is often referred to as the 'contract' between the project manager and the sponsor and as such clearly illustrates the extent of that agreement. It is important for the project manager to fully understand what is expected of them prior to committing to deployment. The PMP acts as a valuable source of clarification in this respect.

Once produced and approved the PMP will guide the project team and act as a baseline from which further measurement and analysis of variation can take place. It is important when conducting performance reviews that the current PMP is used as a reference source.

Typical contents of a project management plan

In essence the PMP should answer the 'why?', 'what?', 'when?', 'who?', 'where?' and 'how?' of the project. The 'how much?' question may also be asked. The size of the project will influence the amount of content of the PMP, which may run into several volumes say for the construction of a large nuclear power station, but may only be several pages for a small simple internal project.

- Why? At this stage that question has really been answered already by the business case. The PMP will therefore reference details from the business case, which can act as an appendix to the PMP.

- What? Contains a specific description of the scope of the project at the first instance and then would become more refined as the project nears deployment. Also contained here would be detail of the acceptance criteria and any constraints that were important to note.

- When? The timeline would be outlined here together with various supporting documentation, such as schedule; showing the timeline for project activities means that all stakeholders are clear on delivery timescales and project life cycle approach.

- Who? The organisation breakdown structure (OBS) would be shown here together with responsibility assignments, reporting lines and role descriptions.

- How much? Considers the budget presented as a cost breakdown structure (CBS) showing how the budget has been allocated to the work. It is likely that the cash flow for the project would be presented for the project duration.

- Where? Logistics of the project location and site conditions outlining any major restrictions or constraints regarding access or particular delivery requirements and security protocols.

- How? Probably the most comprehensive part of the document, which outlines the management strategy for the project. These management plans would contain process steps, template documents, roles and responsibilities, communication requirements and the detailed information necessary to allow those involved in deployment to follow the required process. Specific management plans could exist for the following areas (full descriptions of these areas are contained in sections elsewhere in this guide):

  - risk

  - quality

  - procurement

  - stakeholders and communication

  - safety

  - scope

  - change control procedures

  - cost

  - project controls

  - information and reporting requirements.

This information when assembled together in a self-contained document is now a standard reference for all concerned with the project. The list given may not all be applicable to every project but would be common examples of content.

2.2.1   Learning summary

The section of the guide that you have just read will provide you with the learning necessary to be assessed against the following learning outcome and assessment criteria:

6. Understand planning for success.

6.6 *Explain the relationship between the deployment baseline and the development of a project management plan in linear and iterative life cycles.*

Before starting any work on the project, it is important to have an agreed reference point that can be communicated to all stakeholders involved. That reference is the deployment baseline, which will be formed in the definition phase of the project. The PMP will then represent how that deployment will be managed. The learner might benefit from reviewing Section 2.1.6 Project life cycles to understand the distinct differences between an iterative and linear life cycle and therefore the implications for the PMP. The view of the linear life cycle is to the end of the project and can be planned accordingly, whereas with an iterative life cycle there may only be a need to plan sufficiently to get to a certain point, using the learning gained to that point to then make decisions that may impact the plan for the next stage.

6.7 *Explain the importance of producing a project management plan.*

The PMP is core to any project. It is important that the learner appreciates the extent of such a plan. The PMP sets and clarifies the expectations of all stakeholders who are involved in the project delivery. When approved all processes to execute the plan can be audited and the results fed back to the project sponsor through project assurance. While the PMP is important to provide direction to the project team, it is also a key part of project governance, reflecting how closely the team is delivering the project in relation to the approved plans.

6.8 *Describe the typical contents of a project management plan.*

This should be one of the most straightforward questions for learners to tackle in the exam, as almost every learning section of this guide contains the subject matter that would be part of a typical PMP. Sometimes, in project management terms, the 'plan' is seen as a Gantt chart showing how the project will progress along a timeline. This section should illustrate that a *management* plan is what the PMP is forming, integrating all the essential management processes needed and showing the project teams' intentions of how the project will be managed in all respects, not just the schedule.

MANAGEMENT

2.2.2 Communication

Communication is the process of exchanging information and confirming there is shared understanding. The ability to communicate is a core skill for people working in projects to ensure objectives and requirements are understood, plans and benefits are shared, stakeholders are aligned, teams are motivated and knowledge is embedded.

Communication takes many forms and effective communicators consider not only the message they want to pass on, but also the method (medium) for communicating that message. Decisions about communication methods are made in the context of the target audience, the intended impact and the risks/potential unintended consequences of the approach.

The benefits, to a project, of a communication plan

Effective communication plans include ways to receive feedback and measure effectiveness so that plans can be adjusted to have maximum impact. Taking the time to develop an effective communication plan will yield the following benefits:

- The most appropriate communication media is used – choosing the most appropriate media for delivery of a message is vital to that message being received and understood by stakeholders. Increasing the chances of stakeholder engagement. The communication plan will consider which media is best for which situation and stakeholder, for example, avoiding over reliance on e-forms of communication, which can often lead to misunderstandings and conflicts.

- More focused communication to stakeholders – avoiding mass communication, where receivers are swamped with information, only some of which might be relevant to them. Instead communication messages are planned and tailored to convey the communicator's meaning as accurately as possible to the target audience. If the right information is provided at the right time messages are then more likely to be read by the recipients intended.

- More consistent communication – when communication is planned in advance, all messages will be delivered using a framework that has been agreed and approved in advance. This could for example, involve the assigning of specific responsibilities for communication in the project. The result being that stakeholders do not receive conflicting messages from different areas of the project.

- Communication can be systematically improved – by ensuring that free-flowing feedback channels are planned into the communication structure, communication barriers can be identified allowing improvement actions to be proactively taken to ensure that barriers are eliminated and communication can be conducted more effectively.

- Greater adherence to the organisation's governance and standards – any protocols or standards for communication that are developed in the organisation are important to adhere to for effective communication to take place. The communication plan will take account of any 'norms' in the particular organisation and so circumvent avoidable communication errors, potential conflict or security breaches.

Relationship between stakeholder analysis and an effective communication management plan

All projects have communication plans that build from stakeholder analysis and outline the who, what, when, why and how of two-way communication between the team and the wider stakeholder environment. As soon as a stakeholder has been identified, the analysis process will seek to establish the level of interest and power that stakeholder is likely to possess. This initial view may have been formed by the project team with reference to previous experience or consultation with a subject matter expert. It is not until the communication process starts that the true interest and power of a stakeholder can be confirmed for this particular project situation, which in some cases may be contrary to previous experience.

An effective communication plan will seek to form an engagement strategy, as a result of suitable analysis, by answering some of the following questions:

- What particular message(s) should be communicated to this particular stakeholder?

- Who, in the project organisation, is best placed to carry out this communication?

- What form of message media or method will motivate this stakeholder to engage the most?

- When and how often should communication take place?

- What form of feedback can be solicited or expected?

- What barriers can be proactively identified and acted upon prior to communication taking place?

- Which stakeholders should/should not communicate with each other?

The communication plan allows the essential interactions to take place that are deemed necessary to motivate those stakeholders whose support is needed to achieve desired outcomes. For example, a stakeholder with high power, high interest and positive attitude to the project may need more regular communication in order to keep them engaged and on side, whereas a stakeholder with low power, low interest and positive attitude to the project may need to be monitored and provided with some communication on a more ad-hoc basis. Putting in effort to analyse stakeholder points of view has the dual benefit of building understanding of the issues and developing positive relationships. Managing stakeholders influence relies on these relationships being maintained and can only realistically be achieved through having an effective communications plan.

Factors which can positively or negatively affect communication

Many factors affect the success of communication, from cultural influences to the 'mood' in the team to the method of communication chosen and the language used. Figure 2.2.2.1 shows the difference between face-to-face, voice and words from the receiver's point of view. Project professionals have choices to use written words and symbols, voice and non-verbal signals (body language) when communicating. In face-to-face communication (including video and vlogs), non-verbal communication can have more of an impact than the words used, so being able to control non-verbal signals and create a coherent message are vital.

MANAGEMENT

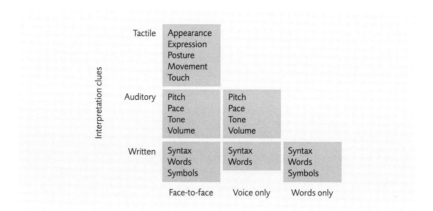

Figure 2.2.2.1 Factors within the medium that can positively or negatively affect a message

Where face-to-face communication is not possible there are advantages and disadvantages. For example, it can be advantageous to be on a conference call if the group is working through feedback in a document, as more focus can be given to the words used and the format of the written information without worrying about visual clues. Disadvantages are that virtual communication runs the risk of the sentiment underpinning what is said being misunderstood.

If the project requires working with virtual teams, there are particular skills needed to ensure that communication between team members is efficient and effective, for example, the ability to include everyone who needs to be involved on a virtual call, simultaneously. The project manager needs to be aware of the specific communication barriers associated with virtual teams, and make sure they understand the various ways to vary communication styles and media to not only connect effectively with on-site team members but virtual team members also. In addition, they need to ensure the appropriate communication mediums are being utilised for the benefit of the project, as well as all team members involved.

A combination of virtual communication methods, including email, video link or conference calling, is necessary when working with remote team members in particular. It's also essential that communication is more precise to ensure that the lack of instant two-way conversation that occurs face to face does not reduce the objective that they want to achieve from the communication opportunity.

Identifying the correct communication for an intended message needs to be properly analysed and implemented effectively to reduce many of the communication risks associated with communication in a virtual team. During the setting up of the team it is worthwhile also considering the training needs of the individual team members. Training both to operate the technology effectively and to fully understand the limitations of such methods are important to heighten awareness and therefore proactively reduce any communication barriers.

There are various factors that can influence communication both positively and negatively; these are outlined in Table 2.2.2.1.

Factor	Positive affect	Negative affect
Use of technical terms (jargon) when communicating	Complex information provided together with technical summaries and supplementary information. Contact established in advance of communication to confirm understanding. Participants are engaged and more fully understand the technicalities of the situation.	Complex information provided without glossary, explanation of terms or supplementary information. Individuals are unable to understand or contribute to the exchange.
Organisational culture and structural hierarchies	Senior people take a more supporting role to junior staff. Inviting them to state their views, reinforcing the presence of an open culture.	Individuals feel intimidated within a mixed audience where senior and junior people are present. Junior staff reluctant to communicate viewpoint.
Time zones and geography	Timing of communication is planned within most common availability. Individuals are compensated for occasions when time needs to be spent out with normal working periods.	Individuals having to work outside their normal working hours. May not be available for regular communication.
Physical and environmental aspects of the location (temperature, noise, safety)	A suitable safe environment is chosen that has the necessary facilities to provide reassurance and comfort. Individuals are motivated to exchange ideas and views.	Individuals are unable to hear what's being communicated or are distracted by activity or noise nearby and are unable to focus on messages being given.
Planning of communication	Communication is specific going only to those who need the information. Individuals appreciate the limited volume of data and are motivated and take time to engage with the message received.	Individuals receive messages in an ad-hoc way without any apparent rationale for the communication. No engagement occurs and the content of the message is not observed.

Table 2.2.2.1 Examples of factors that can affect communication both positively and negatively

Understanding how communication can be influenced by a range of factors will ensure that the project manager seeks to proactively manage these factors as much as possible prior to communication taking place. By doing this the communication plan for the project will increase the chances of achieving effective engagement, which in turn improves the chance of achieving objectives by having a positive influence on stakeholders' behaviours.

2.2.2   Learning summary

The section of the guide that you have just read will provide you with the learning necessary to be assessed against the following learning outcome and assessment criteria:

4.   Understand communication within project management.

4.1   *Explain the benefits, to a project, of a communication plan.*

The ability for the project manager and the team to influence stakeholders is vital when seeking to achieve engagement. That influence will never be present if communication is not planned with the stakeholder population in mind. If a review of any organisation's completed projects were to be carried out, with the aim of identifying the factors that had most impact on how well these projects were delivered, at the top of the list would be communication. It is not that communication didn't take place – it most certainly did – but it probably wasn't effectively planned. What learners must appreciate in this section is that the time consumed in carefully planning communication is returned tenfold by the positive impact the execution of that plan will have on the project's success.

4.2   *Explain the relationship between stakeholder analysis and an effective communication management plan.*

Stakeholder engagement and communication are two very closely linked processes in the PMP. The activity of engaging stakeholders is all about communication. The main touch point between the processes comes when stakeholders are analysed. It is at this point that the project team have an appreciation of who might be for or against the project. This knowledge results in the development of a suitable engagement strategy. The catalyst for that strategy is an effective communication plan. Effective engagement requires the project manager to focus on understanding stakeholder perspectives and to address these in order to achieve the intended outcomes. Effective communication creates an environment in the project based on respect, shared values and trust, ultimately leading to a successful outcome for all involved.

4.3   *State factors which can positively or negatively affect communication.*

Learners should appreciate here that the factors that affect communication are not specific to projects and will be most common throughout every part of every organisation. So, a lot of common sense and some experience of good and bad communication situations will be valuable in this area. The same factor can present a positive or a negative influence, depending on what action is taken proactively to anticipate the situation. Lessons learned can be valuable here in trying to pre-empt what factors are likely to have the biggest impact on the communicated messages, negatively and positively.

2.2.3 Risk and issue management

Risk management is a process that allows individual risk events and overall risk to be understood and managed proactively, optimising success by minimising threats and maximising opportunities. All projects are inherently risky because they are unique, constrained, based on assumptions, performed by people and subject to external influences. Risks can affect the achievement of objectives either positively or negatively. Risk includes both opportunities and threats, and both should be managed through the risk management process.

Risk management must be closely aligned to schedule management. Cost, time and resource estimates should always take risks into account. The project manager is accountable for ensuring that risk management takes place. Depending on the size and complexity of the project, a specialist risk manager may be appointed to oversee and facilitate the risk management process.

Each stage in a risk management process

It is important to note that the risk management process discussed here is not applied to the management of general health and safety risks, which is usually excluded from project risk management. Management of these risks is traditionally handled separately through the formation of a safety plan for the project, often with the support of the health and safety function within the organisation. The process of project risk management will focus on individual project risks that, should they occur, will affect the project's objectives. The project manager will also seek to understand the overall risk exposure of the project, so that this can be reported to the project sponsor and other stakeholders.

A typical risk management process is illustrated in Figure 2.2.3.1. The steps are outlined below.

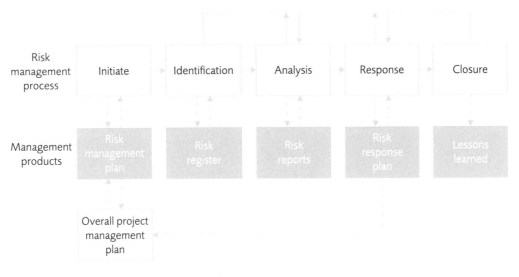

Figure 2.2.3.1 Risk management process and management products

Initiate

The main purpose of this step is to ensure that there is a common understanding of the project to which the risk management process is to be applied. It is important that risk management is not seen by the project team as a burdensome process that will ensure every box is ticked. Instead this step will make sure that the level of process to be used fits the specific requirements of the project.

A key output from the initiate step is the risk management plan, which details how risk will be managed throughout the life cycle. The risk management plan will be an important reference for all stakeholders who require an insight into the risk organisation and control structure and the specific responsibilities for risk management. A number of appendices will also be included such as templates and proformas of the documents necessary to effectively carry out the process. Part of the overall project management plan, the risk management plan makes it quite clear how risk is going to be tackled for the project. In many organisations it may be held as a template in the standard project methodology, although the risk management plan will always be specific to a particular project.

Identification

For this step it is essential that the project objectives are fully understood. The overall appetite for risk of the investing organisation is translated into a set of calibrated impact scales that represent the objectives at risk, and the size of impact that would be tolerable and intolerable. For example, is a high impact on project cost a 5 per cent variance to budget, a 10 per cent variance, or greater? Once impact scales have been defined, the project manager can facilitate the process to identify specific risk events.

There are a number of risk identification tools and techniques available to help facilitate risk identification such as:

Assumptions and constraints analysis – Project definition and planning processes inevitably make use of a large number of assumptions. If these assumptions are recorded, they can be used to identify threats by assessing the probability that each assumption will be met and the impact on the project should the assumption be violated. Constraints can be assessed in a similar manner. In cases where there is a significant probability that a constraint could be relaxed or disregarded, opportunities may be identifiable.

Brainstorming – Brainstorming captures risks quickly, and offers a means of raising enthusiasm for risk management across a team. It can also be used to engage project stakeholders in the risk identification process. An independent facilitator is normally used to ensure that the session is sufficiently well structured and maintains a good pace. Typically, the output of a brainstorm is a list of risks, each described by a phrase or sentence indicative of the risk source.

Checklists – Checklists are usually generated by organisations to reflect the key issues that affect their environment. They are a useful means of preserving the lessons learnt from the occurrence of previous events and they can be incorporated into self-assessment processes or used as a safety net for reviews. However, projects frequently find themselves breaking new ground, so checklists should be used in combination with other, more proactive, risk identification techniques.

Prompt lists – A prompt list is another form of risk identification aide-mémoire, but one that uses headings, usually related to generic sources of risks. The aim of a prompt list is to stimulate proactive and lateral thinking. Prompt lists are therefore a resource that can be used to support other techniques, such as brainstorming. They can also be included in plans or procedures to indicate the breadth of issues that risk management is concerned with. Prompt lists may be structured as a generic hierarchical structure of major risks broken down into components and sub-components to form a risk breakdown structure.

Strengths, Weaknesses, Opportunities and Threats (SWOT) analysis – SWOT analysis comprises a breakdown of the strengths and weaknesses inherent in a project's circumstances that give rise to opportunities and threats – that is, expose it to risk. SWOT may also be useful in risk planning by considering how the strengths and opportunities can be used to reduce the weaknesses and threats. A key advantage of using this technique may be that the project's organisation already uses it for the dissemination of issues associated with other areas of the project and within the organisation to consider marketing and business development functions. Its use would therefore be consistent with integrating the risk management process with such functions, many of which are associated with activities in the earlier phases of projects.

The objective of risk identification is to draw out all knowable risks to project objectives. Risk identification is a creative, divergent process that benefits from the input of a wide range of people using a method that does not restrict or bias their thinking. Working with stakeholders and the team to discuss risk is one area that requires a facilitative approach and a means of providing neutral challenge to address any bias. Workshops are often used for this purpose, although alternative approaches that enable individuals to contribute without any chance of group bias can be more useful.

Once risks are identified they are documented in a risk register. A risk register is a document listing identified risk events and their corresponding planned responses. The term risk log is also used to describe such a document. It provides a standard format in which to record risk information. As a minimum for each risk this information is likely to include the description, causes, probability, impact, mitigation actions, fallbacks, status and the names of individuals with responsibility for the risk's management. Depending on the risk management techniques selected, other data are also likely to be maintained, as appropriate.

Although a risk register can be maintained manually, most projects are likely to use spreadsheet software for this purpose. Such spreadsheets may be designed for a stand-alone PC or for concurrent use by users linked through a network.

When risks are noted on the risk register and to make sense of differing perceptions, it is important to describe risk events clearly, separating causes (facts now or stable planning assumptions), from risk events (situations that may occur), from effects (that have an impact on one or more of the project specific scales already defined).

It is also vital that the correct risk owner is defined for each risk event at this stage in the risk management process. Risk owners are individuals or groups who are best placed to assess and manage the specific risk. Working with the risk owner, the project manager ensures that risks are clearly described in the risk register before moving on to the risk analysis step of the risk management process.

Analysis

The relative severity of identified risks is assessed using qualitative techniques to gain understanding of their individual significance and/or their combined impact on objectives. They can then be prioritised for further attention. Quantitative risk analysis may also be used to determine the combined effect of risks on objectives and for focus on specific risk-based decisions using techniques such as Monte Carlo simulation, decision-trees and sensitivity analysis.

Risk owners will work with the project team to carry out basic qualitative analysis as a minimum to identify and prioritise risk events based on an assessment of the:

- probability/likelihood of occurrence; and

- size of impact on schedule, cost, benefits and potentially other objectives.

Typically, this is presented in the form of risks plotted on a probability/impact grid, as shown in Figure 2.2.3.2.

Probability						
0.9	VHI	0.045	0.09	0.18	0.36	0.72
0.7	HI	0.035	0.07	0.14	0.28	0.56
0.5	MED	0.025	0.05	0.10	0.20	0.40
0.3	LO	0.015	0.03	0.06	0.12	0.24
0.1	VLO	0.005	0.01	0.02	0.04	0.08
		VLO	LO	MED	HI	VHI
		0.05	0.1	0.2	0.4	0.8
				Impact		

Figure 2.2.3.2 Example probability/impact grid to qualitatively prioritise risk events

The simplest way to use the probability/impact grid is on the basis of five degrees of impact and probability ranging from very low to very high. More value can be gained from using the technique by setting agreed risk thresholds for very high risks, medium and very low risks, often described using red, amber and green coloured areas of the grid. Approaches for each of the areas could then be defined in advance; for example, for any risks that would be in the 'red' area (darkest area in Figure 2.2.3.2) the rule might be that these risks must be escalated. It should also be noted that the probability scores for this example are defined using a linear arithmetical scale, whereas the impact scores are on a logarithmic scale. This is common practice to weight very high impact risks higher than very high probability risks.

Response
The risk owner uses information collected during risk identification and risk analysis to determine whether it makes sense to proactively invest previously unplanned time and money to bring the exposure to risk within tolerable levels. Deciding when to take the risk or invest in increasing certainty is influenced by the appetite for risk of the sponsor and ultimately the investing organisation.

If there is a justification for investing time and money proactively to increase certainty, the risk owner makes provision to implement the planned responses (time, resource, cost) and updates the integrated project plan (deployment baseline) accordingly.

Proactive and reactive responses to risk
There are two main types of response to threats and opportunities – a proactive response and a reactive response (Figure 2.2.3.3):

- Proactive response – A planned and implemented response undertaken to address the likelihood of the risk occurring or the size of the impact if it did occur. Responses include avoiding or reducing a threat, or exploiting or enhancing an opportunity. Responses ideally focus on the cause of the risk. Sharing risk in the supply chain is also a type of proactive response. Cost risk may be transferred to another party, for example an insurer, but risks to schedule cannot be transferred.

■ Reactive response – A provision for a course of action that will only be implemented if the risk materialises. Such responses accept the risk but with a contingent response ready to go. Some reactive responses may require funding to be built into the integrated plan because they are designed to monitor the risk and detect changes early.

Figure 2.2.13 Generic response strategies for threat and opportunities

While similarities can be drawn between the risk responses used for threats and opportunities, there is a difference between the two in terms of the language used to describe actions that can be taken in response to them.

In the case of threats, responses should be implemented that reduce the effect of the threats to the extent that the consequences of response actions do not exceed the likely value of risk reduction. In the case of opportunities, the project should aim to improve one or more of the project objectives in such a way that the cost and implications of the response actions do not exceed the likely value of improvement. The aim of any risk response should be to ultimately produce a risk-efficient overall project solution.

Whatever response is chosen, care should be taken to consider the extent to which that response will deal with the risk. There are two types of risks that may emerge as a consequence of a response. They are secondary risks and residual risks.

Secondary risks are new risks that only occur as a result of the response being taken. If a secondary risk occurs the best outcome could be that it is of a lesser magnitude than the original risk, then some progress at least has been achieved. If, however, the secondary risk is of the same magnitude, or greater, than the original risk, the response would be considered ineffective.

Residual risk is the amount of risk remaining after a response has been committed. It is likely that the significance of this risk will need to be assessed on its own merits and a separate response planned to treat the residual risk.

There are several specific ways in which a risk response can be carried out. Examples of risk response for threats are:

Avoidance – Some threats can be avoided by changing objectives or practices so that the cause of the risk can be discounted. For example, a technical threat might be avoided by changing the specification for one of the project's products, or a subcontract threat might be avoided by removing a high-risk company from the tendering process.

Reduction – Responses that reduce the probability of a threat's occurrence usually require that the risk be tackled at source. Such actions are considered as preventive and they can be an effective option for risk control. However, the implementation of preventive action usually requires an investment of cost and management time, and this should be justified by costs versus benefits considerations – that is, the cost of implementing the action should be less than the reduction in the risk's expected value.

Transfer – Risk transfer involves passing on the responsibility for bearing the impact of a threat to another party. An organisation may seek to obtain financial protection through the purchase of insurance. This approach may reduce impact but have no effect on the probability of the event occurring. Risk transfer may only result in an overall reduction to the level of project risk if the party to whom risk is transferred is more capable of managing it. For example, a subcontractor may be used because of its expertise or resources. It is usually not possible, or even desirable, to transfer risk completely, so risk transfer requires a balanced approach that leaves residual risk on both sides.

Acceptance – Where there is no acceptable or economically viable approach to threat avoidance or reduction, residual risk has to be absorbed and its consequences managed.
Time impact may be managed by planning strategies that prevent high-risk activities from being close to the critical path, although this is often not possible. Provision for cost impact should be planned within the budget for financial contingencies. The project should also consider the impact that acceptance of threats will have on its stakeholders and advise them accordingly.

Examples of risk response for opportunities are:

Exploitation – Exploiting an opportunity involves changing the project scope in order to achieve a beneficial outcome for one or more of the stakeholders. If all stakeholders are likely to benefit, this would be a 'win–win' decision, and opposition to such change might be correspondingly low. However, on some occasions to exploit certain opportunities may only benefit one of the stakeholders. Discussion and review may then follow to agree the best way forward.

Enhancement – Enhancing the probability that an opportunity can eventually be exploited requires a proactive response; such a response might be either strategic or tactical. An example of a strategic response would be a decision to develop a design in-house, rather than to subcontract it, in order to retain greater control over future enhancements. Tactical responses involve the identification of improved methods for project delivery.

Share – Organisations involved in the project may collaborate in order to increase the chances of an opportunity being realised. Both parties may have a cost to bear but then will share the benefits if the opportunity subsequently materialises in their favour.

Rejection – Usually if the opportunity is of little value or the work required to gain the result of the opportunity is considered too great a decision not to take advantage of the situation will be chosen.

Closure

The final part of the management process is to ensure that all risks are closed when they have occurred and successfully mitigated, been accepted or that there is no longer a possibility of them occurring. At this stage it is useful to document information about the risk being closed for example any updated risk information, closure rationale, and lessons learned. There are valuable benefits in fully understanding a risk, the approach to analysis, how it was mitigated or what conditions have been met, when closing a risk for future reference.

An aim of effective risk management in any project should be to provide lessons learned to assist future projects in their risk management. Having a prime source of base data, from previous projects, when analysing a new risk provides a greater insight to decide actions to take, risk ownership, as well as improved cost estimates and likely benefits of mitigation plans.

At project closure if there are any open risks remaining, the project manager must ensure that these are communicated to those involved in the adoption phase.

The benefits of risk management

Alongside the introduction of risk management into an organisation, staff should be formally educated about the benefits of risk management, the reasons for its introduction and in the use of the tools and techniques that they will be expected to employ on their projects. Understanding risk management and why it is being introduced will reduce people's scepticism and resistance to its introduction.

Some of the benefits of risk management according to APM's Risk Specific Interest Group *Project Risk Analysis and Management (PRAM) Guide* (2010) are as follows:

- Enables better informed and more believable plans, schedules and budgets:

  As soon as practicable the project needs to plan what needs to be done, together with a prediction of what resources (time, cost, and labour) will be needed to achieve it. The use of risk management to identify risk factors, and to allocate tolerances or contingency in respect of those risks, helps create a more objective description of the tasks and the related budgets and schedules. This gives more credibility to the plans, increasing stakeholder confidence of a positive result.

- Increases the likelihood of a project adhering to its schedules and budgets:

  Clearly, the more realistic the project's plans (schedules, budgets), the more likely it is that the outcome will reflect those plans. Team members who believe that they have a hopeless task and expect to fail, no matter how well they do, will tend to be demotivated. Giving them achievable targets, in which they can believe, will secure greater levels of commitment leading to a higher probability of success.

- Allows a more meaningful assessment and justification of contingencies:

  Many managers apply blanket contingency levels on no better basis than a 'gut feeling'. This often results in over- or under-provision and the ineffective application of scarce resources. Risk management can identify and quantify the amount of contingency required to give an acceptable confidence level, and the risk budget can be actively managed as the project proceeds. The overall budget for the project, and especially the contingency fund, can then be allocated to the prime areas of risk.

MANAGEMENT

- Discourages the acceptance of financially unsound projects:

  The discipline of assessing the impact of possible risks to a project forces realism in the planning stage as risk analysis creates an early awareness of potential obstacles and opportunities. In extreme cases, risk analysis may reveal that a project cannot meet its objectives, is not feasible, or is a potential threat. In these situations, the organisation can decide not to bid or to pull out before resources are too heavily committed.

- Contributes to the build-up of statistical information to assist in better management of future projects:

  The same problems often arise on different projects within the same organisation – even in a company that has good internal communication. This is usually due to the learning curve experienced by many project staff as a result either of transfer to new projects or promotion to new levels of responsibility. Quite often, however, it is because the decision-makers set unrealistic expectations. Formal risk analysis, together with post-project reviews, can provide a wealth of information in a form that can be used as a reference for staff and managers alike.

- Helps develop the ability of staff to assess risks:

  Several benefits may accrue to individuals as a result of being exposed to risk analysis on a project. The simple fact that risk analysis is being undertaken is enough to make people more aware that risks may, and do, exist in their area of influence. As a result, they tend to look out for them not only in the current circumstances, but also when making decisions for future activities. This awareness of risk therefore improves the competence of the people involved in preparing and executing plans. Individuals may assess their own ability by predicting risks and then seeing how this preview compares with reality.

- Facilitates greater risk-taking, thus increasing the benefits gained:

  Calculated risk-taking has always been the basis of success. In the absence of formal risk management, however, the outcome is unpredictable (little more than gambling), and opportunities remain unexploited. By applying formal risk management techniques, with appropriate mitigation and fallback plans, an organisation can take greater levels of risk with lower levels of contingency thus improving the overall return on investment. In addition, the proactive management of risk will remove some of the threats that would otherwise impact on the project and also realise some of the opportunities to improve the project's outcomes.

The key aspects of issue management

In project management, an issue occurs when a problem that is immediate, or is about to occur will breach delegated tolerances for work on a project or programme. Issues require support from the sponsor to agree a resolution. Issues are differentiated from problems that are dealt with on a day-to-day basis by the project manager and team.

There is often a tendency to mix up the identification, analysis and management of risks with issues. They are related but are not the same thing. Issues may develop when particular risks or groups of risks actually occur and the mitigation actions that have been put in place to deal with these risks are insufficient to such a degree that it requires escalation to the next level of management for resolution. If risks occur and the contingencies that have been reserved are consumed to the expected degree, then that is not an issue. Issues happening now may also be causes of new risks, or result in assessment of risk likelihood and/or size of impact to change. It is understandable that a project manager might prioritise the management of issues (problems now) over the management of risks (potential problems or opportunities), but a project where this is continually the case would suggest an underlying concern with project plans and controls.

There is a process used to manage issues which ensures that:

- When an issue is identified it is logged in an issue register/log and analysis is performed quickly to understand the nature of the issue, its causes and impacts if it is not resolved. The prioritisation of issues is based on the impact on success criteria and benefits for the work taking into account the relative priorities of scope, quality, time, cost and benefits in the business case.

- Issues are escalated to the sponsor, who may, in turn, escalate them to the governance board for resolution.

- Actions are assigned to the person or group who is best placed to address the issue and identify and implement a resolution in a timely manner.

- Issues that result in changes to scope or any other part of the baseline plan are progressed through change control. As part of integrated planning, the limits of delegated authority are established and formal change control is required when these tolerances are breached.

- The management of issues is tracked from identification through to resolution and closure, including any change control and replanning of the deployment baseline and project management plan.

The issue management process is a simple concept. However, there are barriers to effective adoption that range from a lack of time or reluctance from the project team to identify and escalate issues early, to an inability of the governance board to make an informed decision that addresses the root cause of the issue rather than treating the symptoms. Issue management is an important project control and effective implementation can be enhanced by engaging members of a project management office (PMO) to help facilitate the necessary resolution.

The role of contingency planning in projects

Contingency is resource set aside for responding to identified risks. Contingency is needed to match the gap between the 'un-risked' (deterministic) plan and the desired level of confidence. In addition to contingency for known risks (sometimes referred to as the risk budget), some organisations also hold a management reserve to make provision for unidentified risks (sometimes referred to as 'unknown unknowns') or for those identified risks that have very low likelihood of occurrence but would have a very high impact if they did occur.

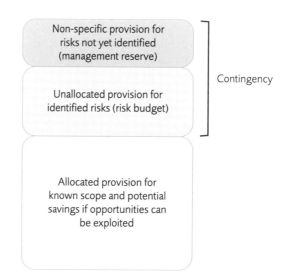

MANAGEMENT

Figure 2.2.3.4 Provision for known and unknown risk

Contingency is most typically expressed as:

- Monetary value – an allowance for dealing with impacts on cost or financial benefit.

- Time – an allowance for dealing with impacts on schedule.

When using an iterative life cycle and timeboxes, it may be relevant to think of contingency in terms of scope/quality, i.e. resource set aside to complete outputs to the desired specification. Timeboxes may also incorporate lower priority items that can be sacrificed to secure emerging priorities.

If it is normal in an organisation to perform probabilistic risk analysis using Monte Carlo simulation, then confidence levels in plans will typically be expressed in terms of probabilities. For example, the P90 cost (the outturn cost of the project with a 90 per cent confidence level based on the uncertainty and risk considered), or the P50 schedule (the end-date that the analysis predicts there is a 50/50 chance of achieving).

In other organisations, the qualitative risk analysis can be used to predict confidence levels with lower precision, for example by looking at the expected value of the risks in the risk register or making an experience-based judgement.

In all cases, contingency is clearly identified, for example as an identified line item in a budget, an additional timeboxed iteration in a schedule or as a buffer to protect a critical chain of activity. Contingency is not 'hidden' extra time or money to deliver planned scope.

It is normal for contingency to be held at different levels to deal with different sorts of risk and to support management of the contingent funds/time. Most organisations will proportion the contingency between the project manager, project sponsor or programme manager and the governance board. Allocation of contingency reflects the level of control desired.

2.2.3   Learning summary

The section of the guide that you have just read will provide you with the learning necessary to be assessed against the following learning outcome and assessment criteria:

10. **Understand risk and issue management in the context of project management.**

10.1 *Explain each stage in a risk management process (such as identification, analysis, response, and closure).*

Keeping the risk conversation alive is crucial to the ongoing delivery of any project. The risk management process is iterative to reflect the dynamic nature of project-work, capturing and managing emerging risks and reflecting new knowledge in existing risk analyses and estimates of contingency required. Risk management should never be considered as a stand-alone process; it must always be closely aligned to schedule and resource management, cost management and procurement, to name just a few. Cost, time and resource estimates should always take risks into account. The project manager is always accountable for ensuring that risk management takes place. Depending on the size and complexity of the project, a specialist risk manager may be appointed to oversee and facilitate the risk management process.

It is also important to identify and manage behavioural influences on the risk process, both individual and group, since these can have a significant impact on risk management effectiveness.

10.2 *Explain proactive and reactive responses to risk (such as avoid, reduce, transfer or accept and exploit, enhance, share and reject).*

A very important part of the process is risk response planning, aiming to avoid, reduce, transfer or accept threats as well as exploit, enhance, share or reject opportunities, with contingency (time, cost, resources and course of action) for risks which cannot be managed proactively. The two sets of responses are fundamentally the same, but tailored to minimise the detrimental effect of a threat or maximise the beneficial effect of an opportunity. Once the response has been agreed it will then be implemented. The learner must understand the iterative nature of all parts of the process. For example, assessment or response planning can lead to the identification of further risks; planning and implementing responses can trigger a need for further analysis, and so on.

10.3 *Explain the benefits of risk management.*

Project risk management must contribute, as appropriate, to both business risk assessments and organisational governance requirements. The project manager must be aware of risks that have an effect outside their scope of responsibility, e.g. those that could affect the organisation's reputation. Taking time and effort to carry out effective risk management consumes far fewer resources than only reacting to risks as and when they arise. The project manager will also appreciate that by carrying out robust risk management, focused on the current project, it will ensure not only compliance with governance but a reduced cost base, better relationships with customers and enhanced reputation as a result of fewer headline project failures.

10.4   *Explain the key aspects of issue management.*

There is generally much confusion surrounding risk and issue processes. They are very different from each other. Issue management is the process by which issues can be identified and addressed to remove the threats that they pose. The project must respond to issues, as by their nature they will have an impact on project objectives, that is certain. Risks on the other hand are in the future; they may not necessarily need a response at this time and actually may never happen. An issue is now breaching, or is about to breach, delegated tolerances for work on a project and require support from the sponsor to agree a resolution.

Consider the occasions when issues arise as the project being caught by surprise. Recording such events is essential for learning. A log of all issues raised during a project, showing details of each issue, its evaluation, what decisions were made, and its current status will be valuable as a base reference for future projects.

6.   Understand planning for success.

6.16   *Explain the role of contingency planning in projects.*

The project budget is for doing the work, procurement of equipment and materials and the provision of all aspects to deliver the scope of the project. It is not for managing risk, that should be a separate amount set aside to act as a contingency fund. This can be a financial amount or a time allowance. Without setting aside a separate amount, unknowns, should they materialise will then need to be funded from the project budget, which accounts for why some projects finish over budget. From a monitoring point of view, it is also useful to have this separate amount that can be monitored apart from the budget to gauge how well the project is managing contingency funding specifically. It is important to see that the management of contingency not only links to risk management but also to issue management and change control.

2.2.4 Quality management

'Quality' is defined as the fitness for purpose or the degree of conformance of the outputs of a process, or the process itself, to requirements. Quality management is a discipline for ensuring the outputs, benefits and the processes by which they are delivered meet stakeholder requirements and are fit for purpose. Project quality management includes the processes required to ensure that the project will satisfy the needs for which it was undertaken. It includes all activities of the overall management function that determine the quality objectives, responsibilities for quality and implements them by means such as quality planning, quality assurance, quality control and continual improvement, within the complete project quality management system.

Project quality management must address both the management of the project and the outputs of the project. Failure to meet quality requirements in either dimension can have serious negative effects for some or all of the project stakeholders.

What is meant by quality planning?

The starting point for establishing quality in the project is quality planning, which takes the defined scope of the project (or the next phase or time period in an iterative life cycle) and specifies the criteria to be used to validate that the outputs are fit for purpose and acceptable to the sponsor.

As a result of quality planning, the quality plan will be created and is agreed with the sponsor and wider governance board as a key part of the overall project management plan (PMP). The quality plan sets out the desired attributes of work in scope and how these are to be assessed. To do this, it references applicable regulations, standards, specifications and, in some cases, values of the investing organisation. Most importantly the quality plan will note the agreed acceptance criteria in order to provide guidance to the team about the requirements and essential conditions for the deliverable that they are working on. They also guide the planning of quality control and other assurance activities that are performed to check that outputs meet requirements. It is important to do this after scope definition and before any further planning is carried out, as quality control and assurance activities take time and consume resources that need to be scheduled and costed.

The quality plan documents:

- methods of verifying that the outputs meet requirements;

- pass/fail criteria for each method;

- frequency of the tests, checks or audits that will be carried out;

- requirements for resources needed, for example: particular test equipment; suitably qualified and experienced staff who may be provided by the delivery organisation or a part of the supply chain; stakeholder approvals.

Obtaining stakeholder agreement facilitates the handover of the project's outputs on completion, and planning early how this will be done is a key success factor for project management.

Differences between quality control and quality assurance

Quality control consists of inspection, measurement and testing to verify that the project outputs meet the acceptance criteria defined during quality planning. Quality assurance attempts to build

MANAGEMENT

in quality through the consistent use of standard processes and procedures, supported by training and feedback, quality control is focused on preventing problems being passed on to the internal or external customer. It is important that quality assurance is performed by a person independent of the project whereas quality control can be performed by a member of the project team.

Figure 2.2.4.1 shows how the three elements of quality planning, quality assurance and quality control work together within the overall discipline of quality management.

Figure 2.2.4.1 Quality management as implemented within the project

For quality control to be effective, change control of specifications and test plans are vital so that any modifications are formally authorised, coordinated and communicated.

As part of quality planning, test plans will have been agreed. These include aspects such as:

- sample size of tests, for example, the whole item or a percentage chosen at random;

- test protocols, including resources required – people, equipment – third-party expertise, or facilities;

- independent performance or witnessing of tests, by a regulator or process owner from business-as-usual.

There are many project scenarios where the project outputs are highly complex and technical and where the work to verify conformance of outputs to specifications is extensive. Testing is well established and understood in these scenarios. It is easy to overlook that all projects need to deliver outputs that are fit for purpose and therefore enable the outcomes to be achieved.

Quality assurance activities must be seen to show an independent view of how the project is being managed in relation to adherence to framework and process, and so to be effective must be conducted as soon as the project starts management activity. Quality control on the other hand cannot be applied until the start of delivery of physical outputs. If the output being considered is related to a management process, then quality control could also be applied equally to interim or final outputs, such as reports, processes, communication materials or financial models.

In all quality control activities, decisions need to be made about the degree of conformance of the output (or sample of outputs) tested to the specification and acceptance criteria, and what action to take in the event of non-conformance.

There will be some projects, for example where safety critical products are being built where continuing to use a non-compliant item is unacceptable and rework will be necessary, triggering a change to the plan. In other scenarios, for example in user acceptance testing of a system, some deviations from requirements may be tolerable in initial use and the decision may be to press ahead to 'go-live' with known issues, picking up remedial work at a later point, and driven by the permanent organisation.

Projects deliver a huge variety of outputs and are consequently subject to many forms of quality control depending on the technical nature of the work and the particular requirements of individual industries. The quality control regime for the project is established by the project manager drawing on input from relevant technical experts rather than by reference to generic processes.

2.2.4 Learning summary

The section of the guide that you have just read will provide you with the learning necessary to be assessed against the following learning outcome and assessment criteria:

11. Understand quality in the context of a project.

11.1 *Explain what is meant by quality planning.*

There are three main aspects to this section that can quite easily be differentiated by remembering some key concepts. The first aspect, quality planning is all about setting standards, these apply to the outputs and benefits and the processes by which they are delivered. The former is usually a fixed element outlined by the sponsor (or customer); the latter will be defined by the project manager and the organisations existing governance framework. Quality planning delivers the quality plan, which documents all aspects of quality that have been agreed by stakeholders, and forms a key part of the PMP.

11.2 *Differentiate between quality control and quality assurance.*

The second aspect, quality assurance, answers one important question: is the project actually following the processes and procedures as set out in the quality plan? There is no point in consuming resources to form a plan if the project then follows a different route. Assuming the project is following the plan – and here is the third aspect – is that action creating an output that meets the acceptance criteria? Quality control will now confirm if that acceptance has actually been achieved. Quality control is the least flexible of the processes, as the result is pass or fail. Whereas with quality assurance the processes could be getting followed to a degree and yet still deliver an acceptable output. Whatever the result from quality control, it is important to ask why? The answer to this question provides the pathway to improvement.

2.2.5 Procurement

Procurement is the process by which products and services are acquired from an external provider for incorporation into the project.

The purpose, typical content and importance of a procurement strategy

The procurement strategy sets out the high-level approach for securing the goods and services required from external suppliers to satisfy project needs. It is informed by decisions made on strategic sourcing and leads to the development of the procurement element of an integrated project management plan (PMP).

Decisions to make on questions with the sponsor and wider governance are:

- How much risk should be retained in the project or programme and how much shared with suppliers in the supply chain?

- On a continuum from transactional to collaborative, what type of relationship is desired with different suppliers, and why?

The complexity of the work, the capability of the team, the client/owner's appetite for risk and the life cycle approach chosen inform these decisions, as does the analysis of the market in the sourcing strategy. The resulting procurement strategy for the project considers the following main areas:

- make or buy decision;

- use of single, integrated or multiple suppliers;

- conditions and forms of contract;

- methods of supplier reimbursement;

- types of contractual relationships;

- supplier selection process.

Make or buy decision

Once the scope of the project becomes known, it is then possible to gain an understanding of the supply possibilities and help identify the criteria by which the 'make or buy' decision can be made.

A key factor in the organisation's internal capacity is in terms of skills, functions and capabilities. For instance, if there is an under-utilised internal capability, it may well be in the best interests of the organisation to utilise these resources to deliver parts of the project. Those parts that cannot be delivered from within will be sourced from the marketplace, requiring that these providers are assessed for their capability in relation to requirements. In order to assess what can be delivered externally from providers under contract, the 'external potential to provide' must be explored. It is critical to know what the market is capable of delivering and how external providers could contribute to the project, before the project is divided up into contractual packages that external providers may be able to supply.

Use of single, integrated or multiple suppliers

A single supplier route means that one supplier will be chosen to supply all the requirements for a particular commodity to the project. Often this would be referred to as a preferred supplier. The advantages of doing this are that a strong relationship will build up between the supplier and the project team, which might provide additional technical support, the costs of procurement are less, better streamlining of joint systems and greater leverage of price in relation to volume. Disadvantages are of course putting all the eggs in one basket, if there are any disruptions to supply or the supplier goes bust it may take time to go through the procurement process to onboard an alternative supplier.

To reduce the risk of supply disruption a multiple supplier route may be chosen instead of single supply. In the multiple supply route, the price leverage to volume benefit gained in single supply may be replaced by looking at ways to encourage competition between suppliers. The main disadvantages of the multi-source approach are increased cost involved in contract negotiation, the amount of management and process execution may be greater, and as each supplier is obtaining a lesser amount of business, they may become less responsive to any requirement for aftersales support.

An integrated supply route could mean that a member of the supplier organisation is actually sitting in the project team alongside those who are actually delivering the project. The advantages of this are the immediacy of the contact, problems can be discussed directly, project to supplier. The supplier also gets an inside view of the project and can gain more knowledge of how to deliver optimum supply. Disadvantages of this approach could be that the supplier is too close for comfort and the project team may feel an awkwardness around discussing other aspects of the project, that are perhaps confidential. Also, if there are service delivery problems, the project team may not wish to express these to their full extent to someone who is in effect part of the same team, leading to slower resolution of service issues.

Conditions and forms of contract

A contract is an agreement made between two or more parties that creates legally binding obligations between them. The contract sets out those obligations and the actions that can be taken if they are not met.

Contracts are covered by contract law. The project manager should always seek specialist advice to ensure that the legal ramifications of any proposed contract are fully understood. The law governing any contract will depend on the applicable jurisdiction. Nevertheless, there are generic principles that are universal in application. For example, there must be:

- an 'offer' made by one party, which is 'accepted' unqualified by the other party;

- an intention to create legal relations between the parties and for the parties to be bound by these obligations;

- a consideration passing from one party to the other in return for the provision of goods or services covered by the contract;

- definite terms, so that it is clear as to what conditions the parties are agreeing;

- legality, with only properly incorporated firms or competent persons entering into the contracts.

In many industries a range of standard forms of contract are available. For example, the Joint Contracts Tribunal (JCT) and the New Engineering Contract (NEC) family of contracts provide standard forms of contract that can be utilised in engineering and construction. The strength of using one of these standard forms of contract is that it will generally take account of established best practice within a particular industry. The weakness is that it may not fully address all the areas required for a particular project application.

Where alterations are made to a standard contract, it then becomes a bespoke contract. A bespoke contract is one that is drafted to suit the specific procurement circumstances. Its strength is that local requirements can be reflected, but this must be traded against the time and cost of producing the document.

The contract itself should contain enough information for the intentions of the parties to be clear. These intentions are set out in the 'contract conditions' and include items such as:

- general information (e.g. who the parties are, description and location of the works or services, legal system that the contract will use, etc.);

- provider's responsibilities for design, approvals, assignment of such responsibilities, subcontracting;

- time – schedule, milestones, completion date;

- quality – testing, defect rectification;

- payment – certificates, release of monies;

- compensation events, change requests, dealing with unforeseen circumstances;

- property – who owns what during the course of the contract, transfer of intellectual property (IP) and copyright;

- assignment and management of risk; the need for insurances;

- how disputes will be managed (e.g. non-performance).

In most circumstances bespoke contracts means that experienced procurement specialists will be competent to write or check contract documentation, including ensuring that there is a clear hierarchy of conditions and precedence, a clear mechanism for performance management, change management and an exit strategy. This means that the need for advice from lawyers can be restricted to unusual or complex issues.

Different methods of supplier reimbursement

Payment mechanisms are a means of achieving the appropriate allocation of risk and of motivating the supplier to perform. Options range from a 'lump sum' or fixed price for a defined scope, where all the cost risk is with the supplier, through to reimbursable contracts where the project pays the supplier on an emerging cost basis.

Intermediate arrangements include 'target cost' contracts, where overspend or underspend is shared in a preordained proportion between parties, or 'bill of quantity' contracts, where actual quantities delivered are measured and valued against agreed unit rates. Penalties and bonus incentives are often used to motivate performance in such arrangements.

Some projects or programmes lend themselves to a procurement strategy whereby the supplier finances the development of a product in return for receiving a fee for its operation for a set period of time. An example would be a contractor building a bridge and collecting the tolls for a fixed period in payment.

The most common forms of supplier reimbursement are outlined below and shown in Figure 2.2.5.1:

- Fixed price – where a fixed price is agreed for a defined scope. If the scope of work is delivered for a greater cost to the supplier, they have to be able to fund that difference. The customer has very low-price control risk, as that has already been agreed; however, the supplier may try and cut corners to achieve the scope within the cost and time constraints of the contract. The customer may therefore experience schedule and technical performance risk, which with this form of reimbursement is very high.

- Cost plus fee – where the customer agrees to pay the costs incurred to deliver the scope plus an agreed fee. There are occasions where this form may be cost plus a percentage, which is usually preferred by the supplier. This is a high-risk contract, overall for the customer, as they agree to proceed with the work, not really knowing what the final cost will be.

- Time and material/per unit quantity – where a price is agreed for a unit quantity of material or time. This is the highest risk contract to the customer as the final cost will not be apparent until the end of the contract. This contract is necessary when the customer has very little idea of the actual scope of the work. The customer risk can be reduced by employing robust contract management to keep track of costs as they are incurred.

- Target cost – where a target sum is agreed in advance by both parties, who expend best efforts to reach that target. If the final cost is less than the target, the surplus is shared between both parties; similarly if the costs are greater, both parties agree to fund the excess. This form of reimbursement is typical where there are opportunities in the work for incentives to apply.

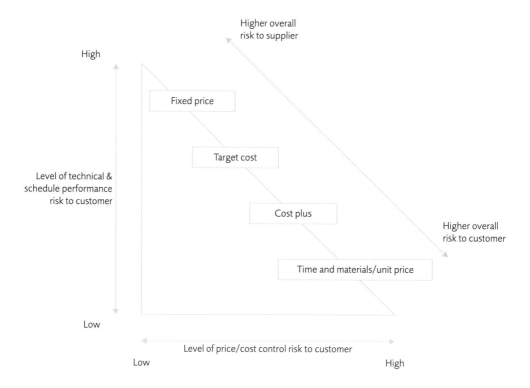

Figure 2.2.5.1 Risk distribution in relation to reimbursement method

Different contractual relationships

In order to deliver the procurement strategy, a number of contractual relationships can be used, for example:

One comprehensive contract – The simplest arrangement contractually is a comprehensive contract in which one supplier is responsible for everything required for a project. Comprehensive contracts have various names. Those used in the construction industry include 'turnkey', 'all-in', 'package deal', 'design-and-construct' and 'EPIC' (Engineer-Procure-Install-Commission). In other industries 'prime contract' is a common description. A risk to the customer is that the entire project depends upon the performance of the one supplier. One comprehensive contract is logical if the customer wishes to place all the responsibility for the project with one supplier and the supplier chosen is able and willing to undertake it satisfactorily.

Sequential contract – This is the sequential use of two or more contractors during a project. For example, in the traditional system for building and public works, one organisation may be employed to design a project and another organisation to construct it. The second contract in such arrangements can be a comprehensive commitment to supply all the goods and remaining services required to complete the project. Starting with a contract for design and development should make it possible for options to be studied and most uncertainties settled before they affect more costly work, such as manufacturing or construction. Detailed and final design can be completed and priced before the customer is committed to many of the later and greater costs of proceeding with the project.

A sequence of contracts has the potential disadvantage that the project team must plan and manage the interactions between the stages, particularly the risk of defaults by one supplier causing claims on the customer from one or more subsequent suppliers. The customer may have a less firm indication of the final cost of the project until the final contracts have been agreed. As a result, no party can plan ahead with any degree of certainty. Additionally, if the construction organisation has problems, they may have a tendency to blame the design, even though the design may not actually be the cause.

Parallel contract – is where a similar scope of work is given to two or more suppliers and they work in parallel to deliver the complete project. For example, a refurbishment contract for a three-story office block where one contractor does the ground floor, another the first and another the second and so on. This type of arrangement is also common in many industries for purchasing goods and services. Communications are direct between the customer and each specialist supplier, but this arrangement requires the customer to manage the relationships between all parties. Separating responsibilities for stages and types of work is logical if requirements are uncertain at the start, or if individual suppliers have limited capabilities or know-how relative to the size or type of work needed for a project.

Customers can use this type of relationship to create competition between suppliers, but this needs to be carefully managed to avoid any compromises of quality or safety.

Sub-contracts – This is where a prime contractor holds the contract and then sub-contracts it to others to complete. The contracts can then be implemented using the same choices reviewed so far for the supplier to purchase goods or services from sub-contractors. Suppliers frequently employ several sub-contractors in parallel, particularly where the project requires the input of specialised goods and services. In most contracts the customer can only communicate formally with sub-contractors through the main contractor. If much of the work for a project is sub-contracted, the customer may have only indirect ability to assess and influence whether it will be completed to requirements on time and to the quality standards set out in the main contract. A customer should therefore consider imposing conditions on sub-contracting when planning the employment of a supplier who is planning to sub-contract any of the work.

Many specialist companies prefer to work directly for the ultimate user of their products and services rather than as a sub-contractor. This provides them with a direct link that may lead to supplying spares or undertaking maintenance work after the completion of the contract. They may not be so well motivated to perform if employed through a main supplier who does not offer the prospect of more work for further projects.

Partnering/Joint Venture – This is where very large projects are completed by a number of suppliers coming together to form a partnership, and may be necessary because the total work is too large or complex for a single supplier to deliver. Often a separate company is set up and each supplier will nominate one of their directors to sit on the board of the joint company.

A supplier selection process

It is important that the supplier selection process is seen to be open to scrutiny, objective and structured to show the best value supplier from a number of suppliers who have been asked to tender for work in the project. A typical supplier selection process is shown in Figure 2.2.5.2.

Figure 2.2.5.2 Stages of supplier selection process

The research step involves identifying the providers that have the required capability. This may be unnecessary where there is already a regularly reviewed and up-to-date approved provider list. Research may result in a long list of potential providers. Pre-qualification seeks to reduce this list by several means. A typical approach is to send out a prequalification questionnaire to gather information from potential providers. This may clarify the production capacity of the provider, their willingness to tender, their financial stability and their technical experience. It may also ask for references for similar work.

The pre-qualification results in a shortlist of providers who will be asked to provide a full bid against a defined set of requirements. Tendering is an important process in its own right and a project manager may need to seek specialist help. It is important that the requirements are clear and all providers are given an equal chance of success.

Records associated with selection should be maintained and archived to contain risks associated with potential challenges by unsuccessful providers. Inputs to the selection process should include an appropriate risk analysis in addition to cost, time and quality considerations as defined in the resource management plan. Where possible, a reserve provider should be identified. For critical goods and services, the contract may be split amongst several providers as a form of risk containment.

Award will involve the negotiation and agreement of a contract to supply goods and services. Attention needs to be paid throughout the whole selection process to ensure that a contract is not casually entered into, and it should be made clear in all meetings and in associated documents that the proceedings are subject to contract. Once a contract is awarded, it is important that the relationship between the project and the provider is actively managed. Although much effort may have been invested in the binding contract, resorting to the contract to resolve disputes should be seen as a last resort. Project managers must regard providers as members of the team and communicate effectively.

Once the goods or services to be supplied by the provider have been delivered and accepted, the contract will be closed. This will involve ensuring that all financial arrangements have been honoured, all changes to the contract have been accounted for, and may involve setting up a maintenance contract to support, repair or upgrade goods provided.

2.2.5 Learning summary

The section of the guide that you have just read will provide you with the learning necessary to be assessed against the following learning outcome and assessment criteria:

9. Understand project procurement.

9.1 *Explain the purpose, typical content and importance of a procurement strategy.*

The procurement strategy is documented in the procurement plan for the project part of the overall project management plan. The project manager will usually be assisted, in procurement matters, with a member of the procurement functional area within the organisation. Whoever has been assigned to support procurement in the project will either be in the team full time, for a large project, or just when required for a smaller initiative.

When a project has a specialist, or unique, requirement it must consider procurement implications as early in the life cycle as is practicable. Waiting until the full approval of the project at the end of the definition phase may, for example, result in tender delays and long lead times having a detrimental effect on the schedule.

9.2 *Differentiate between different methods of supplier reimbursement (including fixed price, cost plus fee, per unit quantity, and target cost).*

At first glance this may seem a complicated area and, in reality, it is; however, from a study point of view there are some fundamental elements that are important. The more the price is fixed, the less cost risk the customer will face; the supplier will be under greatest risk in trying to deliver the scope for the fixed price agreed. When the price is more variable, the customer will now be under more cost risk. Although the scope has been agreed, the customer does not know what the final price will be until the work has been delivered. Why would a customer enter into such a contract? If the scope is difficult to define or where there is lots of uncertainty, there is usually a case for this more flexible type of reimbursement method. If a customer were to offer high-risk work to the market, it would be unlikely to gain much interest from suppliers if it were offered under fixed price conditions. Another example of differences between other methods could include per unit quantity, which allows the buyer to agree a fixed price for 'units' required for the project. However, the buyer might not know how many units are required and therefore the final costs for the project are still uncertain, whereas in a fixed price project the supplier will quote their final price for the work and therefore give the buyer certainty on their final costs.

9.3 *Differentiate between different contractual relationships.*

The main considerations of the most suitable contractual relationship are centred on the size of the project, the number of suppliers available in the market and the amount of involvement the customer seeks in managing the relationship between multiple suppliers. Typically, a project may use a single-supplier route to ensure that there was a simple interface to manage, whereas a project using a multiple-supplier route would have a more complex set of interfaces to manage. This is another area where risk is a factor that will be taken into account in the ultimate decision. Using one main supplier (sequential contract) is putting all the eggs in one basket. If that supplier fails, and if that is in the earlier stages, the whole project will suffer and may be costly to recover. A sequential supply arrangement may be a better option if supplier failure is an identified risk. Often a project when using a single-supplier route may not get the best price available from the supplier; they may get a more competitive price for the resources required from the multiple contractual relationship model. This decision will often depend on the complexity of the item being procured and the number of suppliers in the market.

9.4 *Explain a supplier selection process.*

If suppliers have put together a response to an invitation to tender, there must be an objective process by which that tender will be reviewed alongside other tenders. Suppliers will have consumed resources to produce that tender and it is only good business practice to acknowledge this effort. In some circumstances the purchasing decision may be open to challenge and therefore needs to be as objective as possible. Risk is managed in this part of procurement by using a pre-qualified number of preferred suppliers who may have been audited in advance, or the purchaser has had previous experience of the work that can be delivered by those on the preferred list.

2.2.6 Scope management

'Scope' is the term used in the management of projects to refer to the totality of the outputs, outcomes and benefits and the work required to produce them. Outputs (deliverables) are the tangible or intangible products typically delivered by a project. Outcomes are the changed circumstances or behaviour that results from the use of an output and leads to realisation of benefits. Scope management is the process for identifying, defining and controlling scope.

A high-level scope is typically recorded in the business case in support of the chosen option and its investment appraisal.

How to define scope in terms of outputs, outcomes and benefits

In defining scope, it is important to be clear about the boundaries and interfaces with adjacent projects. This is critical to avoid duplication, conflicts or omission of work within a programme or portfolio, or between other standalone projects or business-as-usual work.

The detailed scope of work emerges from the decomposition of the chosen option to meet the sponsors requirements. Once a solution has been identified that meets the requirements, the scope of the work can be illustrated using a product breakdown structure (PBS). Identifying both products and the work involved in building them is an iterative activity. Where uncertainty about the end products exists, provision must be made for revisiting the PBS and WBS during the project life cycle. The PBS is a hierarchical structure where the main output of the project is placed at the top level. The next level down shows the components that make up the higher level. This process continues to the level of individual products. Each product will have defined acceptance criteria and quality control methods.

For example, if an organisation wanted to undertake an international conference in order to promote its products to new markets overseas, the initial PBS might look like the example shown in Figure 2.2.6.1. The PBS shows what will be delivered; there is no detail provided, as yet, about the actual work required to complete these deliverables.

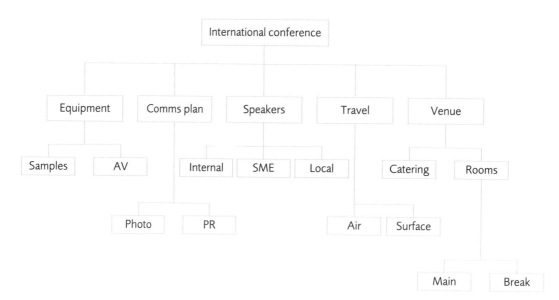

Figure 2.2.6.1 Example PBS for an international conference

Once the exercise of producing the PBS is complete it can then be used to do initial scope verification to obtain stakeholders agreement that the products identified are what stakeholders expect the project to deliver and get a firm agreement to that effect. At this stage it is hoped that stakeholders would also advise on what products are in or out of scope. Scope verification will continue, at various points, throughout the project until the deliverables have been finally handed over and formally accepted by stakeholders. Clearly defining what is in and out of scope prevents the risk of misunderstanding at a later point in the project that may lead to emerging issues and change requests. Incomplete scope definition is a common cause of time delays, cost growth and benefit reduction.

Following the categorisation of the project to create products, the project manager is able to direct those products to the most suitable technical resource for more detailed scope definition. This results in the baseline scope of work to be defined through a work breakdown structure (WBS) which will detail the activities which will be scheduled and resourced to meet all the requirements and benefits (Figure 2.2.6.2).

Figure 2.2.6.2 Example WBS structure derived directly from the PBS

At the lowest level of the WBS, work packages will exist that contain the activities to be performed to allow estimating, scheduling and resource assignments necessary to do the work and ultimately deliver the output. Where the objective is well understood and has a tangible output (e.g. in construction and engineering), it is usual to define the scope as accurately as possible at the beginning of the life cycle.

Where the objective is less tangible, or subject to significant change, e.g. business change or some IT systems, a more flexible or iterative approach to scope is needed. In projects using an iterative life cycle, it is equally important to structure the scope of work and record the assumptions. The difference in this scenario is that the most important requirements are prioritised through a process of stakeholder engagement and these are then translated into a target scope of work to be achieved within a fixed time window with defined resources. Subsequent iterations may alter the scope based on accumulated experience, acquired insights and emerging priorities.

In the WBS each work package will have a coded reference in order to be tracked within the business management systems of the organisation. Any estimated costs related to the delivery of that work package, such as people, equipment, materials or any other resource required, can then be recorded using this coding structure. The resulting structure is the cost breakdown structure (CBS), a hierarchical breakdown of a project into cost elements. The CBS provides a financial view of the project and splits the project scope into its individual cost components, which can be related back to the original budget. The CBS will reflect the financial coding used for project accounting and any booking codes associated with each element of the project.

The work packages in the WBS are reviewed and decisions are made about who in the project will take responsibility for carrying out the work, supervising activity and reporting progress. The structure of the project organisation is vitally important for the effective performance of key activities and to support the efforts of the whole project team. The organisation breakdown structure (OBS) describes the structure of the project organisation required to complete the work-packages in the WBS. This is useful particularly when work will be performed by business staff seconded to the project or by specialist teams working on more than one project. It is also important for individuals themselves to know where they are situated in the structure and their reporting responsibilities.

The way in which an organisational breakdown structure is used to create a responsibility assignment matrix

The WBS and OBS can be used in a combined way to create a communication device known as a responsibility assignment matrix (RAM). This ensures that the people who are going to do the work are fully aware of the work they have been assigned, together with their position in the project organisation. The functional line managers in the delivery organisation would also consult the RAM to confirm the work that has been assigned to their people. There are resource management systems commercially available that can allow the functional manager to approve assignments depending on individual availability and departmental workload. A common coding structure can be applied to the RAM as shown in Figure 2.2.6.3.

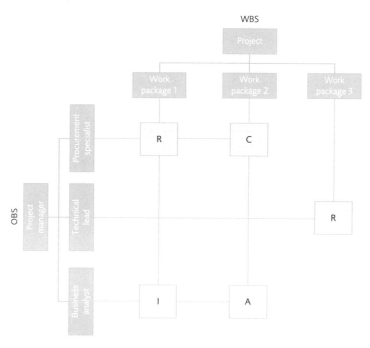

Figure 2.2.6.3 Responsibility assignment matrix (RAM) showing RACI coding

When the RAM is coded in this way it can also be referred to as a RACI matrix where:

(R)   Responsible – conducts the actual work/owns the problem;

(A)   Accountable – approves the completed work and is held fully accountable for it;

(C)   Consulted – is included in decision making and holds a primary supportive role;

(I)   Informed – is kept informed of progress and results.

The RAM provides a clear and concise summary of tasks or deliverables, the specific responsibilities defined within the project procedures, and the level of accountability or contribution expected from named roles or individuals within the project.

2.2.6.1 Requirements management

In all cases, specific project objectives and requirements are informed by the success criteria and benefits desired by stakeholders. Requirements are the stakeholders' wants and needs and must be clearly defined with acceptance criteria. Everyone involved in carrying out requirements management must ensure that:

- there is a clear linkage between benefits, project success criteria, project objectives and project requirements;

- requirements are clear, unambiguous and expressed as simply as possible.

High-level requirements are defined during the concept phase of the project life cycle. These need to be detailed enough to make an investment decision (i.e. whether or not to proceed to the definition phase).

Requirements management is the process of capturing, assessing and justifying stakeholders' wants and needs. It requires the capture of requirements via a structured process. This process should incrementally break down the requirements in a hierarchical manner, considering different conditions and scenarios. The requirements, once defined, must be validated with the project sponsor and/or key stakeholders to ensure the full scope has been captured.

How to establish scope through requirements management processes

Requirements management is an ongoing process that is maintained throughout the project life cycle. These requirements become the principal project deliverables. Thus, it helps to define the project scope. This allows the project team to understand the exact deliverables of the project and how the work will be structured to meet the requirements and deliver the scope.

The gathering of requirements is the first step, it can be done in any number of ways. It ranges from personal interviews, surveys and workshops, to focus groups, modelling and simulation. Some methodologies, including agile approaches, are designed to enable the continuous gathering and refinement of requirements on the assumption that the stakeholders may not be sure of their needs.

Analysing requirements combines information from functions such as schedule management and investment appraisal, with specific value-based techniques such as function analysis and function cost analysis. The result is a thorough understanding of requirements and the value they contribute to the overall objective. This step of the process also tests any assumptions made as part of the analysis primarily providing feedback to stakeholders, building consensus and generating ideas. The results of the analysis are communicated through individual consultation or group workshops. This leads to a debate about functionality and alternative ideas. The product owner has a vital role in ensuring that requirements are always seen relative to business needs and advises on the acceptance criteria necessary to achieve this. The result is a baselined set of options for functional requirements. These can then be used to examine the value of alternative solutions during solutions development. Value represents the amount of benefit that will accrue from the requirement and could be used to justify its priority – how important is this requirement compared to the others.

Sometimes, more requirements are requested than it is feasible to deliver, so a prioritisation exercise is needed to highlight the most essential requirements and justify why the chosen requirements should be the ones that are baselined. A common prioritisation technique is the MoSCoW approach:

(M) Must have

(S) Should have

(C) Could have

(W) Won't have.

If using an agile methodology, the 'could have' and 'should have' requirements would be sacrificed if at any time the project was predicted to go over budget or be late. The 'must haves' would only be reduced as a very last resort. In the worst case scenario the project would deliver only the 'must haves' in the form of a minimum viable product (MVP). The main benefit of the process is to ensure that essential requirements are understood as an input to the work to select the optimal solution and then define the detailed scope of work to be delivered with acceptance criteria. This level of rigour mitigates the risk that in later life cycle there is dispute between the project and the organisation about completion and transition of the deliverables into use.

2.2.6.2 Configuration management

Configuration management encompasses the technical and administrative activities concerned with the creation, maintenance, controlled change and quality control of the scope of work. A configuration is the functional and physical characteristics of the final deliverable as defined in technical documents and achieved in the execution of project management plans.

At its simplest, configuration management involves version control of documents and information, but the discipline of configuration management is a more complex endeavour in projects where the design of the solution is multifaceted, combining multiple technical disciplines and a wide range of asset types. The product breakdown structure (PBS), plus detailed descriptions of each product, becomes the project configuration. Once this is baselined it is subject to formal change control and configuration management.

In agile projects the initial configuration will be very flexible and updated frequently. The lack of a full and detailed configuration at the start makes configuration management of vital importance in such a highly dynamic environment.

How to manage scope through configuration management processes

The configuration management process encompasses the following five activities, as shown in Figure 2.2.6.4:

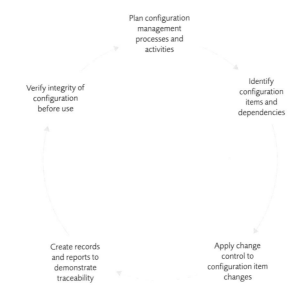

Figure 2.2.6.4 Activities involved in configuration management of an output

Configuration management planning – A configuration management plan describes any project-specific procedures and the extent of their application. The plan also identifies roles and responsibilities for carrying out configuration management. The configuration management plan will often form part of the quality management plan but may be separate in large or complex projects.

Configuration identification – This involves breaking down the project into configuration items and creating a unique numbering or referencing system for each item. A configuration record is created for each item, which will record the current version and subsequent changes to the item.

Configuration control – Configuration control ensures that all changes to configuration items are controlled. It is important to identify the interrelationships between configuration items to enable this.

Configuration status accounting – This provides records and reports that relate to a deliverable and its configuration information. It enables traceability of configuration items throughout their development. Users can consult the configuration record, which will provide an updated account of the status of the item, showing all changes to the current reference point, when these changes were made and who has taken responsibility for creating the latest version.

Configuration verification audit – This is used to determine whether a deliverable conforms to its requirements and configuration information. At a minimum, a verification audit is undertaken at the end of a life cycle phase, when a deliverable is finished, or at the point of transitioning the output into use; however, audits could be carried out throughout the life cycle during change control to ensure management products were being used in line with their current configuration status.

The key outputs of a well-controlled configuration management process are:

- confidence that the current version of any configuration item is known, be that a document, drawing, software or any other asset; and

- documented traceability between versions of each configuration item.

Configuration management is very closely aligned with change control. Together, these two processes ensure that deliverables meet the required specification, any changes are beneficial changes and there is a complete audit trail for the development of each deliverable.

While the configuration is primarily concerned with the products of a project or programme, it should also be applied to key management documents. For example, documents such as the business case and project management plan should be subject to version control and audit to ensure that they are fit for purpose and all changes are recorded.

As work is completed, responsibility for maintaining deliverables passes to business-as-usual. The project or programme management team is responsible for ensuring that configuration management information is suitable for transfer to those who will be maintaining the products long after the project or programme has been closed.

2.2.6.3 Change control

Change control is the process through which all requests to change the baseline of a project are identified, evaluated and approved, rejected or deferred. Change requests may arise as a result of issues that develop in the management of the work, or from external sources such as new stakeholder requirements, new regulations or changes in the context that result in the original plans being no longer viable. The change request should make it clear what the change is and who has requested the change and why.

Managing requests for change effectively is a proven success factor in project management, the alternative being a potential escalation of problems as changes are adopted without analysis of their impact on other parts of the solution or deliverables. It is of particular importance when the project is part of a larger programme or portfolio because the consequential effects of unmanaged change may be far-reaching within the planned change environment and to business-as-usual activities.

At some point a detailed evaluation should be performed by the project team to make a detailed impact assessment of what would need to change as a result of the change request, including understanding the impact on the project success criteria. This assessment will consume a degree of resources, especially if it is a complex change request. It is assumed that prior to the detailed evaluation an initial evaluation has occurred to understand if the project should be considering such a change at all.

Different stages of a typical change control process

Managing change requests in a controlled way enables the sponsor and other stakeholders to:

- understand the implications of variations on the forecasted outcomes of the work;

- influence the decision of how to respond in the context of their objectives and appetite for risk.

Figure 2.2.6.5 outlines the steps in a typical change control process. In scenarios where change is implemented without formal authorisation, the project manager adopts a retrospective process, which is often seen as unnecessary bureaucracy; however, this is needed to enable realistic forecasts.

A change register (or log) records all changes identified or requested from whatever source and whatever their status

Change Log

Raise change request

External stakeholders or internal to project

Update change log

Approval process

Initial evaluation

The change is initally reviewed to considered if it is worthwhile evaluating in detail or should be rejected at this stage

Configuration management ensures most current version and change history of information is provided

Provide information

Detailed evaluation

Detailed evoluation considfering the impact on baseline success criteria, benefits, scope, quality, time, resources, costs, risks, stakeholder engagement or any other criteria important to achieving the business case

Recommendation is made to the sponsor and/or wideer governance board to approve, reject or defer the change. The sponsor is accountable for ensuring a decision is made and communicated

Deferred

Rejected

Approved

The options for change are defined as defer (request for clarification or additional information), reject (the risks or costs to change exceed the value the change will provide), accept (the extra value the change is creating is worth the cost of implementing the change)

Update change log

If a change is approved, plans are updated to reflect the change. Configuration record of items affected and version updated accordingly

Update baseline and budgets

Implement change

Implement the necessary actions and monitor through to completion

Update reports

Communicate change

Figure 2.2.6.5 Stages of a typical change control process and relationship with configuration management

In certain circumstances, it is appropriate to implement a change freeze on a project where no further changes are considered, as to do so would jeopardise the achievement of the project objectives. In some industries, schedules of rates form the basis of pricing changes in advance of implementation. This eliminates the need to negotiate a price between contractor and client. Uncontrolled change in a contractual environment often leads to claims that may have to be settled in court.

Agile projects make change control an integral part of the development process. Each development iteration starts with a planning meeting that clarifies and prioritises the function addressed in the iteration. Some of these features may be changes to existing features but are considered alongside all the others.

2.2.6 Learning summary

The section of the guide that you have just read will provide you with the learning necessary to be assessed against the following learning outcome and assessment criteria:

1. Understand how organisations and projects are structured.

1.2 *Explain the way in which an organisational breakdown structure is used to create a responsibility assignment matrix.*

The organisational breakdown structure (OBS) shows the hierarchical structure of the project. It is common that the project manager will be at the head of that structure. In a large project this may be the project director and individual project managers of the main areas of the project reporting into this position. The OBS is valuable for communicating the reporting structure for the project to all stakeholders. Once the tasks in the work breakdown structure (WBS) have been assigned to positions within the OBS, a responsibility assignment matrix (RAM) is created. The RAM will now be used to communicate to those who have been assigned work and also to communicate to their line management that one or more of their people have been assigned work.

7. Understand scope management.

7.1 *Explain how to define scope in terms of outputs, outcomes and benefits (including use of product, cost and work breakdown structures).*

There are important reasons why a structured approach to scope definition is necessary particularly at the earliest stages of a project. It is at these stages that the project manager and team have most influence over the project and where change is most manageable. If the project team can't get scope defined and agreed at this stage, the longer the project continues, the higher will be the cost to change and the less chance there will be to deliver a satisfactory outcome for stakeholders. Using the key structures is useful for communicating to stakeholders but also internally can act as a check for the project team to be confident that all activities and work has been assigned. Nothing has been overlooked.

7.2 *Explain how to establish scope through requirements management processes (such as gather, analysis, justifying requirements, and baseline needs).*

Not every project will need or wish to use a requirements management process. It is very much in the domain of an agile methodology however the discipline and overall approach could be applied to most projects. The linear life cycle is getting most of its value at the end, when the project is delivered. The agile project will attempt to draw value out of an iterative life cycle at various points during the overall project's delivery. Being able to measure that interim value depends on having deep knowledge of what the project is delivering in terms of segmented requirements equating to measurable value and priority for the whole project. Requirements management allows that decision making to be planned into the life cycle through the MoSCoW prioritisation technique.

7.3 *Explain how to manage scope through configuration management processes (such as planning, identification, control, status accounting, and verification audit).*

The simplest way to think about configuration management is version control, which may sound too insignificant to warrant its own process. However, there have been many projects that were thought to be complete, except when handed over major elements didn't fit, other parts weren't connected, diameters of pipes couldn't be matched up. This was not the fault of the original design but that the design had changed, this change was not followed through to consider the effect on other items, was then approved and thought to be implemented effectively. The big problem here is of course that configuration issues don't tend to come to light until the point at which the output is being put into operation. At that point the cost impact is at its greatest, not only in terms of rework but in lost operational time when the product has to come out of service to be rectified.

7.4 *Explain different stages of a typical change control process (such as request, initial evaluation, detailed evaluation, recommendation, update plans, and implement).*

Probably one of the most straightforward of all project management processes, yet uncontrolled or poorly managed change is still one of the most common reasons why projects fail to meet their success criteria. It is not that the process doesn't exist; it is getting everyone to follow it. Time consuming, too bureaucratic and delaying the decision are some of the common reasons given for not following the process. Change control should be considered as an opportunity to deliver a product in the best way possible to meet the success criteria for the project.

Learners should note the relationship change control has with configuration management. There are two major touchpoints between the two processes. When conducting the detailed evaluation, change control is dependent on receiving the most current information to allow the best decision to be made. Status accounting shows the most current configuration that can be reviewed. Thereafter when the change is implemented, those who have made the decision to change must ensure that all configuration items affected are now updated and the new versions that have been created are now recorded as the current version. All previous versions will now be inaccessible for others or be labelled as 'superseded'.

2.2.7 Leadership and teamwork

Leadership is described as the ability to establish vision and direction, to influence and align others towards a common purpose, and to empower and inspire people to achieve success. There are many theories of leadership and the subject can be approached in a variety of ways. One simple approach to understanding different leadership styles is the comparison of transactional leaders and transformational leaders.

Transactional leaders ensure that requirements are agreed and that the rewards and penalties for achievement, or lack of it, are understood. It is an exchange process to do with setting objectives and plans: 'do this and you will be rewarded thus'.

In contrast, transformational leaders do everything possible to help people succeed in their own right and become leaders themselves. They help those people to transform themselves and achieve more than was intended or even thought possible.

How leadership impacts on team performance and motivation

By definition, the project environment is one of change. New teams come together to achieve objectives and are disbanded when the work is complete. As a consequence, the project manager should focus on different aspects of leadership throughout the project life cycle and set the pace accordingly.

Early phases may require expertise in influencing stakeholders and creating vision, and need a more transactional style with the project team. As the work progresses, the leadership focus shifts to maintaining momentum, responding to change and applying a more transformational approach.

The position of leader is granted by followers who make the decision to follow. That decision will be influenced by the leader using an appropriate style of leadership that takes account of both the situation and the readiness of people to follow. Team members' willingness to follow will vary according to their levels of motivation and ability, as well as their loyalties, priorities and the context of the situation.

Leaders must be aware of their team members' motivational requirements in order to manage their approach to individuals flexibly. The motivation of individuals is the subject of many theoretical models, such as those proposed by Maslow, Herzberg and McGregor.

Maslow's hierarchy of needs

Abraham H Maslow was an American psychologist who first presented his hierarchy of needs in his publication 'A Theory of Human Motivation' (Maslow 1941). He described the various levels of motivational needs in terms of physiological, safety, belongingness and love, esteem and ultimately self-actualisation as shown in Figure 2.2.7.1. His theory described the pattern that people move through depending on the environment and circumstances they face at any particular time.

A motivational leader could observe their team members behaviour on the basis of Maslow's theory and understand their level in the hierarchy. Individuals will have a tendency to look at the level above to gain the strongest motivation. Once a level is fulfilled, it ceases to continue motivating and it is likely the next level up will take over the motivational drive.

Figure 2.2.2.1 Maslow's hierarchy of motivational needs
Source: *Motivation and Personality*, 3rd ed by Abraham H. Maslow, eds Robert D. Frager and James Fadiman © 1987

Herzberg's two-factor theory

Frederick Hertzberg (1923–2000) proposed the 'two-factor theory' of human motivation. According to his theory people were influenced by two factors: motivators and hygiene factors. Achievement and psychological growth were considered motivators, whereas salary, working conditions and company policy were considered hygiene factors. One way to think about hygiene factors is to never assume that if a member of the team comes to work every day, they must be motivated; it could be just because hygiene factors are in place. That person, while not experiencing motivation, is probably not de-motivated; they are indifferent, neither motivated or demotivated.

Douglas McGregor's theory X and theory Y

McGregor's observations about how managers perceive their team members and the resulting management style can provide project leaders with a high-level view of their team members. McGregor (1965) identified two polar opposite views of how team members could be perceived by their leaders. 'Theory X' assumes that people are not motivated and dislike working. This view results in a very structural autocratic style of leadership. Accordingly, management must actively intervene to maintain control and get things done. Organisations where this type of leadership style is prevalent tend to be top heavy, with managers and supervisors required at every stage of productive activity. There tends to be very little delegation of authority and control remains firmly centralised.

At the opposite end of the spectrum 'Theory Y' assumes that employees are willing to work, self-motivated and creative, and happy to accept greater responsibility. It assumes that workers require a more participative style of leadership based on trust that is more decentralised. In organisations where Y-type individuals prevail, people at lower levels of the organisation are more involved in decision making and actively seek out greater degrees of responsibility.

Why it may be necessary to change leadership styles to effectively support the management of a project

Leadership is needed at all levels within a project-based setting. The sponsor communicates the vision to the project team, sets high-level expectations, involves team members in decisions and provides actionable feedback. The project manager should fully understand how to get the best out of each person and provides direction and support for them. Team members share responsibilities and work collaboratively. All leaders must provide timely and constructive feedback and be receptive to feedback provided to them by members of the team.

Figure 2.2.7.2 Factors that contribute to variance in leadership styles

Leaders need to adapt their style and approach to the needs of the team and the work that needs to be accomplished, this is called Situational Leadership®. There are some situations when the leader needs to be directive, for example, to address an issue that threatens the achievement of objectives. A mentoring or coaching style is appropriate when there is time to focus on development of the team as well as goal achievement. For much of the time when the team is established and working well, the leader delegates responsibility for achieving activities to team members, only intervening if evidence arises to suggest that performance is not to agreed expectations. Leadership in a project context is usually performed with limits on the leader's position power requiring them to adopt a style that builds team and wider stakeholder commitment.

Situational Leadership® provides choices of leadership style. Is there a best choice? The answer is a qualified yes providing that the leader takes account of two aspects. First, criticality of the situation – the more critical the situation the more the leader may have to exert control and take a directing style. Communication between leader and team is short, sharp and commanding. Second, skills and motivation of the team members – the greater the team's abilities the more the leader can empower the team to complete tasks, perhaps adopting a more delegating style as shown in Figure 2.2.7.2.

For a leader to consider a Situational Leadership® approach they need to have a good background knowledge of the individual team members skill levels and some insight into their levels of motivation. In addition, they need to have a developed degree of situational awareness to make quick reliable assessments of the nature of the situation and implications for any delays in response.

Characteristics and benefits of effective teams and teamwork

A team is a group of people working together in collaboration or cooperation towards a common goal. Teams in projects are temporary, formed for the specific purpose of delivering defined outputs and outcomes. Their transitory nature brings challenges not experienced in business-as-usual teams.

The establishment of a team will initially involve the selection of individuals based on their skills, behaviours and attitudes. Teamworking is most effective when people with complementary skills and behaviours are committed to a common objective and method of working.

Groups of people with a common aim are called a team on the assumption that the people will not only cooperate with each other but also collaborate to innovate and perform. Leading a group of people so they can become a high performing team is skilled work and some would argue the most important skill that all project managers must develop. Teams do not develop merely by working together – the right context needs to be created for teams to do their best work, and this is not a one-time effort, as team members leave or new ones start, requiring constant attention to ensure that things are going well. Team leaders in this respect can emerge from all parts of the organisation.

It takes time and resources to develop an effective team; however, there can be valuable benefits as a result, such as:

Improved quality of output – In an effective team each team member takes the quality of output personally. They may for example be quite distant technically from the actual point of output delivery but take time to understand the part they play in the production chain to ensure the standard expected by stakeholders is what is being delivered. Teams that work well together are, therefore, essential in improving service and meeting the needs of stakeholders.

More effective communication – As a team develops, individual relationships within it also develop. Communication between individuals becomes more open, and issues are discussed more freely, ensuring that there can be timely solutions agreed before any chance of conflict can arise. This open environment motivates individuals to be more comfortable trying new ways of doing things and asking questions about things they don't understand.

Increased productivity – One common aspect of effective teams is that the team achieves more as a team than the team members would on an individual basis. Within the team the workload is shared equally among members and distributed according to each member's skills and strengths. With focused collaboration team members will not only monitor their own progress but also the progress of others in the team. If one area is proving more difficult, the team will agree how the total resource can be distributed to overcome the problem. Ultimately, tasks are completed faster and more efficiently, thereby increasing overall team productivity.

Improved motivation – When the team collaborates to reach a goal, they can feel a greater sense of accomplishment in the achievement of a positive result that they may not have been able to achieve had they been working alone. This, combined with a sense of belonging, appreciation and recognition, can drastically improve team members self-esteem and morale. Team members find more satisfaction in their work and experience less stress, resulting in the overall team experiencing a much-reduced turnover rate.

Greater degree of innovation and problem solving – Teams are better able to produce more creative, innovative and practical solutions to problems than someone working alone. During workshops and meetings team members are comfortable to present ideas, during brainstorming sessions, knowing that they will not experience any criticism from other team members. This encourages others to feel more confident about coming up with unique and more creative ideas. Risk is seen to be shared. Individuals working alone may decide not to bear such risk and so only consider the safest solution.

In general teamwork has benefits to both the individual team members themselves and any organisation seeking to deliver multiple projects and programmes. Teamwork creates collaboration in the workplace, which can result in more flexible work schedules, particularly when team members are cross-trained to cover for each other's skills and strengths. It's also important to note that flexible working is increasingly being considered as a way to help improve productivity and develop a better work–life balance for employees.

Factors which impact on the leadership of virtual teams

One of the strengths of project-based working is being able to access the best people with the most appropriate skills. Achieving this can pose challenges when the best people for the team are in different places and separated by time zones. Widespread access to virtual communications technology has led to a proliferation in the number of virtual teams, often with virtual stakeholders. It is becoming the norm in many teams to have at least one person who is remote from the others. Even when most team members are co-located, it makes sense to treat this as a virtual team, so that all have the same access and opportunities as far as possible.

While virtual teams can work really well, there are challenges too. It is more difficult to build deep relationships and trust virtually than it is in person. It is much harder to detect the first signs of conflict developing, and then to resolve the conflict. It is harder to gel as a team if members cannot see each other and do not have the sort of informal conversations that happen naturally over coffee or by the water-coolers. All of this makes the project more difficult, but not impossible. Project professionals leading virtual teams need to consider all these factors and work out how to overcome them.

To be effective, a successful virtual team will need more than reliable technology. Figure 2.2.7.3 shows aspects of virtual leadership development. The model starts in the centre, developing a facilitative, virtual leadership mindset, approach and leadership style, then establishing how best to work with remote team colleagues and stakeholders. What are their preferences? What are their skills? How can trust be built and maintained throughout the project or programme? It is important to agree norms for communication, taking everyone's preferences into account.

Figure 2.2.7.3 Steps in development of virtual leadership

After these steps, technology is relevant. Pros and cons of audio and video, network security, availability of equipment and connectivity are just some of the considerations. Collaboration tools, chosen to suit all of the virtual team, help with work outside of meetings. Virtual meetings benefit from a facilitative approach and ensuring that the meeting starts off with everyone clear about how the virtual process will work in practice.

The final stage in developing virtual leadership is to master the complexities of virtual teams, for example, working across wide time zones and diversity of culture, mother tongue and generation. As ever, understanding the perspective of and listening to each member of the team bears dividends.

Factors which influence the creation, development and leadership of teams

A particular challenge for the project or programme manager is the responsibility for delivering the intended outputs and outcomes when they may have had little say about who joins the team and whether the chosen team members have the right skills and attributes.

This makes the ability of the project manager to develop and lead teams of vital importance. The simplest project has people who take on the roles of sponsor, project manager and team members – even if they are part-time roles as part of a wider job. Iterative and agile projects may involve small dedicated teams including a product owner or on-site customer.

As projects get larger, the project manager role is typically supported by specialists in aspects of project-based working, for example, schedulers, cost estimators, risk facilitators, communication specialists or business change leaders. Some team members may span multiple organisations, for example, suppliers, partners or customer/client staff as members of the deployment team. Additional skills to develop and lead the team across organisational and cultural boundaries are needed in this situation.

Some teams are co-located in the same geographic area. Where this is possible there are distinct benefits from the ability to share a physical space where plans and progress can be visualised and close working relationships can be developed.

For teams to be effective it is important that team members are understood as individuals in terms of their capabilities, their preferences, their cultural norms and expectations as well as the social dynamics between team members. By paying attention to team development project managers can create positive working cultures that enable high performance of the team and an increased chance of success.

As soon as a team forms it is unlikely, at that stage, to achieve the performance levels that match the individual capabilities of the group members. Psychological researcher Bruce Tuckman observed that teams will typically go through different stages of maturity over time before reaching their optimum performance levels. The Tuckman model (Tuckman, 1977) identified five stages a team will progress through, from when the team is formed to when the team is disbanded.

An important aspect of this model is that the team does not pass through these stages naturally. Progress through each stage is facilitated by effective leadership actions. The team leader has a key role in helping the team move through these stages as efficiently as possible and readdressing stages as new team members join or others leave. The Tuckman model is shown, in action, in Figure 2.2.7.4. and outlines the stages as:

Forming – This is the first point of contact that team members have with each other. Their knowledge of the project or environmental circumstances is very limited. Team members are naturally guarded. At this stage the leader will ensure that they communicate clear goals and objectives, creating an inclusive and coordinated environment.

Storming – The team now starts to understand that they will be unable to achieve goals as individuals and that cooperation is expected. It is at this stage where personalities start to influence how team members inter-react with each other. The biggest issue at this stage is conflict created through competition and potential disagreements. If conflict is not managed it can cause the team to reverse to forming, team members close down and reduce communication. The leader has a strong role to ensure differences are aired and conflict resolved in a positive way.

MANAGEMENT

Norming – If conflict is resolved successfully the team start to become much more cooperative with each other as they start to focus on the tasks required to achieve objectives. This stage is very much felt by the team as a need for balance; team cohesion is important but not to the detriment of getting the work done. The leadership priority at this stage is to provide process, clear roles and responsibilities and timely feedback.

Performing – The team is now delivering the targeted performance. Creative problem solving and motivation is at its highest level. The leader will ensure performance is maintained by promoting openness, honesty and the development of trusting relationships. Now that the team has experienced achievement it is likely that this will continue; however, it can't be taken for granted. The team could actually revert to one of the earlier stages, usually in response to change, such as team members leaving and new people joining or changing the scope of the tasks. The degree of reversal depends on the scale of the change but also the strength of the leader. Strong leadership means that even with a large-scale change, the team may only revert to norming for a short time before returning to performing. The opposite is also true. For example, under weak leadership a small change can cause the team to completely collapse, returning all the way to forming.

Adjourning – This was a stage that Tuckman identified several years after developing the original four-stage model. This stage acknowledges the efforts of the leader in preparing team members for the end of one team and the start of a new team in the future. Providing feedback on individual performance, liaising with functional management and recognising achievement are just some of the leadership tasks necessary at this stage all with the aim of ensuring that team members are transitioned effectively back into the business or their organisation.

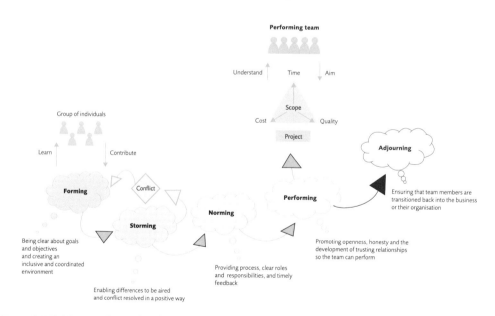

Figure 2.2.7.4 Stages of team development and leadership actions necessary to reach performance

The establishment of a team will initially involve the selection of individuals based on their skills, behaviours and attitudes. When people with complementary skills and behaviours are committed to a common objective and method of working, it is likely that they will be able to reach performing within a reasonable time, even with moderate leadership. Another factor that has also been studied is the influence of different personalities working together and how they might influence team working.

Cambridge psychologist Meredith Belbin produced a model to show how different personalities work together to create an effective team. Belbin described nine social roles (Belbin, 2010) that individuals adopt and the strengths and weaknesses of each. Within a team, one person's strengths balance another's weaknesses. Individuals will perform better in a team context if they are given a role that plays to their strengths. The nine team roles are equally grouped into three clusters, action, social and thinking, as shown in Figure 2.2.7.5.

Action	Social	Thinking
Shaper	Team worker	Plant
Completer finisher	Resource investigator	Monitor evaluator
Implementer	Co-ordinator	Specialist

Figure 2.2.7.5 Belbin's nine social roles

Source: Belbin Associates for the Belbin® team roles', as defined by Dr Meredith Belbin, reproduced by kind permission of www.belbin.com

Action – The Shaper will provide the necessary drive to ensure that the team keeps moving and does not lose focus or momentum. The Implementer will plan a workable strategy and carry it out as efficiently as possible. Most effectively used at the end of tasks to polish and scrutinise the work for errors, the Completer Finisher will subject output to the highest standards of quality control.

Social – The Resource Investigator uses their inquisitive nature to find ideas to bring back to the team. Excellent for communicating from the project to stakeholders. The Team Worker is the diplomat of the team, helping the team to gel, using their versatility to identify the work required and complete it on behalf of the team. The Coordinator's role is necessary to focus on the team's objectives, draw out team members and delegate work appropriately.

Thinking – When the team is faced with obstacles, and needs to be highly creative and good at solving problems in unconventional ways, the Plant provides the necessary support to allow the team to function well. The Monitor Evaluator provides a logical eye, making impartial judgements where required, and weighs up the team's options in a dispassionate way. When the team requires in-depth knowledge in key areas, the Specialist is the member that has distinct strengths in a very narrow area.

2.2.7 Learning summary

The section of the guide that you have just read will provide you with the learning necessary to be assessed against the following learning outcome and assessment criteria:

5. Understand the principles of leadership and teamwork.

5.1 *Explain how leadership impacts on team performance and motivation (using models such as Maslow, Herzberg and McGregor).*

There are two factors that influence a team's performance. They are the skills and abilities of the team members and their motivation. Skills are relatively straightforward to develop. Motivation on the other hand causes managers a lot more difficulty to influence. Sending someone on a training course for example, to build their skill level, is not going to be effective if that person is not motivated. Training should be motivational, but is not seen as a motivator. Instead the project manager may have to take a more creative approach and appreciate some of the deeper aspects of what motivates people. Learners should appreciate here the link between understanding motivation and effective leadership. There are three common models discussed here. In each case focus on the various factors that are involved in understanding motivation rather than the models themselves.

5.2 *Explain why it may be necessary to change leadership styles to effectively support the management of a project.*

Imagine asking a number of people the question: 'Between control and empower, where should the effective manager position themselves?' The most common reply would be: 'in the middle!' Now imagine that the local fire team are called to a blazing building. Where should the fire team leader position themselves? How would they be communicating to the team? How would the team feel about that type of leadership? Still with the fire team, imagine this time they are visiting some premises to conduct a fire audit of the building, checking escape routes, fire extinguishers, training record of fire marshals etc. Where should the leader position themselves now? What has changed? The leadership style has changed because of the changing criticality of the situation. That is the principle of Situational Leadership®. An added factor, combined with the situation is also the skills and abilities of the people who are expected to follow. Lower skilled members of the team will tend to need a more directing approach.

5.3 *Describe the characteristics and benefits of effective teams and teamwork.*

Effective teams achieve more than the sum of their constituent parts, that's clear in every situation. Teams where shared leadership, mutual collective accountability and active problem solving occur are likely to have some of the characteristics of an effective team.

A key aspect of successful project-based working is to be able to bring business expertise into temporary teams and then return those people to the business with enhanced skills and experience, and without losing out in terms of performance review or succession planning. Teamwork helps organisations be more adaptable, in turn individuals also experience benefits from working in a team-based environment, increased motivation, sense of belonging and greater work satisfaction are a few examples.

5.4 *Explain factors which impact on the leadership of virtual teams.*

There are a number of different reasons why virtual teams may arise or become an attractive consideration for organisations. Development of more advanced communication systems make it quick and easy. They also provide an opportunity to reduce management costs by cutting out unproductive travel time. Organisations are also considering ways in which unnecessary travel can be reduced and in turn to reduce environmental impact. This has all meant that in future face-to-face communication opportunities may reduce. However, the leader still needs to lead, but in a slightly different environment. This new dimension to leadership does not change the fundamental principles of leadership but just introduces additional factors that now need to be considered.

5.5 *Explain factors which influence the creation, development and leadership of teams (using models such as Belbin, Margerison-McCann, Myers-Briggs, Hackman, Tuckman, Katzenbach and Smith).*

Putting a number of people in a room and giving them a problem to solve will not automatically turn those people into a team. They may solve the problem but still remain a working group. To become a true team, they will show certain characteristics, have progressed through certain stages and, most important of all, the progress from group to team will have been facilitated by effective leadership. The leader will have recognised the stages of how the team develops over time, illustrated here by reference to the Tuckman model. Another aspect that will influence team creation and development is the individual characteristics of the team members. The Belbin model shows three main clusters of social roles that would influence behaviour in a team.

While there are a number of models referred to in this assessment criteria, learners are urged to maintain focus on the assessment criteria and particularly "factors that influence the creation, development and leadership . . .". Two of the most common models have been chosen to illustrate how the team forms and the different personality types within it. The other models show very similar aspects of teams, perhaps with different names and references. Learners are recommended to research these models for background only, being mindful of the assessment criteria, which is not focused on the models themselves but the generic elements that they all have in common.

2.3 Project delivery

Having the knowledge and skill to be able to influence stakeholders and lead teams has been the emphasis of all the topics in the previous two sections. Communication, negotiation, and schedule and resource optimisation are fundamental management skills that apply universally, regardless of the type of project or programme being delivered. The temporary and constrained nature of delivering beneficial change through project-based working puts particular pressures on these core skills. The communication of relevant information is with people who may not be part of the business-as-usual team. Negotiation is not only formal, with suppliers and partners, but also informal, for example to release scarce resource for project-work. Managing time becomes particularly pressured when juggling multiple urgent and important priorities for different stakeholders.

The results achieved will be proportional to the amount of up-front work, described in this last section and the previous sections topics. Success involves controlling deployment and ensuring that there is good information about progress and performance. This informs correction action and decision-making to ensure that the business case is delivered as well as possible. It is also about rigour in the areas studied up to this point such as issue management, change control, configuration management and quality control – to ensure that good work put into early life cycle planning is not squandered by a lack of attention to detail in implementation.

Controlling deployment requires a detailed focus on monitoring and reporting as well as a commitment to manage risk, issues and change/variations in a disciplined way. The imperative to provide audit trails for assurance, and the opportunity for individual team members and the wider organisations involved to reflect, learn and improve, is an organisational reality for all who work in a competitive environment.

In the final analysis, people deliver projects and strong relationships with people underpin the administrative and bureaucratic disciplines required during deployment. Ultimately engaging and influencing stakeholders, forming, building and leading teams, and the generic skills and responsibilities of being a project professional are addressed with the objective of making it clear that all project-based work relies fundamentally on the ability of people to work together.

This last section of your learning journey includes:

2.3.1   Estimating

2.3.2   Schedule and resource optimisation

2.3.3   Conflict management

2.3.4   Negotiation

2.3.5   Knowledge and information management

2.3.6   Earned value management

2.3.1 Estimating

Estimating uses different methods to produce a prediction of the time and resources required to complete the scope of the work to the defined quality requirements. Depending on the life cycle adopted, estimates may be used to deliver the project to the point of transition into use or may be for the planned working life of the product/service. As time progresses, it is assumed that more is known and therefore estimates become more accurate.

Estimates have multiple purposes:

- to conduct economic analysis for investment appraisals and option selection to support judgements about value for money;
- as an essential input for creating a resourced schedule;
- to enable budget setting and considerations of affordability;
- as the starting point for risk analysis and contingency determination.

Approaches to producing estimates

There is a choice of method to produce an estimate. The actual method adopted will depend on the point in the life cycle where the estimate is being carried out, the time available and the amount of detailed information that exists concerning scope and working approaches.

Parametric

This estimating method uses a statistical relationship between historic data and other variables to calculate an estimate. The specifications of each deliverable are established together with the particular parameters that apply. For example, length of pipe, square footage of floor space or height of wall. Applied to these parameters would be unit rates that are either gained through experience of doing the work previously or using rates that are produced by technical publishers as price books or books of norms. Parametric estimating can be one of the most accurate techniques for determining a project's duration and cost, provided the scope being estimated accurately represents the expected final requirements. When applying published data, care is required to ensure that the actual conditions of the work being estimated are similar to the conditions that have created the norms and take account of skill levels, lost time factors and any physical aspects, such as inclement weather.

Analogous

This comparative method is dependent on data being available of a similar project to the one being estimated. If the historic project was the same size, similar complexity and the method by which the new project is being delivered is the same, then it is accepted that the cost of the previous project becomes the new estimate. It is possible to factor this estimate to take account of known variables. Adding 10 per cent for example to cover the known increases in material costs. When this estimate is produced at the start of the concept phase it is often referred to as an order of magnitude estimate. To carry out this type of estimate the data on previous projects needs to be readily available. It is common that this estimate will provide the basis for the decision to proceed with the project.

Analytical

When the detailed scope of the project has been defined, usually through the formation of a work breakdown structure (WBS) detailed estimates can be produced for labour and non-labour resources to complete the activities in scope. This is often referred to as a bottom-up method in that the task of producing the estimates will be delegated to those who are actually going to deliver the individual pieces of work or work packages. Their individual estimates are then summed from the bottom of the WBS to the top. For this estimating method to be valid the WBS needs to be representative of the work that will eventually be carried out and so a verified WBS is essential to the accuracy of the final estimate. Analytical estimating can only be used to produce a cost estimate and not an estimate of duration. Summing the estimated durations from the bottom of the WBS to the top would not take account of work packages that will be conducted at the same time as others.

Delphi

If estimating is carried out as a group discussion it can be very difficult to avoid individual group members influencing each other as to what the estimate figure should be. To avoid this influence from impacting the estimating outputs the Delphi method can be used. With Delphi, the individual group members, who are tasked with providing the estimates, do this in isolation from each other and submit their independent views to a central focal person who facilitates the exercise. The facilitator then reviews the data and provides a summary report to each member of the group, who then feeds back additional data to build the estimate. Once the facilitator is satisfied that all possibilities have been considered, the exercise is then closed and the output becomes the agreed estimate.

Delphi is not specific to estimating; it is used in a number of different areas in business where there is uncertainty and some future decision is required. The main advantage of Delphi is the accuracy and dependability of the decisions reached, which have been widely shown to be much better than approaches that are less structured.

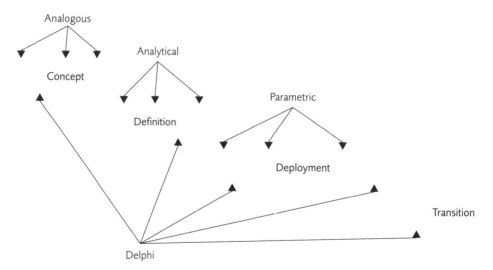

Figure 2.3.1.1 Example of estimating methods used throughout the project life cycle

The reasons for and benefits of re-estimating throughout the project life cycle

As the project progresses project uncertainty will decline and as a result a different estimating method can be applied to verify previous estimates. This increase in accuracy from concept through to implementation is often termed the estimating funnel. Note that as accuracy increases the level of contingency amount should decrease.

In the example shown in Figure 2.3.1.1, initially applied are analogous estimates based on information available about prior projects. Whatever the source of the data, at this point in the life cycle the estimates produced have relatively broad ranges. During definition it is likely that a WBS is available and as verification takes place the duration/work estimating can be carried out for individual assignments. Using work packages improves the estimate accuracy and team member commitment. The overall estimate range has now reduced. During deployment the level of detail at this phase will allow parametric estimating using either published rates or historic data from the organisations own experience. Delphi could be used at any point in the life cycle as it is more a technique to gain consensus rather than to produce an estimate in itself.

Some of the benefits of re-estimating throughout the project life cycle are:

- Reduced contingency reserves – at early stages of the life cycle there is a great deal of uncertainty and a number of assumptions made in order to achieve an estimated value for time and cost. To manage this uncertainty an amount of contingency is reserved. As the project progresses re-estimating will take account of clarification of detail and so a new estimate will be established. As this uncertainty reduces, the level of contingency allowance can also reduce to match the increased certainty.

- Greater involvement of the project team – As the project progresses additional project team members will become part of the project organisation. They can apply their specific technical expertise to the estimating tasks, increasing the accuracy of the estimate. As new team members join the project, opportunities to clarify or validate the scope may become apparent as a result of different perspectives.

- Opportunity to incorporate lessons learned – It is good practice to review stages of work that have been completed to establish actual cost of the work performed in relation to the estimate for that work. Variances and trends can then be incorporated into the estimates ahead with a view to adjusting these incorporating the review findings.

- Increased likelihood of adhering to overall estimate – By re-estimating throughout the life cycle more targeted actions can be taken to respond to anticipated estimating variances, minimising the project-wide effect of variances occurring in specific areas of the project. Adherence in this way provides more confidence to stakeholders of the project's performance in relation to the published estimates.

- Minimising effect of estimating error – If errors are likely to occur it is important that the project team become aware of these as soon as possible during project progression. Re-estimating provides an opportunity for the team to get timely warning of these and so inform stakeholders and take actions necessary to rectify the estimate.

2.3.1 Learning summary

The section of the guide that you have just read will provide you with the learning necessary to be assessed against the following learning outcome and assessment criteria:

6. Understand planning for success.

6.9 *Explain approaches to producing estimates (including parametric, analogous, analytical and Delphi).*

All estimates are predictions of the future and so are fundamentally educated guesses. Project managers can use various approaches and work to make estimates as realistic as possible. External information from suppliers may be used where the supplier is best placed to provide estimates of time and cost. Although the methods cited here have different aspects to them, what they all have in common is reliance on data, and this will impact directly on the estimate produced, its accuracy and relatedness to the project scope actually being delivered. A clear and unambiguous scope definition, together with defined measurable outcomes for all the deliverables and task assignments in the project, are essential prerequisites for a useful estimate to be produced. Any lack of clarity in project scope or uncertain team member assignments, which may be unavoidable depending on the project's current progress, is vital to note when the estimate is produced. Recommended allowances in relation to lack of definition must also be agreed. It is also vital to document assumptions underpinning an estimate to ensure the basis of that estimate is fully understood.

6.10 *Explain the reasons for and benefits of re-estimating throughout the project life cycle.*

An estimate is just that – an estimate. It should not be seen as an exact figure, cast in stone, but it is often seen exactly like that. Re-estimating allows the level of confidence in the estimate to increase, more information is known and those with the technical expertise are starting to get involved and tasked with carrying out estimates for their areas of the project. The estimating task should never be seen as completed. Each member of the project team should be alert to the changing circumstances they may be experiencing as the project progresses and considering how these changes may impact the original estimate for the project.

2.3.2 Schedule and resource optimisation

Time scheduling is a collection of techniques used to develop and present schedules that show when work within a project is planned to be performed. A project schedule can reside within a programme or portfolio schedule and have dependencies on the completion of other projects.

Ways to create and maintain a schedule

Essentially before a project schedule can be created, it is necessary to have a work breakdown structure (WBS), an effort estimate for each task, and a resource list with availability for each resource. If these are not yet available, it may be possible to create an initial schedule, but it will require rescheduling once the required information becomes available. The schedule will be considered an estimate; each date in the schedule is estimated, and if those dates do not have the buy-in of the people who are going to do the work, the schedule will be inaccurate.

In many industries, such as engineering and construction, the development and maintenance of the project schedule is the responsibility of a full-time scheduler or team of schedulers, depending on the size of the project and though the techniques of scheduling are well developed, they are often inconsistently applied throughout industry. In some large organisations, scheduling, as well as cost estimating and risk management, are organised under the project support function.

Many project scheduling software products exist that can do much of the tedious work of calculating the schedule automatically. However, before any member of the project team can use these tools, they should understand the concepts behind the WBS, dependencies, resource allocation, critical paths, Gantt charts and earned value. These are the real keys to planning and scheduling a successful project.

The project schedule is created by defining all the work tasks to be performed taking account of their relationships, estimated durations and the resources required within the project calendar.

The steps in the schedule development process include:

1. Identifying the tasks from the WBS.

2. Estimating the duration (effort) of each task.

3. Determining the logical relationship between tasks (dependencies) in relation to their delivery.

4. Carrying out optimisation of the schedule and testing the logic.

5. Assigning resources that are required to carry out the work.

6. Checking that the defined schedule meets the target success criteria for cost and time.

7. Baselining the schedule and monitoring during its deployment.

Figure 2.3.2.1 shows the scheduling and resource management charts that are created to commmunicate schedule and resource information to stakeholders.

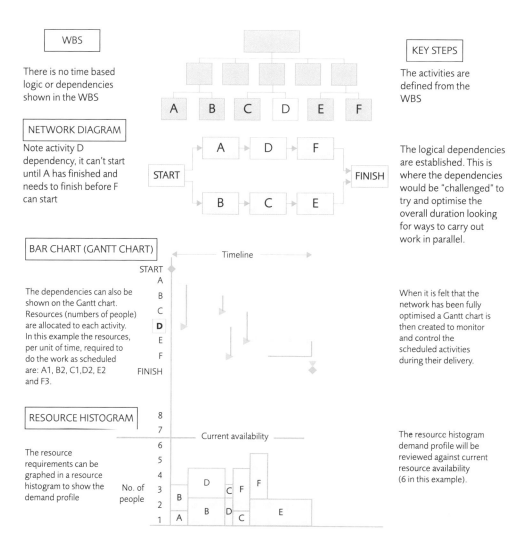

MANAGEMENT

WBS

There is no time based logic or dependencies shown in the WBS

NETWORK DIAGRAM

Note activity D dependency, it can't start until A has finished and needs to finish before F can start

BAR CHART (GANTT CHART)

The dependencies can also be shown on the Gantt chart. Resources (numbers of people) are allocated to each activity. In this example the resources, per unit of time, required to do the work as scheduled are: A1, B2, C1,D2, E2 and F3.

RESOURCE HISTOGRAM

The resource requirements can be graphed in a resource histogram to show the demand profile

KEY STEPS

The activities are defined from the WBS

The logical dependencies are established. This is where the dependencies would be "challenged" to try and optimise the overall duration looking for ways to carry out work in parallel.

When it is felt that the network has been fully optimised a Gantt chart is then created to monitor and control the scheduled activities during their delivery.

The resource histogram demand profile will be reviewed against current resource availability (6 in this example).

Figure 2.3.2.1 Creating a resourced schedule from WBS

Differences between critical path and critical chain as scheduling techniques

There are two principal types of scheduling: critical path and critical chain. The critical path approach places the emphasis on the activities in a project and understanding the shortest time to complete all activities in a logical order. To do this, dependencies (alternatively called precedence relationships) between each activity that forms the scope of work to be completed need to be agreed (Figure 2.3.2.2). Establishing the logic between the activities enables a precedence network to be determined. Then estimates of duration (based on the effort required) can be made. The resulting critical path can be identified as the sequence of activities through the precedence network from start to finish, whose durations, when summed determines the overall duration. It is the longest pathway of activity, other pathways are shorter in their duration and are said to have float (see Figure 2.3.2.3).

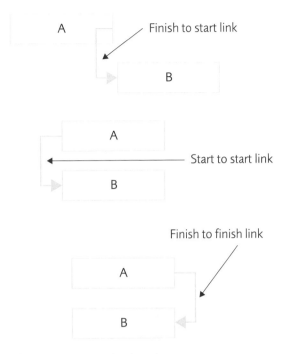

Finish to start link

Start to start link

Finish to finish link

Figure 2.3.2.2 Precedent relationships in critical path analysis

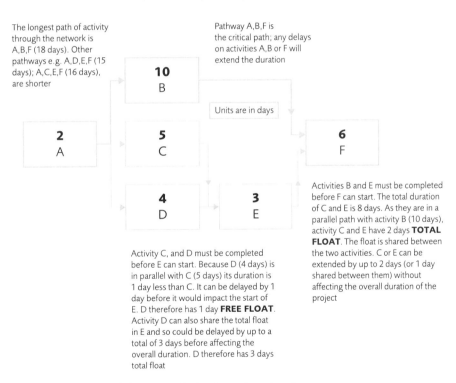

The longest path of activity through the network is A,B,F (18 days). Other pathways e.g. A,D,E,F (15 days); A,C,E,F (16 days), are shorter

Pathway A,B,F is the critical path; any delays on activities A,B or F will extend the duration

Units are in days

Activities B and E must be completed before F can start. The total duration of C and E is 8 days. As they are in a parallel path with activity B (10 days), activity C and E have 2 days **TOTAL FLOAT**. The float is shared between the two activities. C or E can be extended by up to 2 days (or 1 day shared between them) without affecting the overall duration of the project

Activity C, and D must be completed before E can start. Because D (4 days) is in parallel with C (5 days) its duration is 1 day less than C. It can be delayed by 1 day before it would impact the start of E. D therefore has 1 day **FREE FLOAT**. Activity D can also share the total float in E and so could be delayed by up to a total of 3 days before affecting the overall duration. D therefore has 3 days total float

Figure 2.3.2.3 Activity network showing critical path, total and free float

Within a large project, there can be a number of individual schedules to deal with different aspects of the project. The master schedule combines, coordinates and keeps track of all subordinate schedules within the overall project scope.

When using an iterative life cycle, rather than considering scope and quality as fixed and estimating time (and cost), a timebox approach is used – a fixed period of time with determined resources, during which scope is completed to quality as efficiently as possible.

Timeboxes in projects are often sized for a few weeks and some methods refer to these timeboxes as 'sprints'. Timeboxes and an iterative life cycle approach are commonly used to manage technologically novel or risky projects. The project is repeatedly tasked with satisfying requirements, iteratively moving the solution towards a satisfactory conclusion in short, set periods of time. The results of all these techniques are usually presented using a visualisation that shows activities as bars on a timeline, known as a Gantt chart as shown in Figure 2.3.2.1.

The critical chain method, alternatively called 'resource critical path', places the emphasis on the resources (labour and non-labour) in a project, while the critical path emphasises the activities. When the amount of resources are estimated for an activity, there are various aspects that will influence how that activity will be ultimately performed, its resulting duration and its effect on successors. Skills, abilities, tools and motivation are just some of the factors that will influence work rate. Generally if the activity happens to finish early, the activity owner will tend not report completion but instead will use the gained time to either 'gold plate', essentially over-deliver the activity, or catch up with other unrelated activity. If the activity is late then it will have an effect on succeeding activities. The benefit of the task completing early is lost to the project but the effect of the late completion has to be absorbed into the project, the critical chain approach attempts to rebalance this problem.

The simplest critical chain approach takes the estimated duration provided for each activity and reduces this by 50 per cent to create a time contingency, and rather than holding that contingency within the estimate for that activity, it is stripped out and included as a buffer for a (critical) chain of activities. (Figure 2.3.2.4).

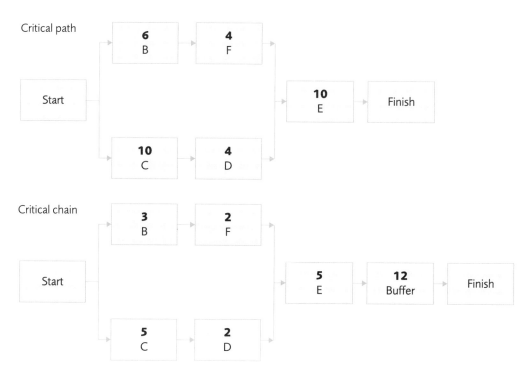

Figure 2.3.2.4 Comparing schedule approaches (activity durations are shown in days)

For this method to work, people and other resources need to be available at the time when an activity can start, and achieving this requires the team and wider stakeholders who may need the same resources for other work to agree on how this will be achieved.

Critical chain depends on a culture being created within the project, where it is accepted that best case estimates will rarely be achieved but on the understanding that all work will be completed as soon as possible and that the buffer for the chain is available to protect the whole project. Using this approach, once resources (people or equipment) are allocated, they focus solely on completing the activity to the required quality standard as quickly as possible. The aim is to overcome the temptation to delay activities or to do extra work when there seems to be enough time. Rather than monitoring start and end dates, the focus is on encouraging resources to gain maximum productivity, regardless of dates.

The rate of consumption of the buffer is used to control the project schedule and subsequent financial performance. In the critical path method the start and finish of activities are the focus for reporting, whereas in critical chain the rate at which the buffer is being consumed is reported to stakeholders, commonly using a fever chart (Figure 2.3.2.5).

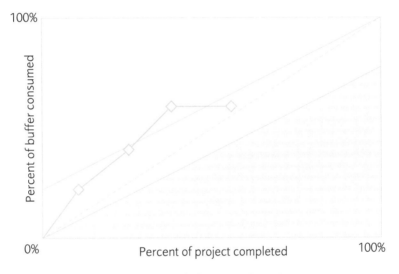

Figure 2.3.2.5 Plotting the consumption of project buffer using a fever chart

Using fever chart reporting it is assumed, for example, that if 50 per cent of the project has been completed, it would be expected that the buffer would have been 50 per cent consumed. Buffer consumption versus project completion is plotted on the fever chart beween pre-defined thresholds. Over or under consumption of the buffer threshold in relation to project progress can be highlighted and actioned or escalated accordingly.

In projects where time is critical, there is empirical evidence that out-of-the-ordinary results have been achieved when critical chain method is used in a more advanced way, taking account of the statistical variations between different activities and relating them to calculation of an optimised buffer. There are examples of projects being able to reduce overall schedules by up to 25 per cent.

How resources are categorised and allocated to a linear and iterative life cycle schedule

Resources are considered as all the labour and non-labour items required to undertake the scope of work to the required quality. Resources can be one or more of the following:

- human (labour);
- plant or equipment;
- materials;
- facilities, such as specialist test sites.

Each of the resources may drive the project pace by constraining the output that can be achieved – for example, a resource cap to a point in time will determine how much work can be completed up to that point. Where resources do constrain the project delivery rate, they are known as 'critical' resources. It is likely that the relative importance of each resource will vary depending on project type, but also from project to project. An important consideration may be the relationship between resources and project logistics. Resources generally require space within which to operate, whereas materials need space to be stored.

When projects are using a linear life cycle, the assumption is that when the schedule is planned initially, all resources are available when required. If, after reviewing the schedule, there are periods where resources are not available, resource management techniques can be applied, such as levelling and smoothing, which can try to fit the scope of work into the resource limit and as much as possible maintain schedule and quality objectives. Ultimately, owever, after all possibilities have been considered and resources are still not sufficient, it is likely that planned completion dates of activities are delayed and overall duration is increased.

Projects using an iterative life cycle ensure requirements are prioritised and implemented within the pre-allocated resources, varying the scope and quality achieved within the timebox, if required. However, if all the scope must be delivered to the specified quality, an extension of time is inevitable, in order to finish on time, specific features may be withdrawn from a timebox and scheduled for a subsequent iteration.

Differences between resource smoothing and resource levelling

The main objectives of resource management are to make sure that all resources are used optimally. There are two basic options available to the project manager: resource levelling and resource smoothing.

Resource levelling (resource limited scheduling) answers the question: 'With the resources available, when will the work be finished?' Levelling is used where resource availability is limited, for example specialists, complex testing equipment or where there might be space or accommodation restrictions. Resource levelling can be achieved in the project by:

- redefining the scope of the activities to be undertaken by the particular resource concerned – in simple terms, this might mean giving some of the work to an under-utilised resource;

- redefining the specification (avoiding if possible, any compromise to the quality of the final product);

- increasing task duration to reduce the overall resource requirements;

- increasing resources on earlier tasks to bring workload forward, such that peaks in the future are reduced – this will have cost, and possibly quality, implications;

- moving activities that are not on the critical path to reduce demand at peak times – i.e. using free and total float to optimise the schedule.

When all levelling options have been considered and a solution is still unavailable, the project duration will extend but hopefully this is will be minimised to the least possible extent.

Resource smoothing (time limited scheduling) is used when time is more important than cost. The objective is to deliver the work within the fixed timescale. This may involve reducing the duration of activities by adding resources – for example, more people – the same number of people working longer hours, or additional equipment, and then trying to get a 'smooth' usage of resources, avoiding peaks and troughs of resource demand and optimising their flow from one piece of work to another.

Resource smoothing needs to be considered on a resource-by-resource basis, particularly if the reason for applying smoothing is in response to a request to reduce the overall duration of the schedule, perhaps as a result of changing time priorities. Applying additional resources to critical path activities is the only way the overall schedule will be impacted. If additional resources were to be applied to activities with float, it would just provide additional float to those activities with no impact on the duration overall. This situation can lead to a build-up of resources, particularly on these critical activities, resulting in large peaks and troughs appearing in the resource demand profile. Applying smoothing will ensure that the additional resources required to meet the new end date are applied on critical activities across the whole schedule rather than in selective areas.

To achieve a smoothed resource profile may require some redefinition of the order of some of the work, where the logic used originally was discretionary not mandatory, for example where work could be done in parallel rather than in sequence. Achieving the optimally resourced schedule can be a creative process requiring multiple iterations to get the best result possible.

There is, of course, a finite limit to the resources that can be put into some tasks due to the nature of the task and the environment. For example, a task involving data entry will be impacted very little by additional resource, if there is only one data input terminal available. If resource really is finite, there are no more hours available from skilled people or no more equipment available, then there is no option but to extend durations and the overall project time to accommodate this (Figure 2.3.2.6).

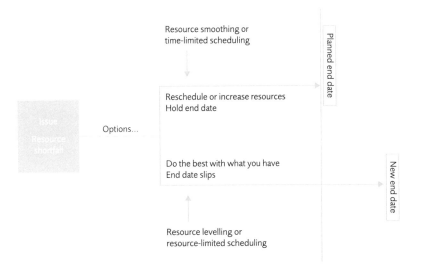

Figure 2.3.2.6 Resource levelling and smoothing options

The result of resource optimising, whether involving the critical chain approach or resource levelling or smoothing of a critical path-based schedule, is a curve that shows the planned deployment of resource (and therefore cost) to complete the scope and quality over time. The example in Figure 2.3.2.7 shows the resource demand profile as a histogram and the cumulative demand as the curve.

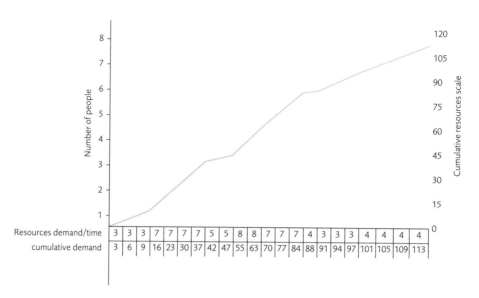

The chart shows the following data table:

Resources demand/time	3	3	3	7	7	7	7	5	5	8	8	7	7	7	4	3	3	3	4	4	4	4
cumulative demand	3	6	9	16	23	30	37	42	47	55	63	70	77	84	88	91	94	97	101	105	109	113

Figure 2.3.2.7 Resource demand profile and cumulative curve

Differences between cost planning for iterative life cycles and cost planning for linear life cycles

Cost planning is an essential part of the project management process, the creation of a justified and credible cost for a project is a good start; however, the forecasted cost alone is not enough to enable project control. In addition, project managers need to understand where costs fall in their schedule to manage resource demand, supplier's payments and funding requests.

The resource optimised schedule is the essential input to cost planning to build up a picture of the cost of the planned resources over time. In some organisations, all resources that will consume costs will be included in the schedule, for example, volume of materials to be used or phasing of purchasing of new hardware to support software development. Other organisations only schedule labour and enter non-labour costs directly into the cost model.

Where subcontracted resources are provided and committed contractually to provide as much labour or other resource as needed to meet the agreed timescales, the budgeted amount is the fixed price of the contract and remains at this level irrespective of actual resource used by the supplier.

Bringing labour and non-labour costs together, the cost profile for the resource optimised schedule is known as the planned value or budgeted cost of work scheduled (BCWS), as shown by the curve in Figure 2.3.2.7. The BCWS is the cost profile against which the project is judged in terms of schedule performance, particularly when using earned value analysis for tracking work and spend.

There are additional cost planning aspects that need to be considered during integrated planning including (Figure 2.3.2.8):

- The relationship between fixed and variable costs – Fixed or non-recurring costs happen once in a project life and contribute a single cost, for example machine setup, site activation, research and development, etc. Variable or recurring costs occur periodically as an event in a project and contribute multiple costs with a cumulative effect, for example, component machining, maintenance at failure events, production line tasks, etc.

- Likely periodicity of funding release by the sponsor and governance board – In an iterative project life cycle, the release of funds may be more frequent due to the close interaction with the sponsor as work is completed in short intervals; whereas in a linear life cycle, funds may only be released at decision gates, when the costs spent to date are understood and costs forecasted for the future are approved through the updated business case.

The level of detail required is dictated by the project phase, more detail is typically necessary in the near term, while later phases of work can be maintained at a higher level of granularity.

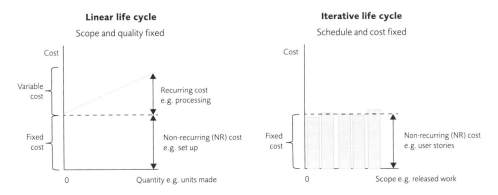

Figure 2.3.2.8 Fixed and variable cost for linear and iterative life cycle approaches

MANAGEMENT

2.3.2　Learning summary

The section of the guide that you have just read will provide you with the learning necessary to be assessed against the following learning outcome and assessment criteria:

8.　Understand schedule and resource optimisation.

8.1　*Describe ways to create and maintain a schedule (including critical path, and Gantt charts).*

There are key steps involved in creating a schedule, each step results in the production of a device that will be used to monitor the project and make control decisions. Most of this documentation is produced by project management software; however, it is of prime importance that the project manager fully understands how it is created and how it is used in the project. Learners should understand the significance of having a verified scope as the solid foundation for any further scheduling process to be conducted. Each element serves a different purpose; the network – optimising the dependencies between activities; the Gantt chart – monitoring the progress; and the histogram – managing resource allocation and availability.

8.2　*Differentiate between critical path and critical chain as scheduling techniques.*

The use of networks to optimise the dependencies between activities and ultimately make the schedule more efficient is not fully understood or practiced. The Gantt chart probably absorbs most attention and general use throughout the project. This section considered two ways in which networks can be used. Critical path, which is the traditional method, developed in the 1930s and focused very much on activities and their durations, the longest path of activity duration being the critical path. Critical chain method was developed in the late nineties when author Eliyahu M. Goldratt's book, *Critical Chain* (Goldratt 1997) showed how this method could produce superior results to the traditional critical path. The focus of critical chain is the resources doing the task rather than the task itself. When resources estimate an activity there will always be contingency built in which will manifest itself in several ways: procrastination, over delivering or multi-tasking. Critical chain strips this time out and uses it at the end of the chain to share amongst all activities. There is a rebalancing effect of the more traditional issues, where delays impact successor activities, but early progress is not reported and so the project gets penalised for delays but does not benefit from early progress.

8.3　*Describe how resources are categorised and allocated to a linear life cycle schedule.*

Resources are categorised in certain ways. The reasons for doing this are related to how these resources accrue their costs. Some will be classed as fixed costs. Regardless of the work that is done in the project, these costs will remain the same; they are often grouped together in a general category as overheads. Variable costs, on the other hand, vary depending on how much work is completed. Each activity will have a total cost for its delivery, which will be made up of the cost of actually doing the work and may also contain a portion of the overhead for the whole project. If that activity is no longer planned to be delivered, its variable cost will be removed from the budget allowance and the portion of overhead spread throughout the remaining work elements.

In a linear life cycle, funds may only be released at decision gates, when the costs spent to date are understood, and costs forecast for the future are approved through the updated business case.

8.4 *Describe how resources are categorised and allocated to an iterative life cycle schedule.*

An iterative life cycle schedule does not start with a full specification of requirements. It may therefore be difficult to understand the resource requirements from the onset. At each iteration, design modifications may be required and new functional capabilities added, potentially requiring resources with specific skills that may not be readily available or currently are deployed in other projects. In cases where such resources are not immediately available, a greater degree of planning is required to ensure that the resource is fully utilised during its available time. Requests for an additional allocation of resources at short notice may be required to reduce any chance of project delays.

8.5 *Differentiate between resource smoothing and resource levelling.*

There are two different problems addressed here; firstly, we don't have enough resource to do the work as scheduled; therefore, we need to move activities to points in the schedule where resources may be underutilised. If activities have float, then our priority will be to move them and hopefully bring our demand for resources into line with availability. If we can do this by using float, we will have successfully conducted levelling, also known as resource limited scheduling. Once we use all the available float and if we continue levelling, the project duration will extend. Attempts will be made to keep any extension of duration to a minimum.

A second problem may exist: we don't have enough time. This could be because the end date has been changed and the overall duration has reduced. In this case we will apply more resources particularly to critical path activities to shorten their duration and therefore the overall schedule. This is an iterative process to ensure we shorten the schedule to the target date and not earlier. It would be inefficient to use any more resource than required. We would want to ensure that the application of additional resource is across the schedule as smoothly as possible and to avoid peaks and troughs in our resource demand. We would have then completed resource smoothing, also known as time limited scheduling.

8.6 *Differentiate between cost planning for iterative life cycles and cost planning for linear life cycles.*

In an iterative approach, the release of funds may be more frequent due to the close interaction with the sponsor as work is completed in shorter intervals. Cost planning will be at its most structured for the iterations that are nearest in time, with lesser attention given to those iterations at much later stages. Feedback from completed iterations will influence cost planning for future work. Remember that in an iterative life cycle, cost planning is fixed and the scope will vary to deliver features within the available costs. In a linear life cycle, funds may only be released at decision gates, when the costs spent to date are understood and costs forecast for the future are approved through the updated business case.

2.3.3 Conflict management

Conflict can be defined as different objectives and attitudes between two or more parties. Conflict resolution is the process of identifying and addressing differences that, if left unresolved, could affect objectives.

Sources of conflict within a project

Conflict arises in the project when there are differing opinions and/or opposing interests between stakeholders that matter to the people involved and are not easily reconciled. Conflict may be associated with the task being undertaken, the process used to perform the task or relationships between people.

At various points in the project life cycle there can be different sources of conflict, as shown in Figure 2.3.3.1.

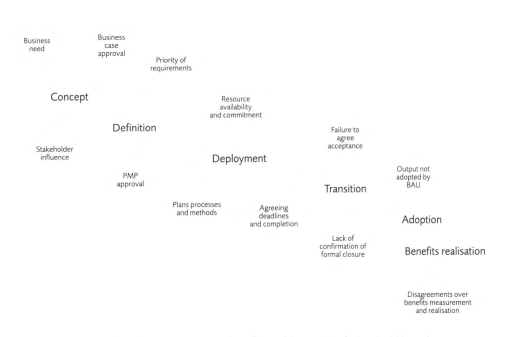

Figure 2.3.3.1 Examples of common sources of conflict within an extended project life cycle

Outside the workplace, people have a choice whether to ignore a conflict or address it. Within the workplace individuals often don't have the same choices as they have in their personal lives. Ignoring the conflict and the people involved is not an acceptable or productive way of safeguarding the success of the project.

Ways in which conflict can be addressed

There are choices that can be made whether to 'manage' a conflict, i.e. prevent it from being an ongoing issue but typically requiring one or other party to lose something of value to them, or to 'resolve' a conflict more equitably, i.e. enable a win-win solution. Taking a conflict resolution perspective, rather than conflict being perceived as negative – an unwanted struggle – conflict should be seen as an opportunity to add value, using an 'everyone-can-win' approach.

A common model to use when considering approaches to the management or resolution of conflict is the one shown in Figure 2.3.3.2. The Thomas Kilmann model encourages people to think about conflict using two dimensions:

- the desire to achieve one's own objectives;

- the desire to help others achieve their objectives.

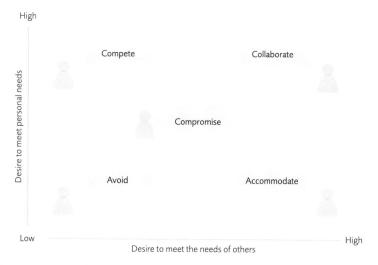

Figure 2.3.3.2 A common model to consider approaches to dealing with conflict

Source: Based on Dr Ralph Kilmann's version of the TKI Conflict Model, © 2009–2018 by Kilmann Diagnostics

Compete ('I am right, you are wrong')

When one party is highly assertive about their own goals and concerns, and tries to further its own interests regardless of the impact this may have on others, it will adopt this battling, competitive style. This particular conflict-handling orientation involves the creation of win-lose situations; the use of rivalry and power-plays to achieve one's own ends; and involves forcing a submission from the other party.

> Uses: May be necessary when quick decisive action is vital (e.g. in an emergency), or *for* important issues where unpopular actions need implementing (e.g. in cost cutting, enforcing unpopular rules, discipline), or *in* issues vital to the organisation's welfare when there is right and wrong solution.

Collaborate ('Let's work together')

Here, both parties in conflict try to satisfy their own goals and concerns but not to the detriment of the other party. It is characterised by a problem-solving stance; confronting differences and sharing ideas and information; seeing problems and conflicts as a challenge. It involves searching for integrative solutions that go beyond just accommodating different points of view. Since the final solution should be advantageous to both parties in that both can gain, this strategy is often referred to as the win-win approach.

> Uses: *When reaching an integrative solution is important. When both sets of concerns are too important to be compromised. To merge insights from people with different perspectives. To gain commitment by incorporating concerns into consensus. To build strong relationships.*

Avoid ('After you – No, after you')

One party may recognise that a conflict exists but chooses to withdraw from it or to suppress it. This style therefore involves ignoring conflicts in the hope that they will go away; putting problems on hold; invoking slow procedures to stifle the conflict; using secrecy to avoid confrontation; and appealing to bureaucratic rules to resolve the conflict. The desire to evade the overt demonstration of a disagreement.

Uses: *When an issue is trivial or more important issues are pressing. When potential disruption outweighs the benefits of resolution. After a period of intense conflict to allow cooling down. When others can resolve the conflict more effectively.*

Accommodate ('You are right, I am wrong')

On occasions, one party may try to appease another and put the other's concerns above their own, perhaps to maintain a relationship. Accommodation involves giving way, submission and compliance.

Uses: *To allow a better position to be heard, to learn and to show reasonableness. When issues are more important to others than self. To satisfy others and maintain cooperation. When harmony and stability are especially important. To allow others to develop when learning from mistakes.*

Compromising ('Split the difference')

When each of the two parties give up some aspect of their concern, then sharing occurs and a compromise outcome is achieved. No-one wins and no-one loses. Instead, parties trade off one advantage for another. In negotiation compromise is required in order for an agreement to be reached. A compromise conflict-handling orientation involves negotiation, looking for deals and trade-offs; and finding satisfactory or acceptable solutions.

Uses: *When goals are important, but not worth the effort or potential disruption of more assertive modes. When opponents with equal power are committed to mutually exclusive goals. To achieve temporary settlements to complex issues. To arrive at expedient solutions under time pressure. As a backup when collaboration is likely to be unsuccessful.*

Sometimes, it is necessary to involve other parties to resolve a conflict, for example, the project sponsor/other stakeholders as part of governance, a neutral mediator (from inside or outside of the organisation) or an arbitration service to prevent the conflict escalating into litigation or industrial action. Projects need clear protocols for escalating conflicts either to project governance, or to the relevant programme or portfolio level and for deciding when the organisation needs to go straight to litigation, or to alternative dispute resolution in order to de-escalate the conflict.

2.3.3 Learning summary

The section of the guide that you have just read will provide you with the learning necessary to be assessed against the following learning outcome and assessment criteria:

4. Understand communication within project management.

4.4 *State sources of conflict within a project.*

The very nature of a project environment lends itself to potential conflict. There are different parties involved, each have objectives and expectations of the outcome, are motivated by different aspects of the project, have varying degrees of influence and they may not be in agreement with each other. Conflict is not necessarily a bad thing, it creates debate and discussion, may show true feelings and allows a direction to be sought. The life cycle of the project has common touch points where there is most likely to be the chance of conflict occurring, as illustrated in this section.

4.5 *Explain ways in which conflict can be addressed (such as Thomas Kilmann Conflict Mode Instrument).*

Investing the time necessary to achieve both one's own and others' objectives is not always the right thing to do – it depends on how much resolving the conflict matters to achieving the objectives and benefits, and the degree to which it is important to build/preserve long-term relationships between the parties involved. Where a win-win is necessary, achieving this needs a high level of skill in facilitation to be able to understand and creatively align goals.

Other skills are important, depending on the conflict management/resolution mode that is desired, for example:

- Assertiveness skills – to stand up for the project and what is required for success.

- Listening skills – to understand the perspectives of the people involved.

- Personal resilience – when the project context is highly charged with many conflicts to manage.

At its simplest, negotiation could be described as a discussion between two or more parties aimed at reaching agreement. There are many situations in the project where some form of negotiation might have to take place on a formal basis or more informally, agreeing the release of a functional expert to support the project, to negotiating large contracts with suppliers and everything in between. The principles of negotiation and the skills needed to make lasting agreements apply to all these situations.

How to plan and conduct negotiations

Planning is vital in negotiation. There is much evidence to show that the more time and effort devoted to the planning or preparation element of a negotiation, the higher the likelihood of a desirable outcome. Each party should define objectives and consider criteria for what they want to achieve and an understanding of their best alternative to a negotiated agreement (BATNA) and how the other party's likely objectives may influence that position. Variables, elements that may need to be adjusted in order to make concessions, need to be identified. Limits are set for these variables to provide the bargaining framework.

It is important in negotiation that people do not bargain over value-based positions (for example, we have never paid more than x for this service before) and instead understand the price that it would be rational to pay for the service being offered. Also, where the negotiation has implications for the wider organisation (or programme/portfolio), the bargaining position reflects this to avoid short-term or local 'good' deals having wider negative consequences.

As shown in Figure 2.3.4.1, the negotiation initial positions are ideally what is preferred, considered as the most favourable positions (MFP). But there will be an understanding from each party that movement is likely. Unless the possibility of movement from the MFP is acknowledged by both parties, negotiation can't take place. The positions of BATNA of the seller and buyer define the zone of possible agreement (ZOPA). These negotiation principles will apply if the negotiation is done face-to-face or in writing.

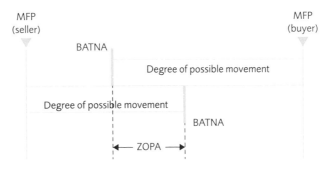

Figure 2.3.4.1 The use of BATNA to form the ZOPA range

Note that the point of final agreement could actually occur anywhere within the ZOPA range, not necessarily in the middle. What is important is how each party feels about how the relationship has developed and the resulting levels of trust that have been created. This is the foundation for a 'win-win' outcome to the negotiation. In the past, the negotiating skills that were valued were associated with 'driving a hard bargain', and tactics to put pressure on the other party and 'win over the opposition' were seen as valuable. This competitive style of negotiating creates a win-lose environment and a poor ongoing relationship after the negotiations have been completed. It is more common now for negotiators to take a more collaborative approach, using more advanced communication skills, problem solving and building a strong trusting relationship, which will exist after the deal has been done. The collaborative approach to negotiation always views the situation through a 'win-win' lens. This does not mean that organisations do not seek a competitive price for a service, but the price of the service is balanced with an understanding of the value that is likely to be achieved, for example, the ability of the supplier to offer things of value to the purchaser, such as storage of goods on the supplier's site until needed or provide technical insight of similar situations.

To work towards collaboration each party must have good background knowledge of the others' positions. Why is negotiation necessary in the first place? What factors are important in the outcome for each party? The saying 'knowledge is power' is absolutely true in a negotiation. One of the strongest elements is time. If a buyer has a time pressure and lets the seller know about that early on, it is likely for that information to create an imbalance of power in favour of the seller.

Understanding concessions is another critical aspect of knowledge each party must have. How much does a concession cost to give? And how much value does the other party place in receiving that concession? Are just two simple questions, but both carry a lot of weight when it comes to their contribution to a successful outcome. Figure 2.3.4.2. shows an example of how concessions could be traded. There is a common thought that low cost–high value should be given away first. That transaction has now created an expectation from the other party that the next concession will be of greater value than the first – trouble ahead for sure! Perhaps a better first approach is low cost–low value and then building up from that point. Remember that if concessions are given, there is a reasonable expectancy that something of value will be returned. Concessions that should not be given away of course are high cost–low value, they may build the relationship but might have too high an impact on the feasibility of the final deal.

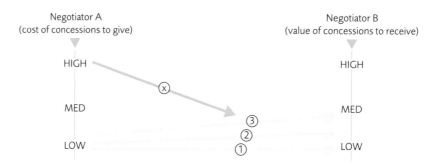

Figure 2.3.4.2 The use of concessions to reach a win-win outcome

Some procurement exercises can be facilitated by an online bidding process although, depending on the type of agreement being negotiated, it may be important for the parties to actually meet face to face.

Follow-up is also vital in order to progress actions agreed and to put in place documentation that will make it clear to all parties of the deal that has been negotiated. This is important to try to minimise future conflict. Where negotiation has been between two legal entities, a suitable commercial contract is needed. The project manager must recognise the limits of their authority and experience in contractual situations and should seek support from their procurement or legal specialists to ensure that negotiated agreements with third parties are defendable in law as well as best value for the investing organisation.

2.3.4   Learning summary

The section of the guide that you have just read will provide you with the learning necessary to be assessed against the following learning outcome and assessment criteria:

4. Understand communication within project management.

4.6 *Explain how to plan and conduct negotiations (including ZOPA, BATNA and 'win-win').*

Many project managers get involved in negotiating on a very regular basis without having gained any training to provide them with negotiating skills. So how could they possibly achieve any value in a resultant outcome? Well, if they did, they would have used common sense, good communication skills, resilience and a respect for the other party that built trust in the relationship. This section discusses three major concepts that commonly exist within negotiation; ZOPA, BATNA and 'win-win' but each will happen by default in most effective negotiating situations. Now at least the learner can recognise them and see the value that their structure can bring to every negotiation outcome.

2.3.5 Knowledge and information management

Information management is the process that includes the collection, storage, curation, dissemination, archiving and destruction of documents, images, drawings and other sources of information.

Effective management of a project relies on accurate and timely information for teams and stakeholders to make informed decisions and fulfil their role in a cost-efficient and effective way. Project documentation should be considered a reliable information source to communicate to all stakeholders and to provide documentary evidence for assurance.

Many organisations have standard forms and tools to use to manage information, potentially supported by a project management office (PMO). Computer software packages exist to optimise data use, including the use of data for project analytics. Gathering and analysing data is vital for an organisation to develop its project management maturity and learning. Standard templates are useful to help with assurance and process improvement, documented in the information management plan, a section of the project management plan and approved by governance.

An information management process

The elements of a typical information management process are shown in Figure 2.3.5.1.

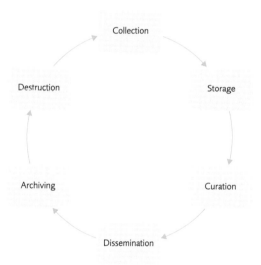

Figure 2.3.5.1 Information management process

Collection

Data received during the life of the project is varied and may be collected in many ways, for example through meetings, from reports on progress and from reviews. The project manager must ensure that there is a uniform filing structure available within the projects document control system to accept this information. It is likely that the organisation will already have predefined document styles and formats to which the project will be expected to comply. Current systems also need to be flexible enough to deal with information that may be collected in a range of formats such as digital, audio or streamed data, as well as traditional paper-based information.

Having an effective way of classifying collected information allows the project team to differentiate information that must be acted upon and is time sensitive rather than information that is simply recording events.

Storage

It is most common that organisations will have a document management system within which information will be stored. Systems like these need to be secured and various access levels created. Data also needs to be classified to establish any legal implications of storing such data. Personal data, for example, has a number of specific legal aspects that are important to understand. The project manager would have to be aware of such legislation and ensure compliance. Non-personal data may also fall under legislative control such as the Official Secrets Act or Freedom of Information Act.

Curation

Data needs to be managed throughout the project life cycle and potentially beyond. Curation makes important decisions about the management of data. When is the data considered obsolete and eligible for destruction? How should it be reliably recorded and structured? Is it in a form that can be used effectively in the future? These are just some of the areas that curation will consider. Data that has been collected has potential value for the organisation, but only if it is ordered and sequenced in such a way that it meets future needs.

Dissemination

Information management and the communication plan interact to ensure that the stakeholders who need information, obtain that information in a timely manner and in a format that enables them to make the necessary decisions regarding the project. This interaction between information management and communication planning is necessary to ensure the right information reaches the right recipients. Stakeholders who receive information that they don't require and get swamped with data, may potentially overlook a vital piece of information that would be useful for them to have. Establishing access rights for all project information is critical to uphold requirements for data protection and to help stakeholders obtain the information they need efficiently.

Archiving

Archived information provides an audit trail of changes. Information that is no longer required will eventually be destroyed, subject to statutory requirements or organisational policy. Despite information being considered eligible for archiving there is still a consideration that it may need to be accessed at some point in the future. As part of curation, an information cataloguing system should help with getting to the required document quickly and easily, without having to trawl through years of possible data.

Destruction

At some point it will be necessary to make the decision to relieve the information management system of the burden of storing lots of data, and commit to destruction. This might be guided by the need for legislative compliance. A data destruction policy will be part of the overall information management plan ensuring that procedures are followed to destroy data to a degree that it cannot be retrieved. This is particularly relevant to information held digitally on storage devices. Procedures will ensure that devices have their contents securely removed, destroyed, or overwritten to an extent that the contents are unable to be viewed.

Factors which would typically be reported on to help ensure successful project outcomes

There are several pieces of information that will be typically reported on throughout the project, and the project manager will use this information in a number of ways to help ensure successful project outcomes:

- performance status – actual or forecast date of achievement for the deliverables;

- schedule status – estimated time of completion for each task;

- cost status – actual expenditure and the committed expenditure to date for each task;

- status of quality progress – changes that might affect the form or function of the task and deliverables;

- risk exposure system – changes in the status of any identified threats to the achievement of tasks, together with any new threats or opportunities;

- exception thresholds and variance reporting – defined triggers will require the task owner to report variations to forecast time and cost at completion and suggest recovery actions.

The project manager will have several uses for this reported information. Schedule status information will be reviewed and the schedule updated. Any variances reported to the schedule for time and cost will be noted and if necessary corrective action will be taken to bring the tasks back onto the appropriate time and cost schedule. The project manager will use information as a basis for reporting to the sponsor and steering group and other stakeholders as indicated by the communications plan.

Information received from the task owners will be formed into a consolidated report. Information from the task owners and teams is received frequently, often weekly, while the consolidated report is required at a longer frequency, often monthly. Reporting of status could trigger an issue that will require escalating to the sponsor and/or steering group. It could also be used as a basis for performance reviews with the teams concerned, particularly with a view to continual improvement, for example when reviewing the quality statistics.

Information from teams could also be used to support valuations of work performed and related payments. This may be linked to an earned value management system. As there will be a significant amount of information analysis to be undertaken in a large project, the project manager may be assisted by the PMO in this task.

The role of knowledge and information management to inform decision making

Whatever life cycle is chosen, what is important is that the experiences of delivering the project are captured and provided to others in a way that will help them make decisions about future life cycle deployment. The nature of a project environment may mean that working practices are imported and exported to match the movement of contracted staff in and out of the project. Practices may be brought from elsewhere and good practice that has been developed within a particular project leaves when the personal contracts finish. The organisation is in a perpetual learning curve and always seems to be starting plans from a blank sheet never really establishing an agreed consistent practice.

Knowledge management is a cross-functional discipline and set of practices concerned with the way organisations create and use knowledge to improve outcomes. Effective knowledge management practices help project teams work better together, utilising existing experience and creating new knowledge. It can be applied within and between projects, programmes, portfolios and organisations and across extended and product life cycles. Working with knowledge, everyone in the organisation can add value by, for example:

- anticipating, understanding and responding to changing conditions;

- avoiding repetition of mistakes;

- generating options and solutions;

- supporting decision-making processes;

- enabling benefit realisation.

Knowledge management activities should be built into the day-to-day management of the project and could include:

- project reviews, ensuring that outputs of such reviews are fully documented and distributed throughout the organisation;

- workshops with facilitated activity focused on areas of the project such as risk, scope and quality performance, for example;

- in-house knowledge portals, where all members of the organisation are encouraged to participate in online discussions and blogs and submit technical queries for others to discuss and contribute ideas or solutions;

- special interest groups (SIGs), where subject matter experts discuss various aspects of the organisation's practice with a view to publishing methodologies and best practice approaches;

- meetings such as lunch and learn, where guest speakers visit the organisation to bring in experience and knowledge as applied in other organisations or industries.

With the availability of common IT programs, knowledge management activities can be performed to good effect and in a most cost-efficient manner. The benefits are not only returned in improved project performance but also in the motivation of all who work in such an environment.

2.3.5   Learning summary

The section of the guide that you have just read will provide you with the learning necessary to be assessed against the following learning outcome and assessment criteria:

6.   Understand planning for success.

6.4   *Explain an information management process (including collection, storage, curation, dissemination, archiving and the destruction of information).*

The actual information required to be produced by any project will vary according to parameters such as the purpose and complexity of the work, standard processes in the investing organisation, or the life cycle and deployment option chosen. Iterative projects place greater emphasis on the discovery and recording of emergent information rather than reliance on pre-approved plans and are likely to employ dynamic modes of capturing such new information. The project must note agreed processes within the information management plan. It will outline the responsibilities for the control and use of information during the project life cycle and beyond.

Where projects are within programmes and portfolios, a reduced administrative burden for projects may exist because information management controls are implemented at the level of the coordinating framework.

6.5   *Explain factors which would typically be reported on to help ensure successful project outcomes.*

Typically, within most organisations' governance framework some form of reporting cycle will exist. It will outline what information goes where and when. Project reporting will use formal and informal reports to communicate the status of the project. The frequency of information could be daily, weekly or monthly. Whatever arrangements have been agreed with stakeholders, the project manager has to understand what type of information is required by stakeholders to provide assurance of a successful outcome.

2.   Understand project life cycles.

2.4   *Outline the role of knowledge and information management to inform decision making.*

A great deal of resources can be wasted when projects find themselves starting the planning processes from a blank sheet, despite having regular experience of delivering similar projects on previous occasions. It's not that the experience doesn't exist, it is just that it is not in a form that can be used directly to the benefit of the project and the team. Knowledge management attempts to develop processes, tools and techniques to build existing knowledge as organisational assets and new knowledge, created through experience is developed to enrich these assets even further. Project reviews, workshops, knowledge portals and meetings should all be considered as part of knowledge management. While these activities may be getting carried out in most organisations, applying knowledge management seeks to formalise the process of harvesting knowledge, maintaining it and making it available to all that need it in a form that allows them to make the best decisions.

2.3.6 Earned value management

Earned value management (EVM) is a project control process based on a structured approach to planning, cost collection and performance measurement. It facilitates the integration of project scope, time and cost objectives and the establishment of a baseline plan of performance measurement.

There are three elements required for any performance measurement: a baseline to measure against; data on actual performance; and an assessment of the implications of the performance to date. Progress monitoring enables meaningful reports to be presented to the sponsor and governance board to enable appropriate decisions to be made to improve performance.

Why a project manager would use earned value management

The approach for progress monitoring will be agreed between the project manager and sponsor. This approach will be deemed appropriate to monitor important aspects of the project, including:

- achievement of planned scope to the required quality;

- motivation and satisfaction of team members;

- performance of contractors and the health of the relationships in the supply chain;

- committed costs and cash-flow;

- changes to the risk profile and impact on time buffers or cost contingency;

- effectiveness of communication with stakeholders.

If EVM is agreed as an approach, then it is useful for all project team members to have a full understanding of how this will be implemented and how performance will be measured and reported in earned value terms. It may be useful to also understand the limitations of earned value in order to clarify to stakeholders what the data being reported represents in relation to actual project performance.

Earned value is represented by the actual budgeted value of the work that has been completed at the point in time that is being measured. For example, a project has a total budget of £1,000,000 and after eight days working, the amount of work that had been completed at that time was measured and verified at 21 per cent complete; the value of the achievement would therefore be £210,000, and this would be the earned value.

Earned value analysis is the optimal way of tracking actual work achieved, compared to how much it has cost to deliver that work, and that shows our current cost performance (are we over- or underspent?). The actual work achieved can also be compared to how long it has taken to achieve that work and that shows our current schedule performance (are we ahead of or behind schedule?). Earned value analysis is superior to separate tracking of spend or work achieved, as it provides opportunities to look at efficiency as cost performance and productivity through schedule performance.

Primary progress and performance tracking are best done by those responsible for the work, although in many organisations with established project controls, monitoring of progress in terms of time, cost and risk is performed in a project management office (PMO). This does not absolve the project manager and team from monitoring progress in other, non-quantifiable, areas of the project, for example, stakeholder and team motivation and satisfaction. Frequency of monitoring and any subsequent reporting depends on the circumstances and is agreed with the sponsor. Monthly monitoring and reporting of time, cost, risk and earned value is appropriate for many projects, but some, for example, turnaround maintenance on a critical asset may warrant weekly, or daily tracking.

The outputs of progress monitoring are typically presented quantitively and the use of 'traffic-light' approaches are common. It is important that areas that are in control or out of control to varying degrees are flagged for attention and potential action. Certain elements of performance may be reported individually or in a dashboard format covering multiple areas of performance. It is important that progress is clearly identified and, in enough granularity, to focus onto any issues and how they should be addressed. Where progress monitoring and reporting highlights issues that cannot be recovered, re-planning is required to establish an amended baseline.

Interpreting earned value data

In order to create earned value data the budget for the project would be shown using an s-curve; this depicts the planned budget for the project as cumulative data plotted against time. It is commonly termed an s-curve as the shape of the graph usually forms an 'S', which shows the cumulative funds that the project expects to consume throughout its duration. The organisation's financial controls find this useful to establish when they are expected to release funds to the project.

At any point in time the s-curve can be viewed and the planned budget for the work that has been scheduled could be plotted. This is referred to as the budgeted cost of the work scheduled (BCWS). Also, at that point in time the actual cost of the work that has been performed (ACWP) could also be shown as an s-curve and could also be plotted at the current time.

The s-curves shown in Figure 2.3.6.1 provide an insight into how much has been spent in relation to the budget. The example shows that more money has actually been spent than was planned at this point in time which could lead to cash flow problems for the project, if it were to continue. As yet there is no earned value data placed onto the axis.

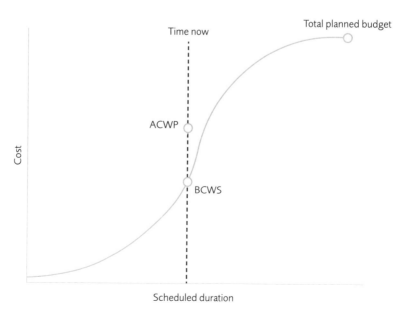

Figure 2.3.6.1 S-curve showing plots at time now for actual cost (ACWP) and planned budget (BCWS)

When the earned value data is plotted it provides a more complete picture of the project's cost and schedule performance and can be interpreted using the standard variances and performance indexes. Performance can be viewed in two ways: cost performance and schedule performance. This data can then be used to forecast future performance.

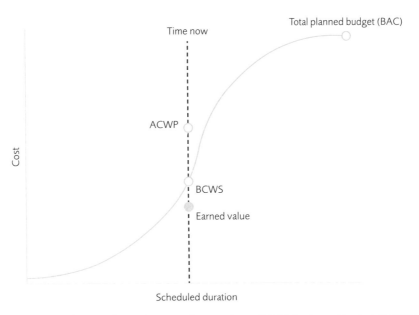

Figure 2.3.6.2 S curve showing plots at time now for actual cost (ACWP), planned budget (BCWS) and earned value

The most important figure needed in the calculation is the earned value figure from the Y axis of the s-curve (Figure 2.3.6.2). This would be a measured value taken from the actual work performed and equated back to the original budget for the work. In earned value terms this is referred to as the budgeted cost of the work performed (BCWP) and will appear in every calculation carried out. Each of the three metrics, BCWP, BCWS and ACWP would be used to give an outline of the current performance and to forecast future performance as shown in Figure 2.3.6.3

Schedule	CURRENT PERFORMANCE	Cost
BCWP – BCWS = Schedule variance (SV) If the project is on schedule the SV would be zero, a negative result behind and positive result ahead of schedule. This value represents the amount of work the project is ahead or behind schedule.		BCWP – ACWP = Cost variance (CV) If spending is equating to production of the same value the CV would be zero, a negative result over and positive under spending. This value represents how much the project is under- or overspent in relation to the value it is earning.
Schedule	FORECASTING FUTURE PERFORMANCE	Cost
BCWP/BCWS = Schedule performance index (SPI) The SPI represents the current productivity of the project. For example, if the above calculation resulted in a figure of 0.89, this would show that the project is 89 % productive. In terms of future performance if the project had a 100-day original duration (OD) and it continued at this rate the final duration could be estimated at 100/0.89 = 112 days.		BCWP/ACWP = Cost performance index (CPI) The CPI represents the current efficiency of the project. For example, if the above calculation resulted in a figure of 1.06, this would show that the project is 106 % efficient. In other words, for every £1.00 the project is spending it is managing to achieve £1.06 in value. In terms of future performance if the project had a £100,000 total planned budget at completion (BAC) and it continued at this rate of efficiency the estimate at completion (EAC) would be £100,000/1.06 = £94,339.62.

Figure 2.3.6.3 Examples of interpretation of earned value data

Those new to earned value often have a difficulty in understanding SV expressed in financial terms bearing in mind that it is a time factor. Simply the SV is showing the value of the work that has been completed in relation to the original work scheduled. It is important to realise that it has nothing to do with cost or spending as far as calculations are concerned. When interpreting the data, keep the two areas, cost and schedule, separate from each other when performing the calculations. Of course, in the actual work site they are probably influencing each other a great deal.

The benefits of using the interpretation of earned value data

When interpreting earned value, the results are only a snapshot of the project at the status time reviewed, which must be thought of as a performance indicator only and may not represent the real pace of the project. The main benefits come from the direction that earned value data may provide, to the project manager, in developing actions that could be taken to remedy the situation.

When earned value data is interpreted effectively, it can provide the following benefits:

- It enables objective measurement of project status to be compiled and communicated to stakeholders providing an easy to understand current status reporting system for the project.

- It establishes a basis for estimating final cost. By using the CPI and the amount of remaining work to be done, the estimated cost of that work can be forecast. When this is added to the costs to date, the final cost for the project can be estimated.

- It enables a prediction for when the project will be complete; use of the SPI allows the productivity of the current work rate to be established. This rate can be calculated for the whole schedule, providing an estimated duration and completion date.

- It supports the effective management of resources; further investigation of the performance data will allow greater visibility of discrete areas of the project that are impacting performance. Resources can be managed in these areas specifically and the earned value results monitored to verify resourcing decisions.

- It provides a means of managing and controlling change; the project-wide impact of change can be verified in advance of the decision, by estimating the performance changes in both cost and schedule performance terms.

2.3.6   Learning summary

The section of the guide that you have just read will provide you with the learning necessary to be assessed against the following learning outcome and assessment criteria:

6. **Understand planning for success.**

6.13   *Explain why a project manager would use earned value management.*

Earned value provides a view of the project that is reasonably simple to produce and provides direction for the project manager in taking action to remedy performance issues. It is, however, very dependent on the accuracy of the data that is being used in the calculations, particularly the measurement of earned value. In some types of work it will be very easy to assess how much has been completed; in other areas perhaps more complex. Earned value uses s-curves, which are a widely understood way of presenting financial data that show the project performance in a way that can be easily understood by stakeholders.

6.14   *Interpret earned value data (including variances and performance indexes).*

The learner should not approach this subject by learning formula. Instead understand the relationship between the three elements involved here. First, the original planned schedule; that's when the project was intended to be delivered and if viewed at a point in time provides the planned work at that time, in earned value terms, the BCWS. Second, how much has it actually cost to get to the status point being measured, the ACWP. Third, how much work has been physically completed, that is the earned value or known as the BCWP. The actual analysis takes two forms: earned value analysed in relation to spending and earned value analysed in relation to the scheduled duration. The indexes can then be calculated and used to forecast the implications of the current performance on the remaining project. By really understanding how the three elements relate to each other, the formula falls into place almost naturally.

6.15   *Explain the benefits of using the interpretation of earned value data.*

Earned value can often be seen as a way of viewing the project 'at a distance'. Project managers will over-rely on earned value data at their peril. It is important then to see the data as indications of performance rather than absolutes. In a large project there can be many anomalies that can make the project look like it is running well, when deep down there are actually fundamental problems that need active attention. Any data that is showing variance in cost or schedule should be investigated in the project as soon as they appear.

3 Self-assessment

3.1 Test questions

These short quizzes are designed to give you a quick insight into your knowledge of each section as you work through the guide and so will give you feedback on your progress. Remember the PMQ exam is not a multiple-choice exam but a written exam. The following questions will help you target potential revision needs for each subject area. Complete the questions in each section. Check your answers at the end of this section.

Section 2 – Short quiz

Chapter 2.1   Initiating a project

2.1.1   Project environment

1   PESTLE analysis covers the following areas:

    A   Political, Economic, Sociological, Technical, Legal, Environmental.

    B   Personnel, Economic, Safety, Technical, Legal, Ecological.

    C   Political, Ecological, Strategy, Technical, Life cycle, Environmental.

    D   Personnel, Ecological, Sociological, Training, Life cycle, Ecological.

2   Which of the following best describes a project's context?

    A   The environment in which the business operates.

    B   The geographic location in which the project is undertaken.

    C   The external and internal business environments, including stakeholder's interests and influences.

    D   Industry and business sector practices.

3   When managing the internal context, the project manager should especially be aware of:

    A   organisational strategy, policies and frameworks.

    B   competitive positioning.

    C   new legislation.

    D   business continuity.

MANAGEMENT

Section 2 – Short quiz   cont.

4   To be fully effective, the project manager:

   A   must take into consideration the internal and external environments.

   B   need only deal with the internal environment since the sponsor will deal with the external environment.

   C   should manage the external stakeholders and external environment.

   D   must liaise with regulating bodies to ensure requirements include the latest legislation.

5   Which type of projects needs to consider environmental constraints?

   A   Construction projects only.

   B   Construction and petrochemical projects only.

   C   All but IT projects.

   D   All projects.

6   What is the main purpose of SWOT analysis?

   A   Evaluate the returns that each project may yield and which option is most favourable.

   B   Provide an established framework for systematically assessing project options.

   C   Consider which project can be completed in the shortest duration.

   D   Provide an established framework to examine the many different factors affecting an organisation and the project.

7   A potential change in national government considered using a PESTLE analysis would be an example of a:

   A   political factor.

   B   economic factor.

   C   sociological factor.

   D   potential change of government would not be considered in such an analysis.

8   What does the term VUCA relate to?

   A   Viability, uncertainty, complexity, acceptance.

   B   Validate, users, criticality, acceptance.

   C   Volatility, uncertainty, complexity, ambiguity.

   D   Variation, unique, consideration, analysis.

9   Why might planning need to be carried out under VUCA conditions?

   A   The new capabilities resulting from a project or programme need to be evaluated in a comprehensive way.

   B   The value the project is planning to deliver is very uncertain to cost and analyse.

   C   There needs to be evidence that the deliverable will meet the full needs of the intended user.

   D   There is inherent uncertainty that makes it difficult to predict and plan with great accuracy.

10   When carrying out a VUCA analysis of project options, which factors need to be considered to identify risks in each option?

   A   Current knowledge, available data and level of confidence in outcome.

   B   Expertise of current project team and amount of available equipment.

   C   Amount of flexibility in the project budget and the degree of estimating accuracy.

   D   VUCA analysis will not identify risks in project options.

NOW CHECK YOUR ANSWERS AT THE END OF THIS SECTION. **YOUR SCORE: /10**

2.1.2   Project, programme and portfolio management

1   Which of the following is a characteristic of a project rather than BAU?

   A   Sustain the organisation to achieve its business purpose and goals.

   B   Repetitive, non-unique product service or result.

   C   Formal line authority over functional unit personnel.

   D   Achieve objectives then terminate.

2   Which one of the following is a consideration of project management?

   A   Making sure that operational management objectives are maintained as projects are delivered.

   B   Planning and executing effective communications within a project.

   C   Measuring business benefits of projects to ensure that in retrospect they have been a worthwhile consideration.

   D   Setting the organisation's standards for excellence in project delivery.

Section 2 – Short quiz cont.

3 Which of the following illustrates why project management is the most efficient way of managing change?

A It provides recommendations for the organisation to follow for employing a consultancy firm who specialise in change management.

B It provides a profile of the skills required when employing project managers.

C It ensures that the head of the organisation will always be accountable for achieving the benefits of all projects undertaken by that organisation.

D It utilises resources as and when required under the direction of a manager with single-point responsibility.

4 Which of the following is not a characteristic of business-as-usual?

A Recruitment of new project managers.

B Operating new production machinery.

C Training of operations staff to become more safety aware.

D Introducing change.

5 When delivering a project, the project manager must balance which of the following constraints?

A Configuration and delivery.

B Time, cost and quality.

C Cost, scope and change.

D Budget, cost and risk.

6 Programme management could be defined as:

A the line management of a team of programme managers.

B the managing of a functional area of the business serving several different projects.

C management of a programme of activities identified in the project schedule.

D management of a group of projects with a common business aim.

7 One of the key benefits of programme management is that:

A it enables every project to be covered by one all-embracing plan.

B it reduces the need to assign priorities to individual projects within the programme.

C dependencies and interfaces between projects can be managed to greater business advantage.

D management time can be saved by grouping projects together under a single distinct programme.

8   Which of the following is a key part of programme management?

A   Benefits management.

B   Network analysis.

C   Work breakdown structures.

D   Operations management.

9   Portfolio management could be defined as:

A   a group of projects brought together to form a strategic programme.

B   the development of expertise and competency throughout the whole organisation.

C   the strategic business plan that is developed to achieve organisational goals.

D   selection and management of an organisation's projects and programmes.

10   Which of the following would best justify the implementation of portfolio management?

A   When more projects that the organisation delivers need to be delivered on time and on budget.

B   The organisation needs to have a stronger focus on realising the benefits from the projects that it delivers.

C   Where there is a need for the organisation's projects and programmes to be more aligned with its key business objectives.

D   When there is a significant one-off project that needs to be delivered that is critical to the organisations business continuity

NOW CHECK YOUR ANSWERS AT THE END OF THIS SECTION. **YOUR SCORE: /10**

2.1.3   Organisation structures

1   What is the main reason why organisations may need to consider a specific structure to deliver projects?

A   Project management cuts across functional boundaries.

B   Project managers are unable to function within traditional departments.

C   There are not enough functional areas within most organisations.

D   The functional structure needs to be changed to a project structure.

2   What is a major strength of the functional structure to deliver a project?

A   Once the project is completed people leave the organisation and are then replaced.

B   It ensures that the project is visible to the whole organisation.

C   People with technical skills are delivering projects requiring those skills.

D   It is very much focused on the project.

Section 2 – Short quiz   cont.

3   Which structure achieves greatest flexibility in the use of human resources?

A   Functional.

B   Project.

C   Matrix.

D   Departmental.

4   In which structure would the project manager's authority be lesser than the functional manager's?

A   Functional.

B   Departmental.

C   Technical.

D   Matrix.

5   What is one of the most important risks an organisation may face when using a product structure?

A   When the project is completed there may not be another project ready at that time to absorb the surplus resources that now exist.

B   When the project is completed that part of the organisation may cease to exist and the people not reintegrated into BAU.

C   When the project is completed individuals may leave the project *en masse* and the organisation will lose accumulated learning.

D   When the project is completed individuals may return to BAU and lose the chance to work together on another equally challenging project.

6   In a matrix structure who is ultimately responsible for delivering the project benefits?

A   Line manager.

B   Project manager.

C   Project sponsor.

D   Functional manager.

7   Which feature of a project structure may make it an effective choice for project delivery?

A   Projects may have their own service functions apart from BAU.

B   Projects have very strong links and free access to BAU resources.

C   Team members report to different managers for different aspects of their work.

D   The head of a BAU functional area will take responsibility for work in that area.

8   One commonly cited disadvantage of the matrix structure is:

A   it makes the project visible to the whole organisation, which impacts confidentiality and trust.

B   individuals moving from project to project become the norm and so reduce overall motivation and morale.

C   once individuals complete their work on the project, they are returned to BAU even though they wish to continue working on the project.

D   individuals can experience a conflict of reporting between line management and project management.

9   For a very high-value, highly complex project, scheduled to take a number of years to complete, the most likely structure suitable to deliver such an initiative would be:

A   project – because a project of this nature would need lots of BAU support ensuring that resources switched focus to this key initiative rather than day-to-day tasks.

B   matrix – because due to its high complexity it would need a pool of suitable resources and a mix of technical specialists to become dedicated to this initiative.

C   project – because it would need clear project management processes, roles and responsibilities so that teams become technically proficient.

D   functional – because this is the only way the project could be passed from department to department, utilising the skills and expertise already available.

10   A structure where the project manager and the functional managers share responsibility for assigning priorities and for directing the work would be best described as a:

A   strong functional structure.

B   matrix structure.

C   balanced project structure.

D   functional BAU structure.

NOW CHECK YOUR ANSWERS AT THE END OF THIS SECTION. **YOUR SCORE: /10**

Section 2 – Short quiz   cont.

2.1.4   Project roles

1   Which of the following statements about the role of project sponsor is false?

   A   A project sponsor is an advocate for the project and the change it brings about.

   B   A project sponsor writes and owns the project management plan.

   C   A project sponsor is able to work across functional boundaries within an organisation.

   D   A project sponsor is prepared to commit sufficient time and effort to support the project.

2   Which statement best describes a responsibility of the project sponsor?

   A   Monitoring progress and use of the project resources.

   B   Analysing the project team's productivity.

   C   Ensuring the benefits of the project are realised.

   D   Planning project evaluation reviews for lessons learned.

3   What is a key role of the project manager?

   A   Coordinating the development of the project management plan.

   B   Conducting benefits realisation reviews.

   C   Reviewing progress against success criteria and checking that the planned business benefits will be achieved.

   D   Authorising any changes to the business case.

4   The group whose remit is to set the strategic direction of a project is commonly known as:

   A   the project management team.

   B   primary users.

   C   steering group.

   D   suppliers.

5   Which stakeholders are likely to form the main part of a project steering group/board?

   A   Project sponsor, project manager and quality manager.

   B   Corporate management, project sponsor, quality manager, project office.

   C   Sponsor, supplier representative, user representative.

   D   Sponsor, project manager and senior project team members.

6   Who in the project is responsible for benefits realisation?

A   The senior management of the organisation.

B   The project manager.

C   The sponsor.

D   The end users.

7   Which of the following roles is primarily responsible for defining goals and creating vision for the operability of the project's outputs?

A   Project sponsor.

B   Product owner.

C   User.

D   Business case owner.

8   When the majority of PMO functions are delivered under the control of the project/programme/portfolio manager, this could be described as a:

A   central PMO.

B   embedded PMO.

C   hub and spoke PMO.

D   matrix PMO.

9   When effectively implemented, what is one of the key roles of governance?

A   Provide confidence that the business case is the best option for the current circumstances and that there will be no changes as the project is being delivered.

B   Provide confidence that the plans that have been developed will guarantee that the project will be delivered on time and to budget.

C   Provide confidence to all stakeholders that projects are being well managed and the most appropriate financial and technical controls are being exerted.

D   Provide confidence to all project team members that their jobs are secure at least from the period of the project start to the handover.

Section 2 – Short quiz   cont.

10   Governance could best be defined as:

A   the framework of authority and accountability that defines and controls the outputs, outcomes and benefits from projects, programmes and portfolios.

B   the framework that structures a review of the project and aids a decision to be made whether to continue with the next phase or stage of the project.

C   the framework that is used for selection, prioritisation and control of an organisation's projects and programmes in line with its strategic objectives and capacity to deliver.

D   the framework used by the organisation and approved by the project board at project initiation that allows the definition of the terms of reference for the project.

NOW CHECK YOUR ANSWERS AT THE END OF THIS SECTION. **YOUR SCORE: /10**

2.1.5   **Business case**

1   Which of the following best describes a project's business case?

A   The definition of why the project is required and the desired benefits.

B   A statement of what the project will deliver in terms of products/deliverables.

C   The reason why the project sponsor wants the project to proceed.

D   A statement as to how the project fits into the long term aims of the project sponsor.

2   What information would be expected as content for a business case?

A   A detailed schedule of the project.

B   An outline of the project management team.

C   An outline of the estimated costs of implementing the project.

D   A detailed breakdown of the scope of the project.

3   Which of the following statements about the business case is true?

A   The business case should always be referred to throughout the project.

B   The business case once written will never change.

C   The business case becomes the project manager's responsibility once the project is in the implementation phase.

D   The business case contains key information on how the project will be performed.

4   The responsibility for development and production of the business case rests primarily with:

A   the project manager.

B   jointly shared between the project manager and project sponsor.

C   the project sponsor.

D   the project steering group/committee.

5   Which of the following would not be considered as part of the business case?

A   Safety plan for the project.

B   Implementation options.

C   Stakeholder identification.

D   Business benefits.

6   What is the importance of having a business case?

A   It allows the sponsor to use the document as a baseline to calculate project slippage.

B   It provides an overview of the project team performance at each stage of delivery.

C   It shows how the project manager is performing in delivering the project.

D   It allows the sponsor to decide on project continuity when used at gate reviews.

7   Which one of the following does not describe the prime purpose of the business case?

A   It defines the strategic direction for the project.

B   It describes the operational impact of project delivery.

C   It shows how the project tasks will be scheduled to achieve the success criteria.

D   It documents the benefits of the various options that have been considered.

Section 2 – Short quiz cont.

8   Which of the following is most true of the business case?

A   It provides details of the overarching approach to be taken to move from the current to a future desirable state using a coordinated and structured approach.

B   It evaluates the benefit, cost and risk of alternative project options and provides a rationale for the preferred solution.

C   It demonstrates the relationship between the costs of undertaking a project, initial and recurrent, and the benefits likely to arise from the changed situation, initially and recurrently.

D   It describes each major element in the work breakdown structure (WBS), describing the work content, resources required, the time frame of the work element and a cost estimate.

9   How does having a business case help an organisation?

A   It provides a documented account of the decisions that have been made and by whom in the planning of the project's finances, ensuring the projects compliance with recognised governance standards.

B   It provides an overview of how the project will deliver the scheduled progress over the period agreed between the project manager, sponsor and other key stakeholders associated with the project.

C   It provides a means by which the sponsor can monitor the project manager's performance in relation to the plans documented in the business case and highlight points at which a change of project manager may be necessary.

D   It provides a recognised framework by which project spending proposals can be recorded, reviewed and audited to learn lessons about how efficiently the organisation is deploying funds to achieve its targeted returns.

10 The monetary value used to judge the value of an investment at a particular discount rate is termed:

A   net present value.

B   internal rate of return.

C   cost benefit analysis.

D   residual profit.

NOW CHECK YOUR ANSWERS AT THE END OF THIS SECTION. **YOUR SCORE: /10**

2.1.6   **Project life cycles**

1   Which of the following is true regarding differences between linear and iterative life cycles?

A   A linear life cycle is best for evolving projects, whereas an iterative life cycle is better for more structured projects.

B   A linear life cycle is sequential, whereas an iterative life cycle repeats one or more phases.

C   A linear life cycle is always longer in duration, whereas an iterative life cycle is always shorter in its duration.

D   A linear life cycle is formally managed by a dedicated project manager, whereas management responsibility is shared in an iterative life cycle.

2   A generic linear project life cycle might include the sequence:

A   definition, concept, design, implementation, transition.

B   concept, definition, deployment, transition.

C   planning, deployment, closing, learning, review.

D   feasibility, planning, deployment, handover, review.

3   One of the main purposes of dividing a project into life cycle phases is to:

A   break the work into controllable blocks in terms of effort and size.

B   ensure the processes are properly maintained.

C   ensure that the workforce is certain of their individual roles.

D   provide a means of producing overall project cost estimates.

4   The primary purpose of a gate review is to:

A   decide if the project is on schedule and within budget.

B   decide if the project manager and team are performing well.

C   decide whether to continue with the project.

D   decide if stakeholders are satisfied.

5   Which of the following might be a probable cause of early project closure?

A   The cost to complete the project is greater than the value achieved so far.

B   The project is on schedule but spent less than expected.

C   The project is expected to yield greater value than stated in the business case.

D   The project manager has resigned and an immediate replacement is unavailable.

MANAGEMENT

6   Which one of the following statements about the project life cycle is true?

   A   The phases in the project life cycle are always the same size.

   B   The same processes are used in each of the project life cycle phases.

   C   The project life cycle has a number of distinct phases.

   D   The project budget is divided equally between each phase of the project life cycle.

7   What might be the most probable reason for a project to close early?

   A   A formal gate review has just been performed.

   B   Stakeholders have asked for a post-project review report.

   C   The project team must attend some formal project management training.

   D   The project is no longer aligned to business strategy

8   Which of the following best describes the sequence of an iterative life cycle?

   A   Definition, concept, evolutionary development, implementation, transition.

   B   Feasibility, foundations, evolutionary development, deployment.

   C   Planning, deployment, closing, learning, review.

   D   Feasibility, planning, deployment, handover, review.

9   One benefit of a gate review process is:

   A   it allows learning from one phase of the project to be passed on to the next phase.

   B   it stops projects that no longer meet the organisation's needs.

   C   it allows procurement to be planned into the project life cycle.

   D   it allows the project team to plan delivery of the next phase.

10   Which one of the following would best describe a post-project review?

   A   It is a personal appraisal for each team member on completion of the project.

   B   It appraises the products of the project.

   C   It considers all aspects of the management of the project.

   D   It involves only the project implementation team.

NOW CHECK YOUR ANSWERS AT THE END OF THIS SECTION. **YOUR SCORE: /10**

2.1.7 **Stakeholder engagement**

1   A project stakeholder could best be described as:

    A   a member of the sponsoring organisation's board of directors.

    B   a key player who is seeking to maximise control over the project outcome.

    C   a person or group who has an interest in or is impacted by the project.

    D   a project team member who has the skills necessary to deliver the project.

2   Stakeholder analysis considers three aspects for each stakeholder, which are:

    A   their interest in the project, whether or not they can influence the project and whether their attitude to the project is for or against.

    B   their level of technical knowledge, whether or not they are able to act as sponsor and if they are available.

    C   experience, position in the organisational hierarchy and number of resources managed.

    D   their interest in the project, whether or not they are a member of the steering group and if they are likely to resist changes.

3   An example of an external stakeholder group could be:

    A   users.

    B   a governmental regulatory body.

    C   functional managers within the sponsoring organisation.

    D   the project team members.

4   One benefit of stakeholder analysis is that:

    A   the communication plan becomes unnecessary.

    B   the stakeholders who oppose the project the most can be 'cut off' to reduce their negative influence.

    C   the communication requirements for each stakeholder can be established.

    D   the stakeholders can be removed from any of the decisions that are being planned.

5   Understanding who stakeholders are and their needs is a key duty of:

    A   the quality manager.

    B   the key users.

    C   the project manager.

    D   the business sponsor.

Section 2 – Short quiz cont.

6 One of the main objectives of stakeholder engagement is to establish stakeholder:

A interests.

B expectations.

C influence.

D involvement.

7 What rule of thumb can be used for ensuring that key stakeholders have been included in the process?

A Make use of widely available templates and predefined structures to ensure a complete spectrum of stakeholders are identified.

B Ask the most influential stakeholders to identify who else they think should be involved in the project.

C Analyse other projects and who their stakeholders are and include them by default.

D Question whose support or lack of it might significantly influence the success of the project.

8 What is the most likely reason a stakeholder may object to the project?

A They have a lack of interest in what the project is trying to achieve as they feel it doesn't really affect them.

B They haven't been involved in choosing what they believe to be a suitable project manager from the candidates available.

C They have misunderstood what the project is trying to achieve and have had very little communication from the project.

D They are a stakeholder in another project and don't have the time currently, to perform the stakeholder role.

9 What is one of the most important aspects to establish about a stakeholder's interest in the project?

A If it is positive or negative.

B If it is regular or intermittent.

C If it is influenced by the project.

D If it is influenced by other stakeholders.

10   What is essential for ensuring the level of stakeholder engagement is maintained throughout the delivery of the project?

A   Stakeholders communicate to each other.

B   The project management plan is established.

C   An effective communication plan is used.

D   All stakeholders are treated equally.

NOW CHECK YOUR ANSWERS AT THE END OF THIS SECTION. **YOUR SCORE: /10**

Chapter 2.2   **Project planning**

2.2.1   **Project management plan**

1   A project management plan could best be described as:

A   an activity on arrow network.

B   a Gantt chart.

C   a plan for the programme.

D   an overall plan for the project.

2   You have been asked to assist in the development of a project management plan for the project. As a minimum what should this plan include?

A   A summary of the project acceptance criteria.

B   CVs of all the team members.

C   Details of previous similar projects.

D   Resourcing details for quality reviews.

3   During the consideration of when and how the development of the project management plan should take place, the objectives of carrying out such an exercise can often appear to be uncertain. As a recommendation the project management plan should be:

A   assembled when all information is available.

B   developed iteratively throughout the early stages of the project.

C   completed in detail before the project is authorised.

D   free from detailed schedule information.

Section 2 – Short quiz   cont.

4   To effectively manage the project the range of documentation may appear to be extensive. However, the document that captures the why, what, where, when, how, how much and who for the project is called:

A   project schedule.

B   project definition and delivery report.

C   end of feasibility report.

D   project management plan.

5   Which one of the following statements about the project management plan (PMP) is considered to be the most important condition of compliance to ensure an effective plan is produced:

A   the project team should not contribute to the writing of the PMP.

B   the PMP should be agreed and signed off by both the sponsor and the project manager as a minimum.

C   the sponsor should maintain ownership of the PMP.

D   the PMP is necessary for effective stakeholder engagement.

6   Which of the following would be considered as the main purpose of a project management plan?

A   To provide a documented account of the outcomes of the planning process.

B   To enable agreement between the project sponsor and project manager with regard to project budget, resource requirements and timescale.

C   To provide a record of how the project was planned for archiving in the organisation's lessons learned.

D   To identify and record the projects intended financial spend over the period of project delivery.

7   What is the agreed reference point that is communicated to stakeholders prior to any work being started?

A   Verified work breakdown structure.

B   Deployment baseline.

C   Configuration record.

D   Business case.

Section 2 – Short quiz   cont.

8   Why is it important to produce a project management plan?

   A   It shows the benefits expected at the close of the project and the specific stakeholders who are involved.

   B   It provides justification for undertaking the project and provides a rationale for the preferred solution.

   C   It sets and clarifies the expectations of all stakeholders who are involved in the project delivery.

   D   It identifies and establishes the most appropriate means of procuring the component parts or services for the project being delivered.

9   When in the project life cycle should the deployment baseline be formed?

   A   Deployment phase.

   B   Concept phase.

   C   Definition phase.

   D   Transition phase.

10   What information would you not expect to see in a project management plan?

   A   Quality management plan.

   B   Financial feasibility analysis.

   C   Risk management plan.

   D   Details of scope.

NOW CHECK YOUR ANSWERS AT THE END OF THIS SECTION. **YOUR SCORE: /10**

2.2.2   **Communication**

1   Three general categories for interpretation of communication could be described as:

   A   email, paper, voice.

   B   tactile/visual, auditory, written.

   C   telephone, computer, microphone.

   D   reception, transmission, interruption.

2   To ensure communication is most likely to be effective in the project, the project manager should:

   A   ensure that everyone is copied on all emails.

   B   insist on a lower level of paper documents.

   C   train project staff in the most up-to-date communication techniques.

   D   develop a communication plan.

Section 2 – Short quiz   cont.

3   Successful project communications will most likely occur when:

    A   the project sponsor takes responsibility for planning all stakeholder communication from the outset.

    B   email is the primary method used in order to get information to stakeholders in a speedy and efficient manner.

    C   a standard project communication format for reports is used to provide feedback to stakeholders.

    D   the different communication needs of each stakeholder group are most fully understood.

4   What is likely to be a benefit to a project of having a communication plan?

    A   The project is more likely to finish on time.

    B   There will be greater adherence to the organisation's governance and standards.

    C   The project will be less susceptible to uncontrolled change.

    D   There will be more focus on what benefits the project will be delivering.

5   What action can lead to more consistent communication in the project?

    A   Only transmitting information that stakeholders have requested ensuring that any excess information is kept to a minimum.

    B   Communication is carried out *en masse* ensuring that all stakeholders get all information.

    C   Communication is planned in advance and all messages delivered use the approved framework.

    D   Communicating information on a one-way basis reducing the need for stakeholders to waste their time providing feedback.

6   One way that communication could be improved in the project is to:

    A   ensure that free-flowing feedback channels are planned into the communication structure.

    B   ensure that communication is carried out as much as possible, transmitting as much information as possible.

    C   target only those stakeholders who seem to show a valid interest in the project.

    D   avoid planning communication too much so that messages are not seen as rigid and complex.

7   What is a factor that is important when communicating as part of stakeholder engagement?

   A   Planned communication will help to establish the level of interest and power a stakeholder is likely to possess.

   B   Planned communication will increase the number of stakeholders who are likely to have an interest in the project.

   C   Planned communication will reduce the power of stakeholders who are likely to have an interest in the project.

   D   Planned communication is likely to reduce the number of valid stakeholders who have an interest in the project.

8   What could be considered a significant barrier to communication?

   A   Use of body language.

   B   Having formal meetings.

   C   Attitudes, emotions and prejudices.

   D   Use of informal communication channels.

9   If planning a meeting likely to be attended by stakeholders with widely different knowledge and experience, what practical proactive measure could the project manager take to reduce the impact of communication barriers?

   A   Ensure that the meeting room was reserved for a longer period than normal.

   B   Have a number of meetings where some would be technical and some non-technical.

   C   Aim for a common level of discussion avoiding highly technical discussions.

   D   Ensure that a glossary of technical terms was made available in advance.

10   What might be considered a disadvantage of virtual communication?

   A   Digital communication links never seem to work as required.

   B   Communication being misunderstood.

   C   There is no method for providing feedback.

   D   This method of communication tends to be time consuming.

NOW CHECK YOUR ANSWERS AT THE END OF THIS SECTION. **YOUR SCORE: /10**

Section 2 – Short quiz cont.

2.2.3 Risk and issue management

1 While providing support to the project and attending a risk management workshop the following statements were noted. Which one of these could be considered as a risk to a project?

A We have never done a project of this kind before.

B We might not have sufficient people with the right experience to undertake the project.

C We always find that design verification takes longer than planned.

D We have never worked in that country before.

2 On examining a particular risk in the project there is some uncertainty amongst the project team of how important this risk is to the project. How would you advise the team on how the significance of the risk is to be determined?

A By assessing its probability of occurrence.

B By assessing its impact on project objectives.

C By assessing both its probability of occurrence and its impact on project objectives.

D By assessing its effect on the business case.

3 What is the main benefit of using a risk register in the project?

A It records risks, their impact and the responses being adopted.

B It records risk ownership and how issues are being managed.

C It assesses the impact and probability of risks taking place.

D It directs the team in how the management of risk in the project should be conducted.

4 A member of your team has described being involved in a risk event. Which one of the following would best describe such an event?

A An action or set of actions to reduce the probability or impact of a threat or to increase the probability or impact of an opportunity.

B The plan of the response to risks.

C An uncertain event or set of circumstances that if realised would influence project objectives.

D A risk identification workshop.

5 Which one of the following statements about project risk is true?

A Risk is always beneficial to the project.

B Risk is neither beneficial nor detrimental to the project.

C Risk can be beneficial or detrimental to the project.

D Risk is always detrimental to the project.

6   A typical risk management process would follow the steps:

   A   identification, assessment, planning, response.

   B   assessment, analysis, management, response.

   C   assessment, planning, managing, response.

   D   identification, planning, response, managing.

7   Who would be typically described as the person or organisation best placed to deal with a risk?

   A   Risk manager.

   B   Sponsor.

   C   Project sponsor.

   D   Risk owner.

8   As part of the risk management process the capture of threats and opportunities to the project objectives are referred to as:

   A   risk assessment.

   B   risk avoidance.

   C   risk exposure.

   D   risk identification.

9   Which one of the following would be expected to form the main part of a risk assessment?

   A   Deciding on the approach to project risk management.

   B   Evaluating the risk in terms of severity and relative importance.

   C   Deciding on how to respond to the risk and who should implement the response.

   D   Deciding if the risk is a threat or opportunity.

10   The implementation of risk management on a project requires a cost allocation from the project budget. Which statement describes the most representative return from such an investment?

   A   A benefit to the project if potential opportunities are realised.

   B   The cost of dealing with a risk should it occur is usually greater than the cost of managing that risk.

   C   Risk management in the project facilitates team building.

   D   It allows the organisation to assure stakeholders of project compliance with regard to risk management.

NOW CHECK YOUR ANSWERS AT THE END OF THIS SECTION. **YOUR SCORE: /10**

Section 2 – Short quiz   cont.

2.2.4   **Quality management**

1   How is 'quality' best defined?

   A   The process of evaluating overall project performance on a regular basis to provide confidence that the project will satisfy the relevant quality standards.

   B   The fitness for purpose or the degree of conformance of the outputs of a process or the process itself to requirements.

   C   A discipline for ensuring the outputs, benefits and the processes by which they are delivered, meet stakeholder requirements and are fit for purpose.

   D   The satisfaction of stakeholder needs measured by the success criteria as identified and agreed at the start of the project.

2   While carrying out quality management for the project you have been assigned the task of determining the quality standards that are applicable and how they should apply. Which part of quality management would best describe this activity?

   A   Quality planning.

   B   Quality assurance.

   C   Total quality.

   D   Quality control.

3   To be considered effective, how should quality management be used in the project?

   A   To ensure compliance.

   B   To ensure quality standards are met.

   C   To ensure the required process needs of stakeholders are met.

   D   To ensure both the project outputs and the processes meet the required needs of stakeholders.

4   During project deployment which process will provide confidence that the project will satisfy the relevant quality standards?

   A   Quality assurance for the project.

   B   Strategic Business Planning for Quality (SBPQ).

   C   Total quality planning.

   D   Total quality management (TQM).

5   What is the most likely result of providing effective quality management in the project?

A   The project outputs will have been delivered.

B   Conformance to the outputs and processes will result in a fit-for-purpose product.

C   The project management plan will have been followed.

D   Customer expectations will have been exceeded with both outputs and processes.

6   You have been asked to review the project's quality management plan and in particular the elements of the plan most relevant to quality control. Which one of the following will be your primary focus for consideration?

A   The development of a strategy for the management of quality in the project.

B   Supplying the client with evidence of control to ISO 9000:2000.

C   A review of whether underlying processes and ways of working are leading towards product deliverables of the right quality.

D   The agreed methods of inspection, measurement and testing to verify that the project outputs meet acceptance criteria defined during quality planning.

7   What would be the most direct symptom of poor quality in the project?

A   The project not using compliant management processes.

B   The customer refusing to take delivery of the finished product.

C   The failure of a quality assurance audit.

D   The project finishing over budget.

8   The characteristics of a product that determine whether it meets certain requirements are known as the:

A   product criteria.

B   acceptance criteria.

C   quality criteria.

D   success criteria.

9   The question "Is the project actually following the processes and procedures as set out in the quality plan" would be answered by?

A   Quality alignment.

B   Quality control.

C   Quality assurance.

D   Quality improvement.

Section 2 – Short quiz   cont.

10   Which of the following provides the project manager with a formal overview of project quality?

A   Design reviews.

B   Project definition reports.

C   Quality audits.

D   Historical experience.

NOW CHECK YOUR ANSWERS AT THE END OF THIS SECTION. **YOUR SCORE: /10**

2.2.5   **Procurement**

1   Procurement could best be described as:

A   an outline of the deliverables required by the project.

B   a process by which the resources required by the project are acquired.

C   an outline of the resources required for the project.

D   a definition of who should be the best supplier of goods to the project.

2   Preparation of contracts, selection and acquisition of suppliers and management of the contracts would be items recorded in the:

A   responsibility matrix.

B   work breakdown structure.

C   business case.

D   procurement strategy.

3   One key principle a project manager should follow when carrying out procurement is to:

A   ensure the same suppliers are used in each project to maintain consistency.

B   always use the supplier who will offer the lowest price.

C   always bring in specialist help for support.

D   always use an objective process when selecting suppliers.

4   Which of the following would best describe a contract?

A   An agreement made between two or more parties that creates legally binding obligations between them.

B   An invitation for a supplier to tender at the lowest price.

C   A stage or work package carried out by a chosen supplier.

D   An accepted completed work package.

5   Consideration of the organisation's internal capacity in terms of skills, functions and capabilities would be most relevant in what situation?

A   To identify the most suitable supplier from a tender list.

B   To verify a suitable warranty is supplied with goods.

C   Considering a make or buy decision.

D   Considering the operational use of goods or services.

6   What are the implications of deciding on a single supplier route?

A   Only one supplier has bid for the work in response to an ITT.

B   One supplier will be chosen to supply all the requirements for a particular commodity to the project.

C   A supplier will not sub-contract any of the work to others.

D   The project will be guaranteed to deliver on time and on budget.

7   A situation where a member of the supplier organisation is sitting in the project team alongside those who are actually delivering the project must mean that:

A   there is a particularly competitive marketplace for that supplier.

B   a contract is not yet agreed and signed; when this happens the supplier will return to their own site.

C   there is a distinct lack of trust between customer and supplier in the project.

D   an integrated supply route has been chosen as part of the procurement strategy.

8   What is the best way of avoiding supply disruption?

A   Choose a multiple supply route rather than single.

B   Build up very large stocks of inventory.

C   Get written guarantees from suppliers.

D   Pay more for the commodity upfront to gain more favour when goods are in short supply.

9   Which of the following is true with regard to a time and materials contract?

A   The customer experiences high level of price/cost control risk.

B   The customer experiences low level of price/cost control risk.

C   The customer experiences high level of technical and schedule performance risk.

D   The customer experiences both high level of price/cost control risk and technical, schedule performance risk.

Section 2 – Short quiz   cont.

10   What are the missing steps? A supplier selection process could be: research, ___, tender, ___, manage, close.

A   review, contract.

B   purchase, select.

C   pre-qualification, award.

D   agree, deliver.

NOW CHECK YOUR ANSWERS AT THE END OF THIS SECTION. **YOUR SCORE: /10**

2.2.6   Scope management

1   What aspect is important to clarify when conducting scope definition?

A   The number of products contained in the PBS.

B   The boundaries and interfaces with adjacent projects.

C   Who is going to perform the work.

D   When the work is going to be performed.

2   How are outputs best described?

A   The changed circumstances or behaviour that results from their use.

B   The work packages developed in the WBS for the project.

C   The realisation of benefits at the end of the project.

D   The tangible or intangible products typically delivered by a project.

3   The combination of which two structures creates the responsibility assignment matrix (RAM)?

A   OBS and CBS.

B   OBS and WBS.

C   PBS and CBS.

D   WBS and CBS.

4   The purpose of using the MoSCoW technique in requirements management is to:

A   ensure that must have requirements are given the top priority for delivery.

B   identify the scope of the project at a deeper level.

C   ensure that all stakeholders get what they want from the project.

D   highlight when areas of the project will be delivered.

5   If using an Agile methodology what actions might be necessary for 'could have' and 'should have' requirements?

A   They need to be given a special priority to ensure that they are definitely delivered.

B   They should have the best resources allocated to ensure they are most efficiently delivered.

C   The project could be extended if the delivery of these requirements were proving more difficult than expected.

D   They would be sacrificed if at any time the project was predicted to go over budget or be late.

6   How is it determined if a deliverable conforms to its requirements and configuration information?

A   A configuration management plan is produced.

B   A configuration identification reference is allocated to the deliverable.

C   A configuration verification audit is performed.

D   A status accounting report is produced.

7   A key output of a well-controlled configuration management process is:

A   documented traceability between versions of each configuration item.

B   that the project is most likely to meet its success criteria.

C   documented evidence of all project changes: proposed, authorised, rejected or deferred.

D   an agreed point after which no further changes to scope will be considered.

8   Configuration management could best be described as:

A   the process through which all requests to change the approved baseline of a project are captured, evaluated and then approved, rejected or deferred.

B   the system to ensure that all changes to configuration items are controlled and the interrelationships between items is identified.

C   the technical and administrative activities concerned with the creation, maintenance, controlled change and quality control of the scope of work.

D   a report of the current status and history of all changes to the configuration, together with a complete record of what has happened to the configuration to date.

Section 2 – Short quiz   cont.

9   What is the main reason for an initial high-level review of a change request?

   A   To consider if the change is feasible to evaluate at this stage.

   B   To establish who might be the best stakeholders to be involved in the change.

   C   To ensure that the change request is considered as soon as possible.

   D   To implement the necessary actions to ensure the change has a smooth implementation.

10   Managing change requests in a controlled way enables stakeholders to:

   A   understand the implications of variations on the forecasted outcomes of the work.

   B   reduce the amount of individual change requests that are received from stakeholders.

   C   increase the speed at which the decisions to change are made and then implemented into the project.

   D   allow stakeholders to quickly decide on which change requests to control less and fast track.

NOW CHECK YOUR ANSWERS AT THE END OF THIS SECTION. **YOUR SCORE: /10**

2.2.7   **Leadership and teamwork**

1   Which one of the following statements is true about work that is delegated by the project manager to key team members?

   A   The project manager would no longer control the work.

   B   The work must be approved by senior line management.

   C   It does not reduce the project manager's accountability for that work.

   D   It can be carried out without recourse to other on-going project work.

2   In order to build an effective team, the project manager should:

   A   organise 'off-site' team building events.

   B   focus on team selection techniques.

   C   ensure that the team are situated at the same site.

   D   clearly define roles and responsibilities.

3   Which one of the following characteristics would best describe an effective team?

   A   A group of specialist individuals working on key tasks within the project.

   B   A number of people working on both business-as-usual activities and project work.

   C   A number of people working collaboratively towards the same goal.

   D   A group of people working on a number of different projects within the organisation.

4   Which one of the following aspects would be most important for the project manager to consider in their approach to building and maintaining a team?

A   Let new team members find their own level within the team.

B   Provide focus by cutting links with departments during the project.

C   Ensure the effective induction of new members to the team.

D   Try to ensure that all team members have a similar personality.

5   A leader who ensures that requirements are agreed and that the rewards and penalties for achievement, or lack of it, are understood, could be described as a:

A   transformational leader.

B   hierarchical leader.

C   situational leader.

D   transactional leader.

6   Which one of the following would best describe the most effective leadership ability?

A   The ability to provide inspiration and empowerment to team members.

B   The ability to have a thorough technical expertise of aspects of the project.

C   The ability to communicate clear objectives to team members.

D   The ability to be flexible and sensitive to each individual team member's needs.

7   What is the key purpose of leadership?

A   Provide ongoing support and personal development to individual team members.

B   Develop the technical strategy to achieving business objectives.

C   Establish vision and direction, to influence and align others towards a common purpose.

D   Establish and maintain control over how the project team performs tasks.

8   What aspect can cause a team to move from 'Performing' to 'Forming' (i.e. backwards)?

A   Change.

B   Risk.

C   Delegation.

D   Monitoring and control.

Section 2 – Short quiz   cont.

9   According to McGregor if a person was assumed to be not motivated and disliked working, they would be referred to as a:

A   theory Y.

B   theory X.

C   hygiene factor.

D   safety risk.

10   What can be a challenge when leading virtual teams?

A   Each team member is usually in a different time zone and so cannot have simultaneous discussions with other team members.

B   Individual skills are more difficult to assess in a virtual environment.

C   It is more difficult to build deep relationships and trust virtually than in person.

D   It is difficult to identify how much attention each team member is paying to the task being discussed.

NOW CHECK YOUR ANSWERS AT THE END OF THIS SECTION. **YOUR SCORE: /10**

Chapter 2.3   Project delivery

2.3.1   Estimating

1   What aspect of the project will have greatest influence on the estimating method being used?

A   The point in the life cycle where the estimate is being carried out.

B   The overall budgeted value of the project being estimated.

C   Whether the project is likely to proceed or not.

D   The amount of acceptable estimating tolerance that exists.

2   What is the prime advantage of using a parametric estimating method?

A   Accuracy.

B   Ability to deal with detailed information.

C   Independence from historic data.

D   Speed.

3   Which of the following statements about estimating is true?

A   Post-project reviews are a prime source of estimating data.

B   An estimated cost for a project must be within +/- 10 per cent to be of any use.

C   If you cannot estimate task durations within 20 per cent there is no point in developing a schedule.

D   The project manager should always add 10 per cent to other people's duration estimates to allow for natural optimism.

4   The project you are working on has chosen to produce an estimate by use of a detailed work breakdown structure (WBS). What estimating method is this approach commonly known as?

A   Comparative estimating.

B   Bottom-up/analytical estimating.

C   Strategic estimating.

D   Parametric estimating.

5   The concept that describes how estimating accuracy changes through the project life cycle is termed:

A   estimating risk.

B   estimating funnel.

C   normal values.

D   parametric estimating.

6   What is the estimating method that uses data of a similar project as the basis for the estimate?

A   Evaluative estimating.

B   Risk-based estimating.

C   Analogous estimating.

D   Analytical estimating.

7   When the project progresses through the life cycle, which one of the following aspects would be expected to occur?

A   Accuracy of the estimate reduces and the level of contingency requirement increases.

B   Accuracy of the estimate increases and the level of contingency requirement reduces.

C   The accuracy and level of contingency requirement both increase.

D   The accuracy and level of contingency requirement both reduce.

8   What is one of the main characteristics of the Delphi method of estimating?

A   The individual group members use a statistical relationship between historic data and other variables to calculate an estimate.

B   The task of producing the estimates will be delegated to those who are actually going to deliver the individual pieces of work or work packages.

C   The individual group members, who are tasked with providing the estimates, do this in isolation from each other.

D   The individual group members identify the optimistic, likely and pessimistic values and then calculate a mean value.

Section 2 – Short quiz   cont.

9   What is a likely benefit of re-estimating throughout the project life cycle?

   A   The project will be much more economically viable.

   B   The business case is justified to a greater degree.

   C   Overall project duration is reduced.

   D   Reduction in contingency reserves are achieved.

10   What estimating method is most commonly used in the definition phase of the project life cycle?

   A   Analogous.

   B   Analytical.

   C   Parametric.

   D   Delphi.

NOW CHECK YOUR ANSWERS AT THE END OF THIS SECTION. **YOUR SCORE: /10**

2.3.2   Schedule and resource optimisation

1   The critical path on a project network is:

   A   the shortest path in duration through the network.

   B   the path with the most float.

   C   the path with the most activities on it.

   D   the longest path in duration through the network.

2   The critical path in the network diagram shown below is:

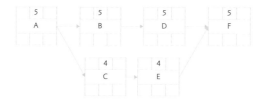

   A   A C E F

   B   A B D F

   C   A C D F

   D   A B E F

3   In the above network diagram, which of the activities have total float?

   A   C and E.

   B   B and D.

   C   A only.

   D   E only.

4   The diagram below shows the relationship between task A and task B.
     According to this diagram the dependency shown is an example of:

TASK A   **TASK B**

A   Finish to start.

B   Finish to finish.

C   Start to finish.

D   Start to start.

5   Which of the following best describes the concept of total float?

A   The value of the earliest finish of an activity subtracted from the latest
     finish of the previous activity.

B   The value of the latest finish of an activity subtracted from the earliest start
     of the same activity.

C   The amount an activity can slip without affecting the overall duration of
     the project.

D   The amount an activity can slip without affecting the start of the next
     activity.

6   In a situation where time becomes more important than cost the project
     manager should first attempt to:

A   remove resources from critical tasks.

B   perform time-limited scheduling (smoothing).

C   redefine the critical path.

D   perform resource-limited smoothing (levelling).

7   To maintain the scheduled duration when resources are limited, resource
     levelling should firstly attempt to:

A   never exceed pre-determined end date.

B   schedule activities within the limits of their float.

C   extend the activity duration.

D   minimise the use of overtime.

MANAGEMENT

Section 2 – Short quiz cont.

The Gantt chart below should be used for answers to questions 8, 9 and 10. It shows the scheduling of seven tasks (A–G) and their daily allocation of resources over a nine-day period. Activities B and F have total float to the extent as indicated by the dotted line.

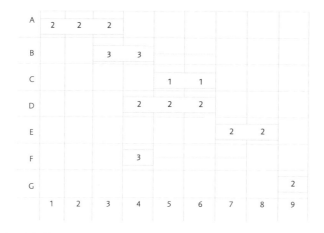

8   Which of the possible actions would be considered the best application of resource smoothing?

   A   Double the amount of resources applied to activity B, reducing its duration to 1 day.

   B   Delay activity F to start on day 5 and finish on day 7, reducing to 1 resource per day.

   C   Extend the overall schedule duration by 3 days and start the project on day 3.

   D   Double the amount of resources applied to activity E, reducing its duration to 1 day.

9   If the total number of resources available is limited to 6 per day, what would be the most efficient way to deal with this constraint?

   A   Increase the project budget to acquire additional resources.

   B   Extend the overall project duration by 3 days.

   C   Move activity B and F to the extent of their float.

   D   Move activity F only to day 5.

10   If resource levelling was being considered to be applied to the schedule, which activities would be initially considered for this technique?

   A   All activities would be considered.

   B   Activities B and F would be initially considered.

   C   Activities A, C, D, E and G would be initially considered.

   D   There is not enough information provided to make such a decision.

NOW CHECK YOUR ANSWERS AT THE END OF THIS SECTION. **YOUR SCORE: /10**

2.3.3   **Conflict management**

1   In general terms what is the most likely reason for conflict to arise in the project?

    A   Projects mostly employ contractor project managers and so there is constant change of leadership in the project.

    B   There are lots of tasks to be completed and members of the project team must be forced to meet critical deadlines even though they are thought to be unrealistic.

    C   Everyone in the project is jostling for position and it is only the strongest that survive.

    D   There are differing opinions and/or opposing interests between stakeholders that matter to the people involved and are not easily reconciled.

2   A common model for helping to manage conflict considers what two dimensions?

    A   The desire to achieve your own objectives; the desire for others to achieve their objectives.

    B   The amount of knowledge you have; the amount of knowledge others have.

    C   The time available in your own situation; time available in others' situations.

    D   The amount of power you have; the amount of power they have.

3   Which of the following is likely to be most effective in a conflict situation?

    A   Bypassing the source of conflict.

    B   Use of structural power.

    C   Exploring differences.

    D   Offering a financial incentive.

4   Which of the following is true about conflict management?

    A   An effective project manager should seek to eliminate conflict.

    B   All conflict should be avoided and so lessen impact on the team's performance.

    C   Levels of conflict can vary throughout the project life cycle.

    D   Levels of conflict are the same throughout the project life cycle.

Section 2 – Short quiz   cont.

5   When might competing be an appropriate approach to resolve conflict?

   A   When quick decisive action is vital.

   B   When it is important to reach an integrative solution.

   C   When an issue is trivial.

   D   When a better position should be allowed to be heard.

6   'Splitting the difference' is an example of which conflict management approach?

   A   Accommodating.

   B   Collaborating.

   C   Competing.

   D   Compromising.

7   In which circumstances is conflict most likely to occur?

   A   When work starts on the deployment phase.

   B   When parties work together for the first time.

   C   When the business case is being approved.

   D   When the project management plan is being created.

8   When should the project manager start implementing a conflict management approach?

   A   Once all suggestions have been presented by the team.

   B   When one or more team members lose credibility with others.

   C   Once the project manager's power base has been established.

   D   As soon as conflict appears evident.

9   Why is conflict likely in a project environment?

   A   Team members know that the project will end at some point and so are naturally anxious about their future careers.

   B   Team members lack any familiarity with what the project is actually delivering and so are fearful of discussing any aspect of the project with others.

   C   Team members have varying degrees of influence and they may not be in agreement with each other.

   D   Team members lack trust in the project manager and so challenge every decision that is made.

10   What skill is important for the project manager to have if they are to manage conflict successfully?

A   Listening.

B   Controlling.

C   Empowering.

D   Managing.

NOW CHECK YOUR ANSWERS AT THE END OF THIS SECTION. **YOUR SCORE: /10**

2.3.4   **Negotiation**

1   Which of the following is true with regard to planning for a negotiation?

A   It is very difficult to plan for a negotiation until the negotiation has started and the parties get to know each other's wants and needs.

B   If too much time is spent on planning the negotiation, the time for the negotiation to take place will be markedly reduced.

C   The more time and effort devoted to the planning of a negotiation, the higher the likelihood of a desirable outcome.

D   The most effective planning technique is to plan while actually doing the negotiation in order to be most flexible to the situation.

2   What is the significance of BATNA for the parties negotiating?

A   It shows which party has most control.

B   It signals the end of the negotiation.

C   It defines the zone of possible agreement (ZOPA).

D   It means that there is unlikely to be a deal.

3   Which area of the project is most likely to require formal negotiations to be necessary?

A   Scheduling project activities.

B   Acquisition of goods and services for the project.

C   Monitoring and controlling project activity.

D   Implementing configuration management.

4   Which essential task should be carried out at the end of a negotiation?

A   Taking note of the names of the participants.

B   Arranging follow-up meetings.

C   Recording all agreements and commitments made so far.

D   Reviewing the capacity of the project to accommodate the terms agreed.

Section 2 – Short quiz   cont.

5   The foundation of a win-win outcome for a negotiation is:

   A   the amount of power that one party has gained over another regardless of the final outcome that has been agreed.

   B   the time it takes for each party to recover any losses as a result of the negotiation terms and agreement reached.

   C   the relative value that one party has achieved in relation to the terms that have been achieved as a result.

   D   how each party feels about how the relationship has developed and the resulting levels of trust that have been created.

6   What is most important for a negotiator to understand about their concessions?

   A   The cost to give the concession and the value to the other party.

   B   What concessions are likely to be offered by the other party.

   C   How the other party will hide their concessions.

   D   The number of concessions that might need to be offered.

7   The first concessions traded should be:

   A   low cost, high value.

   B   high cost, low value.

   C   low cost, low value.

   D   high cost, high value.

8   BATNA is:

   A   best agreement and no agreement.

   B   best alternative to a negotiated agreement.

   C   broad arrangements for terms in agreement.

   D   build, achieve, trade, negotiate, analyse.

9   What is essential for the project manager to be aware of when negotiating?

   A   They must recognise the limits of their authority and experience in contractual situations and should seek support from their procurement or legal specialists.

   B   They must ensure that a negotiated agreement occurs even though the terms may not be the most favourable.

   C   They should focus the negotiation on not giving any concessions at all costs, otherwise it will be considered a failed negotiation.

   D   They need to always ensure that the negotiation occurs in a neutral environment, otherwise they will feel disadvantaged from the start.

10   Which of the following could be the best example of a concession?

    A   Buy one get one free.

    B   A large discount offered early on.

    C   Storage of goods on the supplier's site until needed.

    D   Making sure that the supplier pays for lunch.

NOW CHECK YOUR ANSWERS AT THE END OF THIS SECTION. **YOUR SCORE: /10**

2.3.5   Knowledge and information management

1   The prime role of a project information management system is to:

    A   provide information to the sponsor as and when required.

    B   make decisions about control and coordination of the project.

    C   report on all detailed aspects of the project.

    D   support the decision-making process.

2   Project reporting is for the benefit of:

    A   the project manager.

    B   the project sponsor.

    C   the project management team.

    D   the project support office.

3   The project manager will be expected to produce reports containing which of the following information:

    A   progress against schedule, expenditure against budget and performance against quality plan.

    B   feasibility of the project options currently being delivered.

    C   business case progress and the risks that will have an impact on its achievement.

    D   how benefits are going to be realised once the project has been delivered.

4   The main purpose of project reporting is to ensure that:

    A   the same information is sent to all stakeholders.

    B   the project uses the methods of communication required by the sponsor.

    C   the project communicates to stakeholders in the most effective way possible.

    D   the project complies with the organisation's information management policies.

Section 2 – Short quiz   cont.

5   What is the primary function of knowledge management?

A   To develop processes to audit the project to assess the level of knowledge required by the project delivery team.

B   To ensure that everyone working in the project is assessed to establish their current knowledge levels.

C   To ensure that everyone in the project is trained to the maximum knowledge levels possible.

D   To develop processes, tools and techniques to build existing knowledge as organisational assets.

6   When in the project would it be most likely for archiving of project documentation to take place?

A   After a baseline plan has been created.

B   During project closeout.

C   When the scope has been verified by the users.

D   After completion of each phase of the project.

7   In a typical information management system what part of the process follows storage?

A   Dissemination.

B   Destruction.

C   Curation.

D   Archiving.

8   In a typical information management system what part of the process makes decisions about the management of the data?

A   Dissemination.

B   Destruction.

C   Curation.

D   Archiving.

9   How should the project manager avoid the 'send to all' syndrome?

A   Only send information to those stakeholders who have specifically asked for it.

B   Avoid sending information to most stakeholders.

C   Reduce the amount of information to a bare minimum.

D   Ensure that there is sufficient interaction between information management and communication planning.

10   What must the project manager consider most when planning the destruction of information?

A   That information should be destroyed but a master copy must always be kept on file.

B   That destruction occurs in line with legislative compliance.

C   There is no need to destroy information after a five-year period.

D   That information stored on digital media doesn't need to be destroyed.

NOW CHECK YOUR ANSWERS AT THE END OF THIS SECTION. **YOUR SCORE: /10**

2.3.6   **Earned value management**

1   What is one of the main reasons that a project manager would use earned value?

A   It is the optimal way of ensuring that activities are scheduled efficiently to deliver the project requirements.

B   It shows where requirements have not yet been identified and so areas of the project that could be susceptible to high levels of change.

C   It is the optimal way of tracking actual work achieved, compared to how much it has cost to deliver that work.

D   It identifies where quality deficits are likely to occur throughout the delivery of the project.

2   How is earned value represented in the project?

A   The actual cost of the work that has been completed at the point in time that is being measured.

B   The actual budgeted value of the work that has been completed at the point in time that is being measured.

C   The budgeted value of the work that has been scheduled to be completed at the point in time that is being measured.

D   The number of days of work that has been expended at the point in time that is being measured.

3   How is cost performance measured in earned value terms?

A   The actual number of tasks that are at least 50 per cent behind schedule.

B   The actual work achieved compared to how much it has cost to achieve that work.

C   The actual cost compared to the planned budget.

D   The actual work achieved compared to how long it has taken to achieve that work.

Section 2 – Short quiz   cont.

4   The schedule performance index is defined as:

    A   the ratio of work accomplished versus work planned, for a specified time period.

    B   the difference between the budgeted cost of work performed and the actual cost of work scheduled.

    C   the difference between the budgeted cost of work performed and the budgeted cost of work scheduled.

    D   the percentage of calculations that resulted in an activity being placed on the critical path.

5   A cost comparison between what has been earned and what has been spent is termed:

    A   cost benefit analysis.

    B   cost performance index.

    C   cost variance.

    D   cost of capital.

6   The ratio of earned value over actual cost is termed:

    A   cost variance.

    B   schedule performance index.

    C   schedule variance.

    D   cost performance index.

7   If a project had a CPI of 1.09 what would this indicate about the project's current status?

    A   It was nine per cent ahead of schedule.

    B   It was currently overspent.

    C   It was nine per cent underspent.

    D   It was over budget.

8   If a project's current SPI was 0.84 and this performance was planned to continue until the project finished, what could be deduced from this information?

    A   The project is likely to finish on time.

    B   The project is likely to finish early.

    C   The project is likely to finish late.

    D   The project is likely to finish underspent.

Questions 9 and 10 refer to the following diagram.

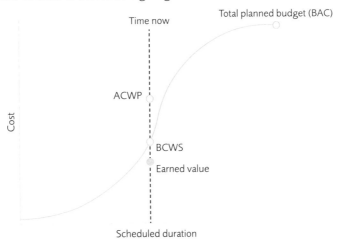

9   In the diagram shown above what could be concluded about the current schedule performance of the project?

   A   The project is behind schedule and overspent.

   B   The project is behind schedule and under budget.

   C   The project is ahead of schedule and overspent.

   D   More information about the actual work completed is needed before the schedule performance can be analysed.

10   In the diagram shown above and if the current performance were to continue to the end of the project, what would be the most likely outcome?

   A   The project will finish late and be underspent.

   B   The project will finish early and be underspent.

   C   The project will finish early and be overspent.

   D   The project will finish late and be overspent.

NOW CHECK YOUR ANSWERS AT THE END OF THIS SECTION. **YOUR SCORE: /10**

3.4.1 Short quizzes answers

Check your answers in each section. For any that are not correct, read over that section again and ensure that you more fully understand the subject area.

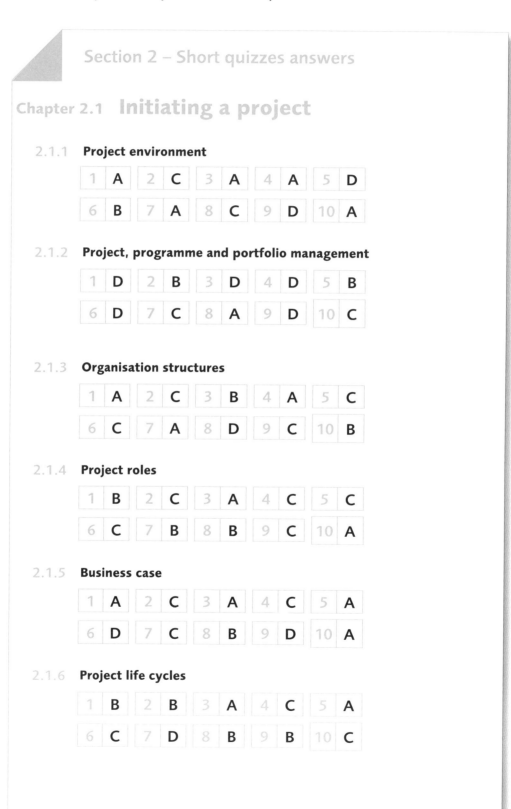

Section 2 – Short quizzes answers

Chapter 2.1 Initiating a project

2.1.1 Project environment

1	A	2	C	3	A	4	A	5	D
6	B	7	A	8	C	9	D	10	A

2.1.2 Project, programme and portfolio management

1	D	2	B	3	D	4	D	5	B
6	D	7	C	8	A	9	D	10	C

2.1.3 Organisation structures

1	A	2	C	3	B	4	A	5	C
6	C	7	A	8	D	9	C	10	B

2.1.4 Project roles

1	B	2	C	3	A	4	C	5	C
6	C	7	B	8	B	9	C	10	A

2.1.5 Business case

1	A	2	C	3	A	4	C	5	A
6	D	7	C	8	B	9	D	10	A

2.1.6 Project life cycles

1	B	2	B	3	A	4	C	5	A
6	C	7	D	8	B	9	B	10	C

2.1.7 **Stakeholder engagement**

1	C	2	A	3	B	4	C	5	C
6	D	7	D	8	C	9	A	10	C

Chapter 2.2 **Project planning**

2.2.1 **Project management plan**

1	D	2	A	3	B	4	D	5	B
6	B	7	B	8	C	9	C	10	B

2.2.2 **Communication**

1	B	2	D	3	D	4	B	5	C
6	A	7	A	8	C	9	D	10	B

2.2.3 **Risk and issue management**

1	B	2	C	3	A	4	C	5	C
6	A	7	D	8	D	9	B	10	B

2.2.4 **Quality management**

1	B	2	A	3	D	4	A	5	B
6	D	7	B	8	C	9	C	10	C

2.2.5 **Procurement**

1	B	2	D	3	D	4	A	5	C
6	B	7	D	8	A	9	A	10	A

2.2.6 **Scope management**

1	B	2	D	3	B	4	A	5	D
6	C	7	A	8	C	9	A	10	A

2.2.7 **Leadership and teamwork**

1	C	2	D	3	C	4	C	5	D
6	A	7	C	8	A	9	B	10	C

Chapter 2.3 Project delivery

2.3.1 **Estimating**

1	A	2	A	3	A	4	B	5	B
6	C	7	B	8	C	9	D	10	B

2.3.2 **Schedule and resource optimisation**

1	D	2	B	3	A	4	B	5	C
6	B	7	B	8	B	9	D	10	B

2.3.3 **Conflict management**

1	D	2	A	3	C	4	C	5	A
6	D	7	B	8	D	9	C	10	A

2.3.4 **Negotiation**

1	C	2	C	3	B	4	C	5	D
6	A	7	C	8	B	9	A	10	C

2.3.5 **Knowledge and information management**

1	D	2	C	3	A	4	C	5	D
6	B	7	C	8	C	9	D	10	B

2.3.6 **Earned value management**

1	C	2	B	3	B	4	A	5	C
6	D	7	C	8	C	9	A	10	D

3.2 Exam practice questions

The questions outlined in this section will give you some insight into the types and structure of questions that could be seen in the PMQ exam. Your paper will have 16 questions, which could be drawn from any of the 11 learning outcomes and you are required to answer any 10 questions for the PMQ exam. Try and put together an answer for each of the questions and then check the material to identify the main points of the answer.

Please note that the questions are not actual questions released by APM, or that will appear in any PMQ exam, but you will find that they are very similar. There is also a sample PMQ paper released by APM; again use this to practice prior to sitting the exam.

You can check back and review your answers against what you have learnt in this guide. There are no model answers to the sample questions published in this guide, or by APM. But you can find helpful hints and tips in the *Exam Techniques* document, available from apm.org.uk/qualifications-and-training/project-management-qualifcation.

Specification for a PMQ examination question

Each question:

- is worth 50 marks;
- is allocated 15 minutes to answer;
- will address one learning outcome and allow candidates to demonstrate their knowledge and understanding in relation to that learning outcome;
- will clearly indicate where a specific number of answers are required;
- will be subdivided into two parts, each of which will:
    address the same learning outcome;
    be identified using lower case letters, that is a and b;
    clearly show the marks allocated.
- will stand alone and not rely on an answer from another question in the examination paper.

Command Verbs

Candidates must become familiar with the definition of different command verbs, which will be used in the syllabus and assessments. A command verb itself is simply an instruction to do something. It is suggested that candidates are familiar with these words if they are to provide the required depth of response to an assessment.

Differentiate – Recognise or determine what makes something different.

Describe – Give an account, including all the relevant characteristics, qualities and events.

Explain – Give an account of the purpose(s) or reason(s).

Interpret – Translate information/data into another form to aid understanding, to demonstrate understanding or to inform a future action.

Outline – Set out the main points/characteristics.

State – Express the details without elaboration.

Learning outcomes, assessment criteria, study guide subject areas and example questions

Learning outcome	1. Understand how organisations and projects are structured.
Study guide subject area	**Assessment criteria** (and question examples)
2.1.3 **Organisation structures**	**1.1** Differentiate between types of permanent and temporary organisation structures (including functional, matrix, and project) (Q2b) (Q4a).
2.2.6 **Scope management**	**1.2** Explain the way in which an organisational breakdown structure is used to create a responsibility assignment matrix (Q3 b).
2.1.4 **Organisation roles**	**1.3** Explain the role and key responsibilities of the project manager (Q3a).
	1.4 Differentiate between the responsibilities of the project manager and the project sponsor throughout the project (Q2a).
	1.5 Describe other roles within project management (including users, project team members, the project steering group/board and the product owner) (Q1b).
2.1.4.1 **Project office**	**1.6** Describe the functions and benefits of different types of project office (including project/programme/portfolio management office (PMO), embedded PMO, central PMO and hub-and-spoke PMO) (Q1a).
2.1.4.2 **Governance**	**1.7** Explain why aspects of project management governance are required (such as the use of: policies, regulations, functions, processes, procedures and delegated responsibilities) (Q4b).

Examples of exam questions for this learning outcome

Question 1

Question part (a)	Describe <u>two</u> ways in which a project management office can assist a project manager to successfully deliver a project.
Marks	20 marks (10 marks each)

Question part (b)	Select <u>three</u> of the project roles below and describe their responsibilities throughout the project.
	▪ Product owner
	▪ Project manager
	▪ Project sponsor
	▪ Project steering group
Marks	30 marks (10 marks each)

Question 2

Question part (a)	Explain <u>two</u> differences between the responsibilities of the project sponsor and project manager throughout the life cycle of the project.
Marks	20 marks (10 marks each)
Question part (b)	Explain <u>three</u> characteristics of a matrix organisation structure when used by an organisation to deliver a change initiative.
Marks	30 marks (10 marks each)

Question 3

Question part (a)	Select <u>two</u> phases of the project life cycle and describe a specific activity the project manager would perform in each of the two phases.
Marks	20 marks (10 marks each)
Question part (b)	Explain <u>three</u> steps in the creation of a responsibility assignment matrix. In each step explain who might be involved.
Marks	30 marks (10 marks each)

Question 4

Question part (a)	Describe <u>two</u> characteristics of a functional organisation structure when used to deliver a change initiative.
Marks	20 marks (10 marks each)
Question part (b)	Explain <u>three</u> ways in which a project would be influenced by the implementation of governance.
Marks	30 marks (10 marks each)

Learning outcome	2. Understand project life cycles.
Study guide subject area	**Assessment criteria**
2.1.6 Project life cycles	**2.1** Differentiate between linear, iterative and hybrid life cycles (Q3a).
	2.2 Explain why projects are structured as phases in a linear life cycle (Q1b).
	2.3 Explain the differences between a project life cycle and an extended life cycle (Q1a).
	2.4 Outline the role of knowledge and information management to inform decision making (Q2a).
	2.5 Explain the benefits of conducting reviews throughout the life cycle (including decision gates, benefits reviews and audits) (Q3b) (Q4b).
	2.6 Explain why projects may close early (Q4a).

Examples of exam questions for this learning outcome

Question 1

Question part (a)	Describe <u>two</u> activities that would occur in the extended life cycle and not in the project life cycle. For each activity state who might be involved.
Marks	20 marks (10 marks each)
Question part (b)	Explain <u>three</u> reasons why a project might be structured in phases, following a linear life cycle.
Marks	30 marks (10 marks each)

Question 2

Question part (a)	Describe <u>two</u> knowledge management activities that should be built into the day-to-day management of the project.
Marks	20 marks (10 marks each)
Question part (b)	Explain <u>three</u> reasons why an iterative life cycle might be used to deliver a project rather than a linear life cycle option.
Marks	30 marks (10 marks each)

Question 3

Question part (a)	Explain <u>two</u> differences between a linear life cycle and iterative life cycle.
Marks	20 marks (10 marks each)
Question part (b)	Describe <u>three</u> different types of review that may be carried out during a project and their main purpose.
Marks	30 marks (10 marks each)

Question 4

Question part (a)	Explain <u>two</u> reasons why a project might close early.
Marks	20 marks (10 marks each)
Question part (b)	Explain <u>three</u> benefits of conducting reviews throughout the life cycle of a project.
Marks	30 marks (10 marks each)

Learning outcome	**3.** Understand the situational context of projects
Study guide subject area	**Assessment criteria**
2.1.2 Project, programme and portfolio management	**3.1** Differentiate between projects and business-as-usual (BAU) (Q1b).
	3.2 Differentiate between project management, portfolio management and programme management (Q1a).
	3.3 Outline the relationship between programmes, projects and strategic change (Q4b).
	3.4 Describe situations where the use of programme management may be appropriate (Q4a).
	3.5 Describe situations where the use of portfolio management may be appropriate (Q2b).
2.1.1 Project environment	**3.6** Explain tools and techniques used to determine factors which influence and impact projects (including PESTLE, SWOT and VUCA) (Q2a) (Q3a).
	3.7 Explain the impact of the legal and regulatory environment on projects (such as the impact on working conditions, risk management, governance and sustainability) (Q3b).

Examples of exam questions for this learning outcome

Question 1

Question part (a)	Describe <u>two</u> ways in which programme management is different from project management.
Marks	20 marks (10 marks each)
Question part (b)	Explain <u>three</u> key differences between projects and business-as-usual (BAU).
Marks	30 marks (10 marks each)

Question 2

Question part (a)	Explain <u>two</u> purposes of carrying out a SWOT analysis for a project option.
Marks	20 marks (10 marks each)
Question part (b)	Describe <u>three</u> situations where the use of portfolio management may be considered appropriate.
Marks	30 marks (10 marks each)

Question 3

Question part (a)   Explain <u>two</u> ways in which VUCA analysis could be used to assess a project context.

   Marks   20 marks (10 marks each)

Question part (b)   Describe <u>three</u> aspects of the legal and regulatory environment of a project that the project manager should be aware in assessing a project's context.

   Marks   30 marks (10 marks each)

Question 4

Question part (a)   Explain <u>two</u> reasons why an organisation might consider programme management as an appropriate approach to deliver projects.

   Marks   20 marks (10 marks each)

Question part (b)   Explain <u>three</u> ways in which projects and programmes can help an organisation deliver strategic change.

   Marks   30 marks (10 marks each)

Learning outcome	4. Understand communication within project management		
Study guide subject area	**Assessment criteria**		
2.2.2 Communication	**4.1** Explain the benefits, to a project, of a communication plan (Q1a).		
	4.2 Explain the relationship between stakeholder analysis and an effective communication management plan (Q2b).		
	4.3 State factors which can positively or negatively affect communication (Q2a).		
2.3.3 Conflict management	**4.4** State sources of conflict within a project (Q1b).		
	4.5 Explain ways in which conflict can be addressed (such as Thomas Kilmann Conflict Mode Instrument) (Q3b).		
2.3.4 Negotiation	**4.6** Explain how to plan and conduct negotiations (including ZOPA, BATNA and 'win-win') (Q3a).		

Examples of exam questions for this learning outcome

Question 1

Question part (a)	Explain two benefits of a communication plan to a project.
Marks	20 marks (10 marks each)
Question part (b)	Explain three common causes of conflict arising in the following phases of the project life cycle (one cause of conflict from each phase).
	▪ Concept
	▪ Definition
	▪ Deployment
Marks	30 marks (10 marks each)

Question 2

Question part (a)	State four factors that can positively affect communication in the project.
Marks	20 marks (5 marks each)
Question part (b)	Explain three ways in which a thorough stakeholder analysis can assist in the production of an effective communication plan.
Marks	30 marks (10 marks each)

Question 3

Question part (a)   Outline <u>four</u> factors that will increase the likelihood of a win-win outcome to a
                      negotiation.

    Marks   20 marks (5 marks each)

Question part (b)   Describe <u>three</u> approaches that a project manager could take to address conflict in the
                      project team.

    Marks   30 marks (10 marks each)

Learning outcome	5. Understand the principles of leadership and teamwork
Study guide subject area	**Assessment criteria**
2.2.7 **Leadership and teamwork**	**5.1** Explain how leadership impacts on team performance and motivation (using models such as Maslow, Herzberg and McGregor) (Q3a).
	5.2 Explain why it may be necessary to change leadership styles to effectively support the management of a project (Q1b).
	5.3 Describe the characteristics and benefits of effective teams and teamwork (Q1a).
	5.4 Explain factors that impact on the leadership of virtual teams (Q2a).
	5.5 Explain factors that influence the creation, development and leadership of teams (using models such as Belbin, Margerison-McCann, Myers-Briggs, Hackman, Tuckman, Katzenbach and Smith) (Q2b) (Q3b).

Examples of exam questions for this learning outcome

Question 1

Question part (a)   Describe two characteristics of an effective team.

Marks   20 marks (10 marks each)

Question part (b)   Explain three reasons why a leader may have to change their leadership style to support the management of a project.

Marks   30 marks (10 marks each)

Question 2

Question part (a)   State four factors that can impact leadership when leading a virtual team.

Marks   20 marks (5 marks each)

Question part (b)   Using a recognised model explain three stages of team development that might occur after the team has formed.

Marks   30 marks (10 marks each)

Question 3

Question part (a)   Outline <u>four</u> motivational factors that a leader should be aware of when leading their team.

    Marks   20 marks (5 marks each)

Question part (b)   Explain <u>three</u> aspects of leadership that a leader would consider when seeking to maximise the performance of their team.

    Marks   30 marks (10 marks each)

Learning outcome	6. Understand planning for success
Study guide subject area	**Assessment criteria**
2.1.5 Business case	**6.1** Explain the importance of a business case throughout the project life cycle (Q1a).
	6.2 Explain what is meant by benefits management (including identification, definition, planning, tracking and realisation) (Q2b).
	6.3 Explain investment appraisal techniques used by a project manager (including Internal Rate of Return (IRR) and Net Present Value (NPV)) (Q2a).
2.3.5 Knowledge and information management	**6.4** Explain an information management process (including collection, storage, curation, dissemination, archiving and the destruction of information) (Q1b).
	6.5 Explain factors that would typically be reported on to help ensure successful project outcomes (Q8a).
2.2.1 Project management plan	**6.6** Explain the relationship between the deployment baseline and the development of a project management plan in linear and iterative life cycles (Q7a).
	6.7 Explain the importance of producing a project management plan (Q6b).
	6.8 Describe the typical contents of a project management plan (Q5b).
2.3.1 Estimating	**6.9** Explain approaches to producing estimates (including parametric, analogous, analytical and Delphi) (Q3b).
	6.10 Explain the reasons for and benefits of re-estimating throughout the project life cycle (Q5a).
2.1.7 Stakeholder engagement	**6.11** Explain the relationship between stakeholder analysis, influence and engagement (8b).
	6.12 Explain the importance of managing stakeholder expectations to the success of the project (Q7b).
2.3.6 Earned value management	**6.13** Explain why a project manager would use earned value management (Q3a).
	6.14 Interpret earned value data (including variances and performance indexes) (Q4b).
	6.15 Explain the benefits of using the interpretation of earned value data (Q6a).
2.2.3 Risk and issue management	**6.16** Explain the role of contingency planning in projects (Q4a).

Question 1

Question part (a)	Explain <u>two</u> reasons why a project might benefit from having a robust business case.
Marks	20 marks (10 marks each)
Question part (b)	Explain <u>three</u> reasons why information management may support the effective management of a project.
Marks	30 marks (10 marks each)

Question 2

Question part (a)	Explain how the following <u>two</u> investment appraisal techniques can be used to assess the validity of a project:
	▪ Net Present Value (NPV)
	▪ Internal Rate of Return
Marks	20 marks (10 marks each)
Question part (b)	Describe <u>three</u> activities that would be carried out as part of a benefits management process.
Marks	30 marks (10 marks each)

Question 3

Question part (a)	Explain <u>two</u> ways in which the project manager could use earned value to track a projects performance.
Marks	20 marks (10 marks each)
Question part (b)	Explain how each of the <u>three</u> estimating methods could be used to produce an estimate of cost for the project.
	▪ Parametric
	▪ Analogous
	▪ Analytical
Marks	30 marks (10 marks each)

Question 4

Question part (a)   Explain <u>two</u> reasons why a planned contingency may be necessary in addition to the project budget.

Marks   20 marks (10 marks each)

Question part (b)   The table below shows the performance of a 10-month project. The current time is month 4.

Month	SPI	CPI
1	0.92	1.00
2	0.89	1.02
3	0.78	1.15
4	0.77	1.11

Interpret the data shown and explain <u>three</u> reasons why the current performance may exist and suggest response actions that could be taken to reach optimum performance by the end of the project.

Marks   30 marks (10 marks each)

Question 5

Question part (a)   Explain <u>two</u> reasons why an initial estimate may need to be revised throughout the project life cycle.

Marks   20 marks (10 marks each)

Question part (b)   Describe <u>three</u> sections of a typical project management plan.

Marks   30 marks (10 marks each)

Question 6

Question part (a)   Explain <u>two</u> ways in which earned value data may be used to make decisions about changes to the project schedule or budget.

Marks   20 marks (10 marks each)

Question part (b)   Explain <u>three</u> ways in which the project manager would use the project management plan during the project life cycle.

Marks   30 marks (10 marks each)

Question 7

Question part (a)   Describe <u>two</u> ways in which the formation of the deployment baseline differs in a linear life cycle as opposed to an iterative life cycle.

    Marks   20 marks (10 marks each)

Question part (b)   Explain <u>three</u> ways in which stakeholder expectations can be managed in order to ensure project success.

    Marks   30 marks (10 marks each)

Question 8

Question part (a)   Describe <u>two</u> types of information that a project might report and how these might be used to manage project outcomes.

    Marks   20 marks (10 marks each)

Question part (b)   Explain <u>three</u> steps in a process that could be used to achieve stakeholder engagement in the project.

    Marks   30 marks (10 marks each)

Learning outcome	7. Understand project scope management
Study guide subject area	**Assessment criteria**
2.2.6 Scope management	**7.1** Explain how to define scope in terms of outputs, outcomes and benefits (including use of product, cost and work breakdown structures) (Q2a).
	7.2 Explain how to establish scope through requirements management processes (such as gathering, analysing, justifying requirements, and baseline needs) (Q2b).
	7.3 Explain how to manage scope through configuration management processes (such as planning, identification, control, status accounting, and verification audit) (Q1a).
	7.4 Explain different stages of a typical change control process (such as request, initial evaluation, detailed evaluation, recommendation, update plans, and implement) (Q1b).

Examples of exam questions for this learning outcome

Question 1

Question part (a)   Explain two ways in which configuration management would help achieve controlled change in the project.

Marks   20 marks (10 marks each)

Question part (b)   Explain three stages in a typical change control process.

Marks   30 marks (10 marks each)

Question 2

Question part (a)   Describe two breakdown structures used to communicate the scope of a project.

Marks   20 marks (10 marks each)

Question part (b)   Explain three steps in a requirements management process that would help to establish project scope.

Marks   30 marks (10 marks each)

Learning outcome	8. Understand schedule and resource optimisation
Study guide subject area	**Assessment criteria**
2.3.2 **Schedule and resource optimisation**	**8.1** Describe ways to create and maintain a schedule (including critical path, and Gantt charts) (Q1a).
	8.2 Differentiate between critical path and critical chain as scheduling techniques (Q2b).
	8.3 Describe how resources are categorised and allocated to a linear life cycle schedule (Q2a).
	8.4 Describe how resources are categorised and allocated to an iterative life cycle schedule (Q3a).
	8.5 Differentiate between resource smoothing and resource levelling (Q1b).
	8.6 Differentiate between cost planning for iterative life cycles and cost planning for linear life cycles (Q3b).

Examples of exam questions for this learning outcome

Question 1

Question part (a)	Explain two reasons why the project manager should understand the significance of the critical path when reviewing a project schedule.
Marks	20 marks (10 marks each)
Question part (b)	Explain three differences between resource smoothing and resource levelling when used for resource optimisation in a project.
Marks	30 marks (10 marks each)

Question 2

Question part (a)	Describe two ways in which resources are categorised and allocated to a project with a linear life cycle.
Marks	20 marks (10 marks each)
Question part (b)	Explain three differences between critical path and critical chain when used to schedule a project.
Marks	30 marks (10 marks each)

Question 3

Question part (a)   Describe <u>two</u> ways in which resources are categorised and allocated to a project with an iterative life cycle.

    Marks   20 marks (10 marks each)

Question part (b)   Explain <u>three</u> differences in how costs would be planned for a project with a linear life cycle as opposed to an iterative life cycle.

    Marks   30 marks (10 marks each)

Learning outcome	9. Understand project procurement	
Study guide subject area	**Assessment criteria**	
2.2.5 Procurement	**9.1** Explain the purpose, typical content and importance of a procurement strategy (Q1b).	
	9.2 Differentiate between different methods of supplier reimbursement (including fixed price, cost plus fee, per unit quantity, and target cost) (Q1a).	
	9.3 Differentiate between different contractual relationships (Q2a).	
	9.4 Explain a supplier selection process (Q2b).	

Examples of exam questions for this learning outcome

Question 1

Question part (a)	Explain <u>two</u> methods of supplier reimbursement. Choose <u>two</u> from the following:
	▪ Fixed price
	▪ Cost plus fee
	▪ Per unit quantity
	▪ Target cost
Marks	20 marks (10 marks each)
Question part (b)	Explain <u>three</u> elements of a procurement strategy and why these are important for effective procurement to the project.
Marks	30 marks (10 marks each)

Question 2

Question part (a)	Describe <u>two</u> different types of contractual relationships that an organisation might choose to procure goods or services for the project.
Marks	20 marks (10 marks each)
Question part (b)	Explain <u>three</u> steps in a supplier selection process for a project.
Marks	30 marks (10 marks each)

Learning outcome	10. Understand risk and issue management in the context of project management	
Study guide subject area	**Assessment criteria**	
2.2.3 Risk and issue management	**10.1** Explain each stage in a risk management process (such as identification, analysis, response, and closure) (Q2a).	
	10.2 Explain proactive and reactive responses to risk (such as avoid, reduce, transfer or accept and exploit, enhance, share and reject) (Q2b).	
	10.3 Explain the benefits of risk management (Q1b).	
	10.4 Explain the key aspects of issue management (Q1a).	

Examples of exam questions for this learning outcome

Question 1

Question part (a)	Explain <u>two</u> ways in which issues might be managed differently from risks.
Marks	20 marks (10 marks each)
Question part (b)	Explain <u>three</u> benefits to an organisation of carrying out formal risk management in the project.
Marks	30 marks (10 marks each)

Question 2

Question part (a)	Explain <u>two</u> ways in which risks to the project can be identified.
Marks	20 marks (10 marks each)
Question part (b)	Explain <u>three</u> responses to risk that the project manager might decide.
Marks	30 marks (10 marks each)

Learning outcome	**11.** Understand quality in the context of a project	
Study guide subject area	**Assessment criteria**	
2.2.4 Quality management	**11.1** Explain what is meant by quality planning (Q1a).	
	11.2 Differentiate between quality control and quality assurance (Q1b).	

Examples of exam questions for this learning outcome

Question 1

Question part (a)   Describe <u>two</u> factors that would be considered when developing an effective quality plan for the project.

Marks   20 marks (10 marks each)

Question part (b)   Explain <u>three</u> differences between quality control and quality assurance when managing a project.

Marks   30 marks (10 marks each)

Glossary

This glossary is made up of terms that you will find in this study guide and is consistent with definitions outlined in the seventh edition of the *APM Body of Knowledge*.

Acceptance criteria The requirements and essential conditions that have to be achieved before a deliverable is accepted.

Activity (1) A task, job, operation or process consuming time and possibly other resources. (2) The smallest self-contained unit of work in a project.

Adoption The optional additional phase in a linear life cycle that facilitates the use of project outputs to enable the acceptance and use of benefits.

Agile A family of development methodologies where requirements and solutions are developed iteratively and incrementally throughout the life cycle.

Analogous estimating An estimating technique based on the comparison with, and factoring from, the cost of similar, previous work. Also known as comparative estimating.

Analytical estimating An estimating technique that uses detailed specifications to estimate time and cost for each product or activity. Also known as bottom-up estimating.

Assurance The process of providing confidence to stakeholders that projects, programmes and portfolios will achieve their objectives for beneficial change.

Baseline The reference levels against which a project, programme or portfolio is monitored and controlled.

Benefit A positive and measurable impact of change.

Benefits management The identification, definition, planning, tracking and realisation of benefits.

Benefits realisation The practice of ensuring that benefits are derived from outputs and outcomes.

Bottom-up estimating An estimating technique that uses detailed specifications to estimate time and cost for each product or activity. Also known as analytical estimating.

Breakdown structure A hierarchical structure by which project elements are decomposed. Examples include: cost breakdown structure (CBS), organisational breakdown structure (OBS), product breakdown structure (PBS), and work breakdown structure (WBS).

Buffer A term used in critical chain for the centralised management of schedule contingencies.

Business-as-usual An organisation's normal day-to-day operations. Also referred to as steady-state.

Business case Provides justification for undertaking a project, programme or portfolio. It evaluates the benefit, cost and risk of alternative options and provides a rationale for the preferred solution.

Business readiness A continuous concern and activity through the life of a project or programme that seeks to understand attitudes to change and any barriers so that people are ready to accept outputs and adopt new ways of working to realise benefit.

Change control The process through which all requests to change the approved baseline of a project, programme or portfolio are captured, evaluated and then approved, rejected or deferred.

Change freeze A point after which no further changes to scope will be considered.

Change management The overarching approach taken in an organisation to move from the current to a future desirable state using a coordinated and structured approach in collaboration with stakeholders.

Change register (or log) A record of all proposed changes to scope.

Change request A request to obtain formal approval for changes to the approved baseline.

Closure The formal end point of a project, programme or portfolio; either because planned work has been completed or because it has been terminated early.

Communication The process of exchanging information and confirming there is shared understanding.

Communities of practice A type of learning network used within and between organisations to maintain, develop and share knowledge.

Comparative estimating An estimating technique based on the comparison with, and factoring from, the cost of similar, previous work. Also known as analogous estimating.

Complexity Relates to the degree of interaction of all the elements that make up a project, programme or portfolio and is dependent on such factors as the level of uncertainty, interaction between stakeholders and degree of innovation.

Concept The first phase in a linear life cycle that develops an initial idea through initial studies and high-level requirements management, and assessment of viability including an outline business case.

Configuration The functional and physical characteristics of a product as defined in its specification and achieved through the deployment of project management plans.

Configuration management Encompasses the technical and administrative activities concerned with the creation, maintenance, controlled change and quality control of the scope of work.

Conflict resolution The process of identifying and addressing differences that if left unmanaged would affect successful completion of objectives.

Context A collective term for the societal and/or organisational setting of a project, programme or portfolio. Also known as environment.

Contingency Provision of additional time or money to deal with the occurrence of risks should they occur. See also risk budget and management reserve.

Continuing professional development (CPD) The term used to describe the requirement for any professional to continually develop their competence.

Contract An agreement made between two or more parties that creates legally binding obligations between them. The contract sets out those obligations and the actions that can be taken if they are not met.

Control Tracking performance against agreed plans and taking the corrective action required to meet defined objectives.

Cost of capital A term used in investment appraisal to reflect the percentage return an investment must deliver to satisfy lenders. Value is only created when the return is greater than the cost of capital. See also weighted average cost of capital (WACC).

Cost planning and control The estimation of costs, the setting of an agreed budget, and management of actual and forecast costs against that budget.

Critical chain A resource-based approach to scheduling, useful when time is critical and derived from the critical path, that protects critical chains of activities with buffers.

Critical path A sequence of activities through a precedence network from start to finish, the sum of whose durations determines the overall duration.

Critical path analysis An activity-based scheduling technique that determines the overall duration of the identified work based on estimates and logical dependencies. The method of determining the critical path.

Decision gate A point in the life cycle between phases that is used to review and confirm viability of the work in line with the business case. Alternatively called stage gates or gates.

Delphi technique The generation of an estimate through individual expert judgement followed by facilitated team consensus.

Deployment baseline The reference levels created as an output of integrated planning and the development of the project management plan.

Earned value A measure of progress that expresses costs committed and work achieved in the same units.

Earned value management A project control process, based on a structured approach to planning, cost collection and performance measurement. It facilitates the integration of project scope, time and cost objectives and the establishment of a baseline plan of performance measurement.

Emergent change Unplanned change that is managed by an organisation through incremental, iterative or evolutionary approaches.

Environment A collective term for the societal and/or organisational setting of a project, programme or portfolio. Also known as context.

Escalation The process by which issues are drawn to the attention of a higher level of management.

Estimate A forecast of the probable time or cost of completing work.

Estimating The use of a range of tools and techniques to produce forecasts of the probable time or cost of completing work.

Event-driven Control actions or reports that are triggered by a specific event.

Extended life cycle A life cycle approach that adds an adoption phase to a linear or iterative life cycle with the purpose of ensuring the accountability and governance of the investment stays with the change teams until change is fully embedded. It provides the missing connection to benefit realisation in a linear life cycle and facilitates cooperation and knowledge sharing between change and business-as-usual teams.

Facilitation An approach to working with groups in a collaborative way to create energy and make it easy for the group to solve problems.

Fixed or non-recurring cost A resource and associated cost that is not influenced by volume of business or quantity, for example a one-off capital cost.

Float A term used to describe the flexibility with which an activity may be rescheduled. There are various types of float, such as total float and free float.

Forecast A prediction of a defined future state, typically related to the duration and out-turn cost of a project or programme.

Funding The means by which the money required to undertake a project, programme or portfolio is secured and then made available as required.

Gantt chart A graphical representation of activity against time.

Governance The framework of authority and accountability that defines and controls the outputs, outcomes and benefits from projects, programmes and portfolios. The mechanism whereby the investing organisation exerts financial and technical control over the deployment of the work and the realisation of value.

Governance board A body that provides sponsorship to a project, programme or portfolio. The board will represent financial, provider and user interests. Members of a governance board oversee deployment and make decisions through the chosen life cycle. Alternatively called steering committee, steering group, project board, programme board, etc.

Handover The point, as part of the transition phase of a linear life cycle, where deliverables are commissioned and handed over to the permanent organisation to adopt.

Host organisation The organisation that provides the strategic direction of the project, programme or portfolio and is the primary investor and recipient of benefits. Used interchangeably with investing organisation and client organisation.

Hybrid life cycle A pragmatic approach to achieving beneficial change that combines a linear life cycle for some phases or activities with an iterative life cycle for others.

Influencing The act of affecting the behaviours and actions of others.

Information management The collection, storage, curation, dissemination, archiving and destruction of documents, images, drawings and others sources of information.

Integrated assurance The coordination of assurance activities where there are a number of assurance providers. It can follow a Three lines of defence model from corporate governance.

Integrated planning The application of management processes that bring together the planning of benefits, success criteria, scope, quality, time, resources, cost, risk, communications, etc, to create the project management plan.

Internal rate of return (IRR) Used to determine the profitability of a potential investment. It is the discount rate that makes the net present value zero.

Investment appraisal The analysis done to consider the profitability of an investment over the life of an asset alongside considerations of affordability and strategic fit. An input to the investment decision.

Investment decision The decision made by the sponsor and governance board that justifies the investment in a project, programme or portfolio. Investment decisions rely on robust investment appraisal.

Issue A problem that is now breaching, or is about to breach, delegated tolerances for work on a project or programme. Issues require support from the sponsor to agree a resolution.

Iterative life cycle A life cycle that repeats one or more of the phases of a project or programme before proceeding to the next one with the objective of managing uncertainty of scope by allowing objectives to evolve as learning and discovery takes place.

Knowledge management The holistic, cross-functional discipline and set of practices concerned with the way organisations create and use knowledge to improve outcomes.

Leadership The ability to establish vision and direction, to influence and align others towards a common purpose, and to empower and inspire people to achieve success.

Life cycle A framework comprising a set of distinct high-level stages required to transform an idea of concept into reality in an orderly and efficient manner. Life cycles offer a systematic and organised way to undertake project-based work and can be viewed as the structure underpinning deployment.

Linear life cycle A life cycle that aims to complete a project within a single pass through a set of distinct phases that are completed serially and span from the development of the initial concept to the deployment of an ultimate output, outcome or benefits.

Management plan A plan that sets out how an aspect of a project, programme or portfolio will be delivered, for example, a configuration management plan. Individual management plans are component parts of the overall project management plan (PMP) that is the output of integrated planning.

Management reserve A sum of money that is part of overall cost contingency to cover the cost impact of unidentified risks, and potentially some already identified very low-probability, very high-impact risks. See also risk budget and contingency.

Milestone A key event selected for its importance in the schedule commonly associated with tangible acceptance of deliverables.

Minimum viable product A product with just enough features to satisfy early users, and to provide feedback for future product development.

Net present value (NPV) The difference between the present value of cash inflow and the present value of cash outflow over a period of time. It is the monetary value used to judge the value of an investment at a particular discount rate.

Network diagram A model of activities and their dependencies used in scheduling. Also known as a Precedence network.

Objectives A generic term for pre-determined results towards which effort is directed. Objectives may be defined in terms of outputs, outcomes and/or benefits.

Opportunity A positive risk event that, if it occurs, will have an upside/beneficial effect on the achievement of one or more objectives.

Organisational culture The unwritten rules that influence individual and group behaviour and attitudes. Applicable at multiple levels of organisation, including national culture or project culture.

Outcome The changed circumstances or behaviour that results from the use of an output and leads to realisation of benefits.

Output The tangible or intangible product typically delivered by a project. Used interchangeably with deliverable and product.

Parametric estimating An estimating technique that uses a statistical relationship between historic data and other variables to calculate an estimate.

Phase The major subdivision of a life cycle.

Planned value The cost profile of a resource, optimised schedule used as the baseline to monitor actual spend and earned value. Alternatively called the Budgeted Cost of Work Scheduled (BCWS).

Portfolio A collection of projects and/or programmes used to structure and manage investments at an organisational or functional level to optimise strategic benefits or operational efficiency.

Portfolio management The selection, prioritisation and control of an organisation's projects and programmes in line with its strategic objectives and capacity to deliver.

Precedence network A model of activities and their dependencies used in scheduling. Also known as a network diagram.

Procurement strategy The high level approach for securing the goods and services required from external suppliers to satisfy project, programme and portfolio needs. See also strategic sourcing.

Product A tangible or intangible component of a project's output. Used interchangeably with deliverable and output.

Product owner The owner of a product who may contribute to decisions concerning the development of a product.

Product life cycle A life cycle approach that adds operation and termination phases to a linear life cycle to reflect the whole life of an asset. Enabling a full asset life cycle perspective encourages engagement with long-term future implications of project-related actions.

Professionalism The application of expert and specialised knowledge within a specific field and the acceptance of standards relating to that profession.

Programme A unique, transient strategic endeavour undertaken to achieve beneficial change and incorporating a group of related projects and business-as-usual (steady-state) activities.

Programme management The coordinated management of projects and business-as-usual (steady-state) activities to achieve beneficial change.

Project A unique, transient endeavour undertaken to bring about change and to achieve planned objectives.

Project-based working A collective term for project, programme and portfolio management. Used interchangeably with management of projects.

Project management The application of processes, methods, knowledge, skills and experience to achieve specific objectives for change.

Project (programme or portfolio) management office (PMO) An organisational structure that provides support for projects, programmes and/or portfolios.

Project management plan (PMP) The output of process of integrated planning for a project or programme.

Project professional The term used to describe those people in roles associated with the management of projects, programmes or portfolios.

Quality The fitness for purpose or the degree of conformance of the outputs of a process or the process itself to requirements.

Quality control Consists of inspection, measurement and testing to verify that the project outputs meet acceptance criteria defined during quality planning.

Quality planning Takes the defined scope and specifies the acceptance criteria used to validate that the outputs are fit for purpose to the sponsor.

Reports (1) The presentation of information in an appropriate format (e.g. management report). (2) A written record or summary, a detailed account or statement, or a verbal account. (3) A term used to refer to a role that is subordinate to another role in an organisation structure.

Requirements The stakeholders' wants and needs clearly defined with acceptance criteria.

Requirements management The process of capturing, assessing and justifying stakeholders' wants and needs.

Resource allocation The process by which labour and non-labour resources are attributed to activities.

Resource levelling An approach used during resource optimisation that delays activities such that resource usage is kept below specified limits. Also known as resource limited scheduling.

Resource management The acquisition and deployment of the internal and external resources required to deliver the project, programme or portfolio.

Resource optimisation A collective term used to describe the methods for ensuring that labour and non-labour resources are matched to the schedule. See also resource levelling and resource smoothing.

Resource smoothing An approach used as part of resource optimisation that involves utilising float, or increasing or decreasing the resources required for specific activities, such that any peaks and troughs of resource usage are smoothed out avoiding extension of the duration where possible. Also known as time limited resource scheduling.

Resources All the labour and non-labour items required to undertake the scope of work to the required quality.

Responsibility assignment matrix A diagram or chart showing assigned responsibilities for elements of work. It is created by combining the work breakdown structure with the organisational breakdown structure.

Return on investment (ROI) An expression of the value of an investment in change based on the gain in benefit relative to the cost.

Risk The potential of a situation or event to impact on the achievement of specific objectives.

Risk analysis An assessment and synthesis of estimating uncertainty and/or specific risk events to gain an understanding of their individual significance and/or their combined impact on objectives.

Risk analysis and management A process that allows individual risk events and overall risk to be understood and managed proactively, optimising success by minimising threats and maximising opportunities.

Risk appetite How much risk investors are willing to tolerate in achieving their objectives. Expressed as risk thresholds or tolerances.

Risk attitude The perception driven choice of a person or group about an individual risk, or overall riskiness of a project, programme or portfolio.

Risk budget A sum of money that is part of overall cost contingency to cover the cost impact of identified risks. See also management reserve and contingency.

Risk event An uncertain event or set of circumstances that would, if it occurred, have an effect on the achievement of one or more objectives.

Risk owner The individual or group best placed to assess and manage a risk.

Risk register A document listing identified risk events and their corresponding planned responses. Used interchangeably with risk log or risk repository.

Risk response An action or set of actions to reduce the probability or impact of a threat, or to increase the probability or impact of an opportunity.

Schedule A timetable showing the forecast start and finish dates for activities or events within a project, programme or portfolio.

Scope The totality of the outputs, outcomes and benefits and the work required to produce them.

Scope management The process whereby outputs, outcomes and benefits are identified, defined and controlled.

Share A risk management response to an opportunity that increases its probability, impact or both by sharing the risk with a third party.

Sponsor A critical role as part of the governance board of any project, programme or portfolio. The sponsor is accountable for ensuring that the work is governed effectively and delivers the objectives that meet identified needs.

Stakeholder Individuals or groups who have an interest or role in the project, programme or portfolio, or are impacted by it.

Stakeholder engagement The systematic identification, analysis, planning and implementation of actions designed to influence stakeholders.

Statement of work An annex to the main body of a contract that defines the detail of deliverables, timescales and management procedures relevant to the contract.

Strategic intent The term used to describe the aspirational plans, overarching purpose or intended direction of travel needed to reach an organisational vision.

Strategic sourcing An analysis of the buying strengths and weaknesses of an organisation that enables procurement strategies to maximise buying advantages and respond to risks of supply disruption.

Success criteria The satisfaction of stakeholder needs for the deployment of a project. Note this is a different performance measure to benefits which are focused on the strategic intent and delivering beneficial change.

Sustainability An approach to business that balances the environmental, social, economic and administrative aspects of project-based working to meet the current needs of stakeholders without compromising or overburdening future generations.

Team A group of people working in collaboration or by cooperation towards a common goal.

Temporary organisation (team) A generic term used to describe a specific project, programme or portfolio team brought together specifically to implement project-based work. Used to contrast the organisational structure for project-based work from the permanent organisation.

Threat A negative risk event; a risk event that if it occurs will have a downside/detrimental effect on one or more objectives.

Three-point estimate An estimate in which optimistic best case, pessimistic worst case and most likely values are given.

Time scheduling A collection of techniques used to develop and present schedules that show when work will be performed.

Timebox A generic term used in iterative life cycle approaches to refer to an iteration with a fixed end date that is not allowed to change, thereby adjusting the scope and quality to deliver on time and to cost.

Tolerance A level of delegated permission to vary performance from specified parameters.

Tranche A sub-division of the deployment phase of a programme designed to enable an incremental approach to development of outputs, outcomes and benefits.

Transition The fourth phase in a linear cycle where results are handed over, commissioned and accepted by the sponsor, culminating in formal closure.

Triple constraint A way of describing the fundamental trade-off between time, cost and quality in delivering the scope of a project. Often also called the iron triangle.

Users The group of people who are intended to work with deliverables to enable beneficial change to be realised.

Value A standard, principle or quality considered worthwhile or desirable. In value management terms, value is defined as the ratio of 'satisfaction of requirements' over 'use of resources'.

MANAGEMENT

Variable or recurring cost A resource and associated cost that is influenced by volume of business or quantity, for example a recurring operational cost.

Virtual team A team where the people are separated by geography and potentially time-zone.

VUCA conditions (volatility, uncertainty, complexity and ambiguity) A phrase used to describe an organisational context where there is inherent uncertainty that makes it difficult to predict and plan with great accuracy.

References

Figure 2.1.6.2 Source: *The DSDM Agile Project Framework Handbook*, 2014, https://www.agilebusiness.org. Reproduced with the kind permission of the Agile Business Consortium

Figure 2.2.7.1 Source: *Motivation and Personality, 3rd ed* by Abraham H. Maslow, eds Robert D. Frager and James Fadiman, © 1987. Reproduced by permission of Pearson Education, Inc., New York, New York

Figure 2.3.3.2 Source: Based on Dr Ralph Kilmann's version of the TKI Conflict Model, © 2009–2018 by Kilmann Diagnostics. All rights reserved. Original figure available at http://www.kilmanndiagnostics.com/overview-thomas-kilmann-conflict-mode-instrument-tki

Index